Oppositional Discourses and Democracies

Routledge Studies in Social and Political Thought

For a full list of titles in this series, please visit www.routledge.com

28. Durkheim's Suicide
A Century of Research and Debate
Edited by W.S.F. Pickering and
Geoffrey Walford

29. Post-Marxism
An Intellectual History
Stuart Sim

30. The Intellectual as Stranger
Studies in Spokespersonship
Dick Pels

31. Hermeneutic Dialogue and Social Science
A Critique of Gadamer and Habermas
Austin Harrington

32. Methodological Individualism
Background, History and Meaning
Lars Udehn

33. John Stuart Mill and Freedom of Expression
The Genesis of a Theory
K.C. O'Rourke

34. The Politics of Atrocity and Reconciliation
From Terror to Trauma
Michael Humphrey

35. Marx and Wittgenstein
Knowledge, Morality, Politics
Edited by Gavin Kitching and
Nigel Pleasants

36. The Genesis of Modernity
Arpad Szakolczai

37. Ignorance and Liberty
Lorenzo Infantino

38. Deleuze, Marx and Politics
Nicholas Thoburn

39. The Structure of Social Theory
Anthony King

40. Adorno, Habermas and the Search for a Rational Society
Deborah Cook

41. Tocqueville's Moral and Political Thought
New Liberalism
M.R.R. Ossewaarde

42. Adam Smith's Political Philosophy
The Invisible Hand and
Spontaneous Order
Craig Smith

43. Social and Political Ideas of Mahatma Gandi
Bidyut Chakrabarty

44. Counter-Enlightenments
From the Eighteenth Century to the Present
Graeme Garrard

45. The Social and Political Thought of George Orwell
A Reassessment
Stephen Ingle

46. **Habermas**
Rescuing the Public Sphere
Pauline Johnson

47. **The Politics and Philosophy of Michael Oakeshott**
Stuart Isaacs

48. **Pareto and Political Theory**
Joseph Femia

49. **German Political Philosophy**
The Metaphysics of Law
Chris Thornhill

50. **The Sociology of Elites**
Michael Hartmann

51. **Deconstructing Habermas**
Lasse Thomassen

52. **Young Citizens and New Media**
Learning for Democractic Participation
Edited by Peter Dahlgren

53. **Gambling, Freedom and Democracy**
Peter Adams

54. **The Quest for Jewish Assimilation in Modern Social Science**
Amos Morris-Reich

55. **Frankfurt School Perspectives on Globalization, Democracy, and the Law**
William E. Scheuerman

56. **Hegemony**
Studies in Consensus and Coercion
Edited by Richard Howson and Kylie Smith

57. **Governmentality, Biopower, and Everyday Life**
Majia Holmer Nadesan

58. **Sustainability and Security within Liberal Societies**
Learning to Live with the Future
Edited by Stephen Gough and Andrew Stables

59. **The Mythological State and its Empire**
David Grant

60. **Globalizing Dissent**
Essays on Arundhati Roy
Edited by Ranjan Ghosh & Antonia Navarro-Tejero

61. **The Political Philosophy of Michel Foucault**
Mark G.E. Kelly

62. **Democratic Legitimacy**
Fabienne Peter

63. **Edward Said and the Literary, Social, and Political World**
Edited by Ranjan Ghosh

64. **Perspectives on Gramsci**
Politics, Culture and Social Theory
Edited by Joseph Francese

65. **Enlightenment Political Thought and Non-Western Societies**
Sultans and Savages
Frederick G. Whelan

66. **Liberalism, Neoliberalism, Social Democracy**
Thin Communitarian Perspectives on Political Philosophy and Education
Mark Olssen

67. **Oppositional Discourses and Democracies**
Edited by Michael Huspek

Oppositional Discourses and Democracies

Edited by Michael Huspek

Routledge
Taylor & Francis Group
New York London

First published 2010
by Routledge
711 Third Ave, New York, NY 10017

Simultaneously published in the UK
by Routledge
2 Park Square, Milton Park, Abingdon, Oxon OX14 4RN

Routledge is an imprint of the Taylor & Francis Group, an informa business

First issued in paperback 2013

© 2010 Taylor & Francis

Typeset in Sabon by IBT Global.

All rights reserved. No part of this book may be reprinted or reproduced or utilised in any form or by any electronic, mechanical, or other means, now known or hereafter invented, including photocopying and recording, or in any information storage or retrieval system, without permission in writing from the publishers.

Trademark Notice: Product or corporate names may be trademarks or registered trademarks, and are used only for identification and explanation without intent to infringe.

Library of Congress Cataloging-in-Publication Data
  Oppositional discourses and democracies / edited by Michael Huspek.
    p. cm.—(Routledge studies in social and political thought ; 67)
  Includes bibliographical references and index.
    1. Opposition (Political science) 2. Communication—Political aspects. I. Huspek, Michael, 1950–
  JC328.3.O69 2009
  328.3'69—dc22
                                2009008163

ISBN13: 978-0-415-80389-2 (hbk)
ISBN13: 978-0-415-84978-4 (pbk)

Contents

Tables ix
Acknowledgments xi

Introduction 1
MICHAEL HUSPEK

PART I
The Limits of Imperfect Democracies and How They Are Contested

1 State Ideology and Oppositional Discourses: Conceptual and Methodological Issues 17
PETER JONES AND CHIK COLLINS

2 Ideology, Discourse, and Moral Economy: Consulting the People of North Manchester 40
COLIN BARKER

3 Where State Power and Opposition Collide: Discourses of Labor Protest in a New Market Economy 60
CHARLES WOOLFSON

PART II
State Responses to Oppositional Discourses and Democratization from Below

4 Challenging New Laws with Old Values: Indigenous Resistance to State "Enforcement" of Children's Rights in Ghana 85
JANICE WINDBORNE

viii *Contents*

5 State Power and the Reconstitution of Parental Rights in U.S. Child Custody Mediation 103
LYNN COMERFORD

6 Weaving and Unweaving the Rights of Public Woman: The Case of Telephone Operators at the Turn of the Twentieth Century 118
JANE S. SUTTON

PART III
Sustained Forces of Democratization and the Effectiveness of Oppositional Discourses

7 Vigilance and Solidarity in the Rhetoric of the Black Press: The *Tulsa Star* 135
OLGA IDRISS DAVIS

8 "From the Standpoint of the White Man's World:": The Black Press and Contemporary White Media Scholarship 155
MICHAEL HUSPEK

9 Exposing the Hypocrisies of State Power: The African-American Press and the Holocaust 174
FELECIA G. JONES ROSS AND SAKILE KAI CAMARA

PART IV
Normative Contours of State and Oppositional Discourses

10 The Philosophical Foundations of the Discourse Society 191
DARRYL GUNSON

11 Habermas and Oppositional Public Spheres: A Stereoscopic Analysis of Competing Discourses 212
MICHAEL HUSPEK

12 The Rational Bases of Transgressive Rhetoric 236
MICHAEL HUSPEK

Contributors 255
Index 257

Tables

8.1	Official v. Community Sources	160
11.1	Openly Strategic and Communicative Action	220

Acknowledgments

The editor and contributors of this collection express their gratitude to the *Journal of Intergroup Relations* and its sponsor, the National Association of Human Rights Workers, and the association's president, Willie Ratchford, for granting permission to print in this volume three essays that were published by the journal fall of 2005, vol. 32, no. 3. The three essays, slightly modified for this collection, are: "Vigilance and Solidarity in the Rhetoric of the Black Press: *The Tulsa Star*" (Olga Davis); "The African-American Press and the Holocaust" (Felecia G. Jones Ross and Sakile Kai Camara); "'From the Standpoint of the White Man's World': The Black Press and Contemporary White Media Scholarship" (Michael Huspek). We are also grateful to Blackwell Publishers for permission to print in this volume, in slightly modified form, Michael Huspek's essay, "Habermas and Oppositional Public Spheres: A Stereoscopic Analysis of Black and White Press Practices," which appeared in *Political Studies December* of 2007, vol. 55, no. 4. Further, we are grateful to Routledge as part of Taylor and Francis for its permission to print in this volume seven articles that appear in two special issues of the *Atlantic Journal of Communication*, vol. 14, nos. 1–2 and 3. These include: Colin Barker's "Ideology, Discourse and Moral Economy: Consulting the People of North Manchester" (14, 1–2); Darryl Gunson's "Philosophical Credentials of the Discourse Society" (14, 1–2); Peter Jones's and Chik Collins's "Political Analysis versus 'Critical Discourse Analysis' in the Treatment of Ideology: Some Implications for the Study of Communication" (14, 1–2); Charles Woolfson's "Discourses of Labor Protest in Post-Communist Society" (14, 1–2); Janice Windborne's "New Laws, Old Values: Indigenous Resistance to Children's Rights in Ghana" (14, 3); Lynn Comerford's "Power and Resistance in U.S. Child Custody Mediation" (14, 3); and J. S. Sutton's "Weaving and Unweaving Public Woman: Contingencies of Oppositional Discourse" (14, 3). Special thanks also to Professor Gary Radford, editor of *Atlantic Journal of Communication*, for his enthusiastic encouragement to proceed with this project.

Introduction

Michael Huspek

This collection of essays is premised on the idea that increased democratization of the body politic is a good thing. As democracies become more democratic, they improve themselves and the political well-being of their members. Increased democratization further opens the public sphere to diverse opinion and thereby offers actors an increased stake in deliberative decision-making. Actors can rightly expect that their expressed interests and insights will be genuinely recognized and engaged by significant others, and so they are motivated to seize upon opportunities for meaningful input into matters of import to themselves and their progeny. All this and more creates a positive rippling effect across the political landscape that culminates in better informed and reflexive political action.

The idea of increased democratization and the value it places upon the participatory involvement of actors in political institutions underscores a need for expanded arenas of public discourse. As Benhabib puts it, increased democratization brings with it "the creation of procedures whereby those affected by general social norms and collective political decisions *can have a say* in their formation, stipulation and adoption" (Benhabib 1992, 87, my emphasis). Democracy, on this view, is not simply a matter of aggregated numbers (e.g., what percentage of citizens vote), but rather involves concerted enactment of discursive possibilities where all feel they have a reasonable expectation that their arguments will be heard and taken up by fellow citizens. An emphasis upon the discursive dimension is essential to what theorists have termed deliberative democracy: "a form of government in which free and equal citizens (and their representatives), justify decisions in a process in which they give one another reasons that are mutually acceptable and generally accessible, with the aim of reaching conclusions that are binding in the present on all citizens but open to challenge in the future" (Gutmann and Thompson 2004, 7).

The importance of discourse to democracy points up a tension between the ideal of increased democratization, manifested in expanded deliberative arenas, and the realities of imperfect democracies which often work in ways contrary to the ideal. On the one hand, free elections, proportional representation, and majority rule all testify to the progress of democratic states and, indeed, serve as discursive props for legitimation of existing state institutional arrangements and practices: competing programs of action are debated; the will of the people is expressed through elections; the reins of government are often exchanged; social conflicts are resolved by peaceful means. On the other hand, such outcomes and how they are discursively represented can disguise a tendency of democratic states to suppress some actors' input as a means of protecting or advancing the interests of privileged others: debates over competing programs of action may be only partial and exclusionary of some (perhaps most) potential participants; the will of the people may in fact be little more than an ostensive majority opinion expressed restrictedly in calcified aggregations of electoral result or representational apportionment; claims of conflict resolution may in fact deflect attention away from chronic disparities in how power is distributed.

Emphasis upon discursive dimensions of democracy points to how specific discourses can be used to legitimate state practices, institutional arrangements, and the ideologies to which they appeal. Discourses of the state constitute fields of lawmaking, enforcement, adjudication and all manner of practices associated with governance and, by so doing, establish zones of regulated discursive possibility. They determine who is recognized as valid participant in governance, what is permitted as acceptable discourse, and what counts as a truthful or moral or rational validity claim. Such determinative power weighs extensively on how states secure ostensive consensus-based agreement on the necessity for administrative steering of state apparatuses; it figures into how political actors manage to procure strategic gains and consolidate power in ways that are kept hidden from public scrutiny; and it lays the semantic basis for ideologies that mystify the operations of government and discourage all manner of potential contestation.

The tension between the deliberative ideals of increased democratization, on the one hand, and actually existing imperfect democracies, on the other, can be restated as follows. The democratic deliberative ideal embraces open exchange of viewpoints in public arenas where diverse opinions help to ensure informed and reflexive programs of political action which genuinely reflect the people's will, mediated through public discourse. Imperfect democratic states, in contrast, draw upon discourse-specific truths and meanings that often suppress discursive openness and diversity—a tendency that promotes not a more participatory and educated public but rather one that either is asleep or angry because its viewpoints are neither sufficiently recognized nor engaged.

In light of this tension, it is perhaps unreasonable to expect imperfect democracies to give way to increased democratization without public pressure to do so. As Dryzek aptly states: "the history of democratization indicates that pressures for greater democracy almost always emanate from oppositional civil society, rarely or never from the state itself" (Dryzek 1996, 476). Pressures for greater democracy, that is, usually emanate "from below" and are exerted through expressions of discontent and desire for change by people who have taken to the street or packed assembly halls or have developed long-term strategies whether this is formation of grassroots political organizations or institutions of alternative media. Pressures for greater democracy do not ordinarily seek expression through the ruse of "legitimate" channels as regulated by discourses of the state, but rather are voiced through oppositional discourses.

Oppositional discourses vary widely in terms of their contents and uses, yet they share a number of core characteristics. Perhaps most important, they are actively and openly oppositional. In this regard, they should not be confused with mere forms of resistance. The latter often take the form of secretly encoded reactions to power meant to provide disempowered actors some discursive space, beyond power holders' earshot or watchful gaze, where actors can speak without suffering recrimination. Oppositional discourses, in contrast, are not so much about enabling their users to cope with powerlessness, although at times they do this, but rather are geared toward active and open contestations of the truths and meanings advanced through discourses of the state and other dominant discourses that rationalize powerlessness and the practices that enforce it. Oppositional discourses seek to empower the actors who use them.

Further, oppositional discourses are materially based. They emerge as responses to existing relations of power which, as Jones and Collins have aptly noted, "[are] factual relations between actual people which rest on and are inextricably entangled with such social realities as the ownership of property, wealth, rate and intensity of exploitation, rights and privileges under the law, institutional authority, political organization, and so on" (this volume). Oppositional discourses spring up as political expressions of dissatisfaction with existing relations of power and aim to actively counter how the needs and interests of some have been ignored or discounted as part of the legitimation of those relations. Affirmation of those needs and interests requires, first, a negation of the meanings and truths of discourses of the state that have legitimated their exclusion and then, second, their replacement with alternative meanings and truths. This involves real, openly engaged struggle between discourses of the state and discourses of actors who have been discursively disenfranchised, with meanings and truths, as Barker notes, being both site and means of a struggle that "runs through language, about the language, for control of the language" (in this volume).

Oppositional discourses exert a critical thrust that can potentially enlighten those who have been unreflectively beholden to discourse-legitimated meanings and truths of the state. This involves airing out of contradictions and untruths advanced by discourses of the state, as well as rendering transparent the discursive norms and practices that have kept them hidden. The critical thrust of oppositional discourses may be to strategically counter the state's conscious attempts to deceive the public. But oppositional discourses can also reveal "silences" in public discourse that result in participants' self-deception. Here, we note Jurgen Habermas' idea of systematically distorted communication in and through which actors tend to assume that their communicative norms and practices are open and inclusive when in fact they are closed and exclusionary, and which thereby discourage challenges to prevalent norms, assumptions and practices. Oppositional discourses are meant to roust actors from such ideological slumber; their critical diagnoses invite a sleeping citizenry to consider not otherwise publicized norms of action.

Oppositional discourses often rely upon distinctive rhetorical forms such as jokes, hyperbole, satire and insult that express public sentiment and point to new understandings of people's life conditions and their normative possibilities. This often involves transgression. Those who have raised charges that transgressive rhetoric appears unrealistic or even irrational miss a crucial point, viz., that the rhetorical forms through which oppositional discourses are often expressed are *meant* to appear transgressive—an oftentimes necessary first step toward eliciting public response as a precondition for movement toward consensus on matters ranging from just governance to the modes of rationality to which they appeal. Indeed, oppositional discourses may at times be likened to subversive ways of fictionalizing that draw upon collective imaginaries on route to new social and political possibility. As with other aesthetic forms, the rhetorical expressions of oppositional discourses are not meant to stand alone as, say, might a singular insult or hyperbolic statement. Rather, they are aimed at potential interlocutors in order to provoke new conversations. In this regard, oppositional discourses may at times unearth truths or insights that, long submerged in the subterranean depths of a people's disenfranchisement, can be best brought to light only through actors' willful, active and artful transgressions.

Those who study oppositional discourses rarely fail to appreciate the creativity within people's struggles, the insights they produce, the normative possibilities they offer. On the empirical level, however, oppositional discourses persist in atmospheres of underappreciation, as gatekeepers of legitimated discourses of the state apply multiple rationales for dismissing their potential challengers, obstructing them where they cannot be easily ignored, or absorbing and re-casting them in ways that distort their intended ends. An important role of analysts is thus to illuminate the workings of oppositional discourses by pointing to their critical contents and normative potentials as part of a research strategy that analyzes them in relation to the forces that suppress them. This involves consideration of questions such as:

> What roles do oppositional discourses play in citizen contributions to increased democratization, and how effective are they?
>
> How do states resist pressures to democratize by way of deflection, reconstitution and absorption of the contents of oppositional discourse, and what implication does this have for understanding the overall effectiveness of participatory action?

Can oppositional discourses be sustained over time as countervailing forces against states' structural resistances to increased democratization?

Are there adequate grounds upon which to judge the moral contents of oppositional discourses and to then assess them in relation to discourses of the state?

It may well be that the life of democratic systems—their ability to evolve in ways that clarify its ideals and ways to realize them—hinges upon their responsiveness to voices of criticism and change that emanate from below. In this sense, addressing questions such as those raised above may well assist scholars in understanding the limits and potentials of oppositional discourses, their relevance to political actors, their successes and failures in reaching intended audiences and having lasting effects upon the workings of democracy; but they may also contribute a better understanding of the limits and potentials of democracy itself.

The first section in this collection consists of three essays that treat oppositional discourses as empirical sites where meanings and truths form a double relation with those who use them, being both site of contestation and the primary tools by which to wage the contest. The essay by Peter Jones and Chik Collins, "State ideology and oppositional discourses: Conceptual and methodological issues," emphasizes that discourses should be examined as living phenomena, materially based, and bound up with contexts that are themselves often by-products of discursive acts of control or contestation. The authors advance their work as counter to such schools of thought as Critical Discourse Analysis which tends to pare discourse away from its contextualized uses and treat it as a structured slice of an abstract linguistic system. This kind of abstraction, the authors argue, inflicts fatal damage "upon rational thinking and action when the connections between ideas and life experiences are broken, when the processes of critical thinking and intellectual engagement with real life problems are replaced by the words and word meanings within a verbal system abstracted from communicative practice." With discursive elements so abstracted, we deprive ourselves of an understanding of entire actions or events, the dynamic forces and relations which give discourses their meaning and which are produced as effects of that meaning. As antidote, Jones and Collins call for a more thoroughgoing approach that involves "searching out, piecing together and thinking through a mass of relevant empirical facts" as part of a process that develops historical, theoretical and practical knowledge of the political and ideological aspects of discourse.

The essays of both Colin Barker and Charles Woolfson offer superb illustration of the kind of analysis called for by Jones and Collins. Barker's essay, "Ideology, discourse and moral economy: Consulting the people of North Manchester," presents a vivid demonstration of how oppositional discourses are best "studied in action, as people use it in social life." Specifically, Barker analyzes the dynamics of discursive struggle in public assemblies that involve the Manchester Health Authority and community activists, the former expressing intent to close a local children's hospital, the latter campaigning to save it. The struggle reveals itself to be about saving a hospital, but also much more, as Barker carefully analyzes the collision of two discourses: one combines bureaucratic authority and medical expertise into an ideology of legitimation and control which attempts to disguise the state's placement of monetary interests above the health needs of working-class communities; the other draws upon Manchester citizens' historically rooted moral economy, which includes nonmonetary values, traditions and customs that are geared to protect patterns of social activity, rights and obligations within the community. In this particular case, although the hospital was shut down, Barkers' analysis reveals how a community-based oppositional discourse advanced a "battle cry, or at least a justification for action" that reaffirmed the idea of community, only now made more aware of contradictions between state practices and community rights and how the contradictions might be better combated in future discursive struggles.

Charles Woolfson's essay, "Where state power and opposition collide: Discourses of labor protest in a new market economy," examines the dominant state discourse of "democracy" and "new market economy" in postcommunist Lithuania as a significant means by which the state has rationalized "deterioration in wages and working conditions of labor, and the growth of high levels of unemployment." Woolfson then describes oppositional discourses of labor that have emerged "from below," with special consideration directed toward forms of individualized and desperate protest, personalized protests by way of quiet pickets staged outside MP's homes, and "muted" collectivist discourse of workers who, because of prohibitions against the right to strike, engage in public "walks" during workers' lunch breaks, "sit-ins" conducted at the end of work shifts, and hunger strikes. Woolfson's study is especially adept in showing the strict limits imposed upon discursive action by the state as a means to exclude organized labor from an independent role in civil society and in turn limit its effectiveness within the narrow parameters of the public sphere. At the same time, the study shows oppositional discourses to be flexible and changing—what Baker has termed "a continuous arrival at turning points" within contexts of considerable risk, peril or suspense (Baker Jr., 1999)—that continue to have social resonance for the highly embattled labor movement in Lithuania.

The above essays point to the dynamic qualities of oppositional discourses. They should not be cast as frozen moments in time as structuralists have been wont to do but rather should be treated as ongoing struggles that never quite come to an end. Strictly speaking, victories and defeats are never quite what they may seem. With "defeat," the material relations that prompted an emergent oppositional discourse do not disappear, and so neither do discourses of control and contestation entirely disappear. Insofar as meanings and truths are encoded to represent social actors' life experiences and needs more accurately than dominant discourses of the state, so then even in "defeat" comes actors' heightened awareness of the nature of the struggle and what may be best suited as future stratagems and their expressive forms. So, too, the victories achieved by oppositional discourses may be successful in disruption of discourses of the state, as well as signaling a normative shift in state practices or institutional arrangements. Such victories, however, can be pyrrhic. Despite a state's concessions to challenges posed by oppositional discourses, it may then absorb and refit the contents of those challenges in ways that legitimate extant governing apparatuses. This latter tendency is elaborated in detail in the second section of this collection, which contains the essays of Janice Windborne, Lynn Comerford and Jane S. Sutton.

Janice Windborne's essay, "Challenging new laws as old values: Indigenous resistance to state 'enforcement' of children's rights in Ghana," examines how Ghana's government has trumpeted its response to public calls for state-provided education for all of the nation's children. At the same time, the state's inattention to existing social and economic policies has meant that impoverished families have had to continue to send their offspring into the netherworld of exploited child labor. This is especially the case regarding young girls whose parents, realizing that an education for women in Ghana provides no guarantee of post-educational position or income, submit to a calculus that recognizes the value of child labor over educated citizenship. The Ghanan state thus claims to have been responsive to public pressures to institute a universal right to education, and has incorporated the language of such into its own state-legitimating discourse. But the language exists only on paper. In reality, young girls' life potentials remain severely stunted, a point wholly ignored within the Ghanan state's proud embrace of a human rights discourse.

Lynn Comerford's essay, "State power and the reconstitution of parental rights in U.S. child custody mediations," focuses upon how the state has responded to public criticism of its child custody policies by conferring a new set of selective rights and obligations for parents. Mediation sessions are said to empower women by giving them a voice that had been denied them in the once favored but now discredited adversarial process in courtroom proceedings. Comerford argues, however, that the empowerment is illusory. Her empirical examination of mediation sessions shows that women quickly learn that they must engage in self-censorship as a condition for being assessed by mediators as "balanced" and responsible parents. Women's cries of injustice or willfully advanced counterarguments often tend to be classified by mediators as indicators of hysteria, uncooperativeness, or irrationality, which are then used as basis for mediators' decisions to separate children from their mothers. Comerford concludes that despite the state's self-congratulatory response to feminism's challenges to the male-centered injustices of adversarial processes for assignment of children, the shift to mediation may have been less about correcting injustice and more about the state's need to unclog its overloaded court system.

Jane S. Sutton's essay, "Weaving and unweaving public women: The state's reconstitution of women's rights," focuses upon how the state responded to calls for women's rights to participate in public spaces during the late 19th and early 20th century. Sutton discusses how women's successes in gaining entry and acceptance in public spaces were often made contingent upon their submission to an enforced silence and other muted behaviors. Women were permitted into the workforce, for example, only on the condition that they comported themselves as "agentless speakers," which as suggested by the contradiction within the term, was a very "tricky" task. Perhaps no less "tricky" was the task of traversing public streets on the way to and from the workplace, which required that women endure the scrutinizing gaze and interrogations of patrol officers commissioned to enforce the morality of city streets. The contradiction is patent enough: a state that proclaims recognition of women's right to access public domains; and a regimen of assumptions and practices geared toward keeping women muted when in public domains and invisible when travelling public thoroughfares in order to reach such domains. The contradiction, moreover, seems not to have diminished greatly, as Sutton concludes her essay with an account of late 20th century women employees of a large corporation being shuttled from workplace to home by predominantly male taxi drivers, with women and drivers alike under strict orders by their respective supervisors that they navigate the public streets together under conditions of strict silence.

In order to withstand the tendency of states to absorb and reconstitute oppositional discourses' meanings and truths, the latter often seeks to sustain the effectiveness of its countervailing force in and through alternative institutions. A significant example of this is the historical role of the black press in the United States, its discourse-based oppositions based on the viewpoint of activist communities that the white mainstream press is used as a conduit for advancing the legitimation of state practices. The nature of the symbiotic relationship between state and mainstream media—e.g., the latter's use of state officials as sources and how it privileges officials' truths and meanings—no doubt is at the basis of African Americans being "twice as likely as Hispanics, Asians or whites to believe that the [mainstream] media is responsible for worsening race relations . . . [and that] . . . 62% of blacks are angry at least once a week over how the [mainstream] media covers racial issues" (Newkirk 2000, 18).

Essays in the third section focus upon how the black press has positioned itself as oppositional counterpart and counterpoint to the mainstream press. In its enduring oppositional guise, the black press affirms race- and class-based anger and channels its logic of challenge into constructive and nonviolent political action. It collects and disseminates information not otherwise available in the mainstream press and provides a sounding board for diverse opinions that do not otherwise get aired. It offers critical analysis of state institutions and practices not otherwise found in the apologetics of the white press. And in all these ways the black press offers its readers a sense of empowerment within the community. It educates readers with information, opinion and analyses, drawing upon the truths and meanings that emanate not from governmental officialdom but from the black community. At times irksome, at other times painfully incisive, the black press strikes at the heart of a racially divided nation as it calls attention to stubborn and unrelenting ignorance and hypocrisy. Indeed, were it not for the black press, the presence of such apparent mainstays within the political culture might likely go altogether unchallenged. But they are challenged, as the black press diligently puts them to the test of critical scrutiny in public discourse. By so doing, it lays a semantic groundwork for critique of and active engagement with democratic institutions, thereby acting as both vigilant beacon of citizen solidarity and vanguard for change.

Olga Davis' essay, "Vigilance and solidarity in the rhetoric of the black press: *The Tulsa Star*," details the early 20th century ordeals of the *Tulsa Star* and its editor, A.J. Smitherman, who persisted with great "tenacity and determination" in calling upon black Tulsans to resist the frequent lynching and mob violence directed against them. By reporting often otherwise unreported or underreported events that most concerned black communities in Tulsa and beyond, "the *Star* promoted interstate and intrastate coalition-building efforts, informing [Tulsa's] Greenwood community that other black communities, distant in proximity as they might be, experienced similar atrocities and injustices as a part of the black lived- experience, and reported on the political and rhetorical means they employed to resist the systems of domination." The *Star's* reportage, aimed at the core of racial violence and its toleration and support by the state, did not go unnoticed by white elites and state officials. Smitherman's courage of conviction was lambasted in the white press and his outspoken ideas were castigated as criminal. White rage against the *Star* and its readers helped to fuel the Tulsa riot of 1921 during which a heavily armed white mob, joined by the National Guard, inflicted extensive damage to life and property in the previously industrious and thriving Greenwood community, leaving it "decimated and reduced to a blackened landscape of charred rubble and smoldering lumber, dashed hope and broken dreams."

For nearly two centuries the black press has continually recast itself in the struggle against new and recurrent skeins of racism that course through a nation's social and political fabric. During that time, a dark cloud of often state-initiated or state-supported threats of physical and symbolic violence has hovered over African-American communities. Threats of race warfare, xenophobic hostility, ideologies of racial superiority have made it extremely difficult for black voices to find a hearing in public arenas. Michael Huspek's essay, "'From the standpoint of the White Man's world': The mediated struggle between state power and forces of democratization," emphasizes the extent to which contemporary media scholarship has been complicit in the suppression of black voice. Specifically,

Huspek argues that a "majoritarian bias" has encouraged mainstream media scholars to dismiss the importance of the black press. The bias has been multi-pronged: an uncritical acceptance of an ostensive majority voice and an accompanying underestimation of ideologies that rationalize majority-based exclusionary practices as well as the state's indifference to such; and a devaluation of minority voice along with an accompanying failure to grasp its significance as the basis for ideology critique. This bias and the exclusionary practices it promotes has been a serious shortcoming of contemporary media scholarship. Along with black churches, the black press has been significant originator and purveyor of African-American oppositional discourse. Attention to the black press is vital if we are to best understand how oppositional discourse, conveyed through artfully crafted narratives and a raft of stinging rhetorical tropes, provide readers with the discursive means by which to move beyond the monolithic tendencies of mainstream press reportage and commentary. To the extent that contemporary mass media scholarship has dismissed the importance of the black press, so it has sealed itself off as a discipline from consideration of a crucial discursive counterweight to the mainstream press and the ideologies it advances.

Felecia Jones Ross and Sakile Camara's study, "Exposing the hypocrisy of state power: The African-American press and the holocaust," offers illustration of the critical roles played by the *Chicago Defender* and *Pittsburgh Courier* in relation to the state during the 1930's and 40's. Both authors correct a common misconception that black press news coverage and editorial commentary have been limited strictly to domestic issues. In fact, the two black newspapers commented extensively upon Nazi ideology and practice, and did so at a time when both the state and America's mainstream press had expressed relative indifference to the ongoing horrors then taking place on the European continent. Both black newspapers continued commentary after the United States began to openly acknowledge the Nazis' abuses, but the commentary then shifted to the contradiction of the United States adopting a hypercritical stance toward Nazi practices, on the one hand, while maintaining a conspicuous silence on the systematic violence being waged against a race of people within its own national borders, on the other. In this regard, the study shows that the black press may have offered a more critically thoughtful coverage of the Holocaust than that which was offered by the mainstream press. This consisted of open use of a human and civil rights terminology—a recurrent theme of black oppositional discourse—which had found not nearly as much currency in discourses of the state or the venues by which they were expressed in the mainstream press.

All of the essays in this volume recognize that oppositional discourses play a vital role in exposing the limits of discourses of the state and their ideologically disguised aims. Yet treatment of the tensions between state and citizenry raises questions as to how competing discourses might be critically judged. Are there grounds for arguing that oppositional discourses are morally preferable to the state discourses that they oppose? How might such grounds be best defended? How might they inform critical analysis? And what overall value might such analysis have for our understanding of the workings of imperfect democracies in relation to democracy's deliberative ideals? These questions are addressed in the fourth section of this collection with essays by Darryl Gunson and Michael Huspek which draw upon Jurgen Habermas' discourse-based theory of public sphere practices. Gunson's essay does so primarily by means of theoretical discussion; Huspek's by application of Habermas' theory to oppositional discourses in empirical contexts of democratization.

Darryl Gunson's essay, "The philosophical foundations of the discourse society," expounds upon Habermas' theory of discourse ethics and defends it against some of its critics. This entails developing the idea that the contestation of norms in modern societies requires that speakers defer to a minimal set of universal requirements – what Habermas calls the basis of a communicative rationality – such that speakers construct validity claims in accordance with ideals of truth, rightness, sincerity and comprehensibility, but then also must show a willingness to genuinely engage interlocutors' questions, challenges or counterarguments. Much is at stake here. For if Habermas' theory can be established as articulating that which is already "known" and presupposed by all actors – and Gunson suggests it is – then the theory may be accorded a normative standing and used prescriptively to assess the successes or failings of discursive practices on moral grounds. The significance of Gunson's theoretically informed inquiry should not be underestimated; it very well may move us beyond the problematic idea that discourses are best assessed strictly in terms of their effectiveness in gaining or solidifying power.

Huspek's essay, "Habermas and oppositional public spheres: A stereoscopic analysis," treats sympathetically the normative ideals developed by Habermas and further adumbrated by Gunson, but then raises the following question: If we accept Habermas' theory in its entirety, are there ways by which we can unproblematically apply its normative criteria to concrete instances where the state and oppositional groups compete in their advancement of claims that have persuasion of their audiences as a primary aim? Although Habermas has suggested ways by which this question might be addressed, neither he nor Gunson has delivered on this count—an outcome perhaps bound up with what so far has been a theory in need of empirical filling in. Toward that end, Huspek applies Habermas' theory to an empirical site of oppositional discourses of black owned and operated newspapers in the United States, and he finds that the theory appears to be limited in the way it overestimates the communicative options of discourse users where asymmetries of power are in play. Power holders, for example, may think themselves to be acting in a communicatively rational manner, but the discourses they rely upon may disguise systematic violations of rational norms, thus rendering their users unable to recognize many of their own communicative shortcomings in their dealings with others. So, too, those outside of power, especially in their dealings with power holders, may not have access to forms of discourse that measure up to the normative standards explicated in Habermas' theory; or if they do have access, it is not of a kind that elicits recognition and engagement from power holding others. These are significant shortcomings which suggest that the theory needs to be modified if it is to be adequately responsive to users of discourse in asymmetrical power relations.

In a second essay, "The rational bases of transgressive rhetoric," Huspek focuses upon how transgressive rhetoric as deployed in oppositional discourses is frequently turned against its users as part of a larger strategy to exclude them from public sphere arenas of discourse. The rhetoric of the black press, for example, all too often has been dismissed on account of its purported irrationality. Huspek points out that the transgressive rhetoric of oppositional discourses is used in asymmetrical relations where power holders have systematically withheld recognition and engagement from minority actors. Transgressive rhetoric thus becomes a "last resort" in actors' attempts to achieve genuine dialogue, and so is perhaps best viewed not as irrational but, on the contrary, as a quite rational attempt to gain recognition and engagement in contexts where they historically have been denied. Drawing upon some fundamental propositions of speech act theory, Huspek goes on to argue that actors are morally obliged to respond to requests, pleas and appeals even as they are delivered in a transgressive manner—e.g., through the rhetorical tropes of irony, hyperbole, or insult. Acknowledgement of this obligation is necessary if democracies are to best realize their deliberative potentials.

The essays in this collection demonstrate how relations between oppositional discourses and discourses of the state tend to be antagonistic, rooted in uneven distributions of power and its applications. Power in these relations is not unchecked, however. Insofar as it is manifested in and through discursive forms, it must submit to norms that ensure at least, if nothing else, that its communicative modes of expression do not give way to unbridled violence. Of course, this is not to say that the norms of imperfect democracies are entirely satisfactory to all actors. Nor certainly is it to say that we even fully recognize in what respects the norms are unsatisfactory; for the normative shortcomings of democracies, perhaps especially as they pertain to communicative processes, are frequently hidden from participants' view. In this respect, there is considerable agreement among those who research oppositional discourses that they rightfully deserve scholarly attention: Inasmuch as oppositional discourses are inextricably bound up with actors' experiences of disempowerment, they tend to provide a signally important critical impulse for expanded reflection upon the normative limitations of imperfect democracies and the means by which they may be productively overcome.

REFERENCES

Baker, Jr., Houston. 1999. Critical memory and the black public sphere. In *Cultural memory and the construction of identity*, ed. Dan Ben-Amos and Liliane Weissberg, 264–296. Detroit: Wayne State University Press.

Benhabib, Seyla. 1992. Models of public space: Hannah Arendt, the liberal tradition, and Jurgen Habermas. In Habermas and the public sphere, ed. Craig Calhoun, 73–98. Cambridge: MIT press.

Dryzek, John. 1996. Political inclusion and the dynamics of democratization. *American Political Science Review* 90, 1: 475–487.

Gutmann, Amy and Dennis Thompson. 2004. *Why deliberative democracy?* Oxford and Princeton: Princeton University Press.

Newkirk, Pamela. 2000. *Within the veil: Black journalists, white media*. New York: New York University Press.

PART I
The Limits of Imperfect Democracies and How They Are Contested

1 State Ideology and Oppositional Discourses
Conceptual and Methodological Issues
Peter E. Jones and Chik Collins

PRELUDE

In his "Foreword" to the September 2002 document *Iraq's Weapons of Mass Destruction: The Assessment of the British Government*[1], Tony Blair made the following assertions:

> What I believe the assessed intelligence has established beyond doubt is that Saddam has continued to produce chemical and biological weapons, that he continues in his efforts to develop nuclear weapons, and that he has been able to extend the range of his ballistic missile programme . . . I am in no doubt that the threat is serious and current, that he has made progress on WMD and that he has to be stopped . . . And the document discloses that his military planning allows for some of the WMD to be ready within 45 minutes of an order to use them.

We are interested in how you, the reader, would react to this bit of discourse and so we put to you the following questions, to which we give our own answers later:

- What is your opinion of the claims being made here?
- What considerations would you accept as admissible or relevant in coming to an opinion?

We begin by asking these questions because they immediately get our critical faculties to work on the text. It is this process of critical interrogation of communicative acts that we are interested in and wish to explore. It will be our contention that an informed and engaged critical response to political communication is not, and does not involve, a 'discourse analysis' grounded in what Harris (1996) refers to as "segregational linguistics". We will attempt to explain what we think *is* involved in such a critical response, and examine the implications of our position for the study of language and communication more generally.

INTRODUCTION

In what follows we continue to develop our case against the use made of familiar linguistic methods and techniques in the service of political and ideological analysis by proponents of Critical Discourse Analysis (CDA)—and especially in the work of its leading proponent Norman Fairclough.[2] We argue that the linguistic methods used by CDA actually get in the way of understanding the political and ideological significance of discursive practices and processes. On the one hand, there is broad agreement between us and the practitioners of CDA that a critical approach to communicative acts involves a grasp of their distinctive contribution to specific social practices. On the other hand, we argue that the CDA brand of 'discourse analysis' cannot account for this contribution. This is because that contribution does not involve, as proponents of CDA believe, the instantiation or use of an abstract system or systems of verbal forms, but rather the creation of unique communicative resources as an integral dimension of the practices themselves. Consequently, our own argument is that the contribution that people make, or may make, when they communicate, to a particular action can only be grasped through an exploration of the communicative conduct in its actual place, within the unfolding action, and only in terms which are specific and proper to that action at the relevant conjuncture. Communicative acts, then, are inseparable in form and meaning from the distinctive composition and dynamic of the relevant field of action into which they are pitched. Such acts demand for their skilled production and interpretation the kind of knowledge and insight that will usually only be supplied by experienced, well-informed and critically minded participants in the relevant field—or by analysts who are at least prepared to immerse themselves seriously and critically in the task of detailed reconstruction of the relevant actions and events.

Putting it more simply, a political document, for example, is a matter of politics and a matter for political analysis and judgement. To get at its political or ideological significance we must apply our politically attuned eyes and ears to a concrete analysis of the specific political conjuncture to which the document belongs and contributes in some way; 'linguistic' analysis cannot help us with this. More specifically, as we shall try to show, the critical interrogation and interpretation of political discourse involves searching out, piecing together and thinking through a mass of relevant empirical facts. In other words, to understand and critically respond to communicative practices and products, in whatever domain, we need to know the relevant business inside out.

In everyday life, of course, we do not dispute this principle. We call on the lawyer and not the discourse analyst to find the catch in the fine print, or on the engineer, rather than the linguist, to find the flaws in a blueprint. But it seems as if this principle has been ignored or set aside in CDA in favour of a view in which detailed historical, theoretical and practical knowledge of the relevant spheres is deemed unnecessary to understanding political and ideological aspects of discourse.

CRITICAL DISCOURSE ANALYSIS

Although there have been a number of attempts to ground a would-be critical social theory on premises and methods borrowed from linguistics[3], it is Norman Fairclough's version of CDA (e.g., 1989/2001a, 1992, 1995, 2000, 2001b, 2003) which, in our view, raises most pointedly the issue of the relevance of linguistics to political and ideological critique. While the horizons of van Dijk's (1993) CDA, for example, are limited to commentary on what he calls "elite discourse", Fairclough argues that discourse analysis can serve as "a method for studying social change" (1992, 1). This argument is underpinned by far-reaching claims about the novelty of the processes and trends of social change in "late modernity" (Chouliaraki and Fairclough 1999). Fairclough argues that there have been "important shifts in the function of language in social life" whereby discourse has become "perhaps the primary medium of social control and power". Furthermore, he insists that "the relationship between discourse and social structures is dialectical" in the sense that "as well as being determined by social structures, discourse has effects upon social structures and contributes to the achievement of social continuity or social change" (1989, 3, 37). Fairclough has also acknowledged the centrality of class interests and struggle in social change and has paid homage to Marx's contribution (Fairclough and Graham 2002). For these reasons Fairclough's CDA is of theoretical interest to us and our ongoing attempts to settle accounts with it are perhaps also something of a backhanded compliment to its theoretical sophistication, as well as, and perhaps more importantly, to its influence within the field.

Jones (2004) examines the key historical, political and economic arguments advanced by Fairclough in support of his claims about the role of discourse. Jones's verdict is that the arguments were based either on misconceptions about the workings of particular economic and political processes within capitalist states or on a one-sided or oversimplified general conception of the relations between social being and social consciousness. His conclusion is that "the CDA approach to language involves a mystification of the role of discourse in society. CDA itself, therefore, constitutes an ideological formation" (2004, 119). These issues aside, the justification for applying linguistic procedures to political discourse in the first place can only be that such procedures provide novel and distinctive insights that are essential to our appreciation of the political and ideological workings of the discourse in question. However, Jones argues that Fairclough's (2000) analysis of the discourse of Tony Blair's 'New Labour' in fact amounted to little more than a political commentary on Labour politics and policies from a rather timid reformist perspective. So-called critical discourse analysis, in other words, was just a novel way of expressing particular political opinions. On this basis, it would appear that the distinctive contribution of this kind of discourse analysis is not to be found in any genuine discoveries or insights it makes or offers about political communication but, rather, in allowing particular political interpretations and conclusions to be presented as if grounded in established knowledge and procedures in linguistics, and as "a method in social scientific research" (Fairclough 2001b), rather than as reflecting and expressing particular political predilections and allegiances.[4]

In what follows we build on these arguments in a critical examination of the CDA approach to ideology. However, we will certainly not be able to do justice here to all the ins-and-outs of this difficult problem. Our focus will be on the question of whether a consciously critical, politically engaged response to communicative practices and their ideological implications is achievable by discourse analysis in the CDA sense.

CDA AND IDEOLOGY

CDA justifies itself, as did its Critical Linguistics (CL) forerunner (Fowler et al. 1979; Hodge and Kress 1979), by claiming to offer insights into the workings of ideology. The focus on ideology is justified by its importance among the mechanisms of power and social control in "late capitalism" (Chouliaraki and Fairclough 1999). Thus, for Fairclough, "the exercise of power, in modern society, is increasingly achieved through ideology" (1989, 2).

Proponents of CDA, like those of CL, take the further step of claiming that linguistic or discursive structures themselves convey the ideological punch. As Fairclough puts it, the exercise of power is achieved "more particularly through the ideological workings of language . . . [which] has become perhaps the primary medium of social control and power" (1989, 2–3). Trew, for example, argued that language structures "are the material existence of ideology" and that his customised version of Transformational Grammar could be used "as a means of revealing ideological processes in the production of discourse" (1979, 116). Fowler and Kress offered a "checklist of linguistic features which have frequently proved revealing in the kind of critical linguistics" they had been doing (1979, 198). And Fairclough, too, has adopted this "checklist" approach in his CDA. The checklist is put together using a "framework for linguistic analysis" of lexical and grammatical properties of sentences and texts which "is based . . . on systemic functional linguistics" (2001b, 126, 130–1). Chouliaraki and Fairclough see ideologies as "discursive constructions" and so argue that issues of "power and ideology" are "best treated in terms of relations between the discourse moments of different practices and different orders of discourse", that is, in terms of relations of identity and similarity in the form and meaning of words, phrases and other constructions between different texts (Chouliaraki and Fairclough 1999, 26, 63).[5] In this spirit, Fairclough presents his discussion of 'New Labour' politics as "a book about politics and government that approaches them through language, *as language*" (2000, 5, our emphasis).

There is no space here for a thorough examination of the view of ideology as the main or most potent force in the production and maintenance of exploitation today, a view that has gained wide currency in academic circles for reasons explored insightfully by Thompson (1978) and Anderson (1976, 1983) among others.[6] To cut a long story short, this view, as Jones (2004) has argued, is simply false. We say this, however, not to dismiss the role of ideology in social processes, but to emphasise the need to get things in proportion and see them in their proper place. As an aspect of the relatively peaceable exercise of class rule, ideological domination or hegemony generally relies on the possibility of applying force as a last resort (or as a first resort in the case of 'rogue' or excluded communities, or far away peoples or states whose lives and opinions do not matter). Furthermore, rule by 'consent' is always a partial, precarious and fragile state of affairs, since the maintenance of the very specific social conditions which it presupposes is ultimately outside the control of the ideologists. For that reason, the extent to which ideological means of dominance and control will be effective in deflecting, disarming or containing resistance and opposition in particular circumstances is always an open question, however much mainstream political debate and media production are dominated by propaganda in favour of those who rule. By the same token, it is unwise to judge the degree of ideological 'incorporation' of oppressed and exploited individuals and groups merely on the basis of their everyday compliance, communicational conduct included, with the status quo, since what people say and think in such circumstances is not the best indication of how they will act in changed circumstances nor, indeed, is it always at one with their actual practice. That is why the consciousness of working people, their degree of radicalisation, and their preparedness for political change can ultimately only be judged in the course of events.

The problems with the 'dominant ideology' position are, however, compounded and amplified when ideology is seen in the image of a linguistic system as modelled in a structuralist, "constructivist-structuralist" (Chouliaraki and Fairclough 1999)[7] or "systemic functional" (Fairclough 2001b) fashion. The problems we have in mind are expressed very clearly in the account by Bennett (2003) of what structuralist linguistics has to offer:

> The "objects" of which language speaks are not "real objects", external to language, but "conceptual objects" located entirely within language. The word "ox", according to Saussure's famous example, signifies not a real ox but the concept of an ox.

Bennett elaborates:

This is not to deny that there exists a real world external to the signifying mantle which language casts upon it. But it is to maintain that our knowledge or appropriation of that world is always mediated through and influenced by the organizing structure which language inevitably places between it and ourselves (Bennett 2003, 4–5).

Here we see that the reward we get for adopting this linguistic view of meaning is the opportunity to surrender our faculties for thought and communication to an "organizing structure" placed as an opaque barrier between us and the world by language. Bennett never asks how or why language gets to do this, or how this organizing system might help or hinder us in our actual practical dealings with the world, a world which includes the real ox as well as our relations with it. In any case, the premises of this linguistic approach make the question irrelevant or unanswerable; in life, our immediate connections are not with the world but with language: "reality is always discursively mediated—*we have no access to reality except through discourses*" (Chouliaraki and Fairclough 1999, 136, our emphasis).[8] Thus, whatever our practical dealings and experiences may seem to tell us, the language system is responsible for the way we talk about and conceptualise things. If actual communicative acts are always only expressions of, uses of or instances of, elements within the pre-existing abstract system, then that makes it impossible for communicative or cognitive actions to go beyond the semiotic, and, therefore, ideological limits of the "organizing structure" already in place.

Now, the failings of Saussurean linguistic structuralism have long been known. But these failings are not confined to the idea (obviously false) that all members of the community use the same semiotic system and, consequently, cannot be addressed by allowing "organising structures"—whether we call them 'languages', 'codes', 'lects', 'genres' or 'discourse types'—to proliferate along socio-economic, cultural or occupational lines, since this proliferation merely reproduces the inherent problems of "abstract objectivism" (Vološinov 1973) in ever decreasing circles.

In our view, the main problem with the whole approach is a matter of the fatal damage visited upon rational thinking and action when the connections between ideas and life experience are broken, when the processes of critical thinking and intellectual engagement with real life problems are replaced by the play of words and word meanings within a verbal system abstracted from communicative practice. Hereon it becomes impossible—without being accused of being a hopeless dupe of empiricist ideology—to talk any more about understanding or having an insight into something, or getting to the bottom of things, or, heaven forbid, getting to the truth of the matter.

Accordingly, those who are prepared to view the ideological realm in these linguistic terms have to disconnect ideology from questions of truth and falsity. As Fairclough rightly concedes, "discourse analysis cannot *per se* judge the truth or well-groundedness of a proposition", although it can, apparently, detect ideology provided that we adopt what Fairclough calls the "pejorative view" of it, which he explains as follows:

> In claiming that a discursive event works ideologically, one is not in the first instance claiming that it is false, or claiming a privileged position from which judgements of truth or falsity can be made. One is claiming that it contributes to the reproduction of relations of power (1995, 18).

But this sidestep only appears to get round the problem – since it begs the question of how we can tell if a discursive event "contributes to the reproduction of relations of power" or not. This, we would argue, is the fatal flaw at the heart of CDA. We submit that it is actually impossible to judge the ideological flavour or implications of communicative acts independently of a consideration of the empirical facts of the relevant matter. And this for the simple reason that relations of power, while certainly having to do with attitudes of compliance or resistance as well as beliefs and moral values, are not figments of the imagination or figures of speech but real, factual relations between actual people which rest on and are inextricably entangled with such social realities as the ownership of property, wealth, rate and intensity of exploitation, rights and privileges under the law, institutional authority, political organisation, and so on. How particular communicative practices may impact on or influence such practical social realities is itself, therefore, a matter for factual investigation of the relevant chains of action within which these communicative practices have their place and to which they are connected.

Let us attempt to justify our position by returning to the questions we posed to the reader about the Blair extract:

- What is your opinion of these claims?
- What considerations would you accept as admissible or relevant in coming to an opinion?

For our own part, we would start by addressing the second question. Our first consideration might be the veracity of the claims. In the case of this particular document the claims made are substantially false. It is not just that they turned out to be false when events subsequent to the US-UK invasion and occupation of Iraq conclusively demonstrated the complete absence of "WMD" to even the most fervent believers, but that informed observers knew at the time that the claims were false or grossly exaggerated; the political and military establishment knew that there was no "serious and current" threat. We would also note that the credibility of this document, and of Blair and his case for war on Iraq, suffered a serious blow with the subsequent publication of what quickly became known as the "dodgy dossier", namely a document with the gloriously understated title *Iraq—its infrastructure of concealment, deception and intimidation*.[9] As Channel

4 News immediately revealed on its website, "large chunks" of the dossier "had been lifted word for word", without acknowledgement, from a PhD thesis by Ibrahim al-Marashi. Close textual comparison of the dossier with the plagiarised thesis shows that certain passages had been deliberately altered to beef up the case for war. For example, the original wording "aiding opposition groups in hostile regimes" turned into "supporting terrorist organisations in hostile regimes". Once this plagiaristic tampering had been exposed, close examination of the actual claims made in the dossier became rather pointless since it was clear that its authors simply did not care whether the material was factually accurate.

A second consideration might be the immediate political context into which the document was pitched. Of particular relevance would be the mood within the general public, some sections of the media and a growing band of Labour Members of Parliament, of increasing disquiet about, and outright opposition to, the prospect of an invasion of Iraq. Indeed, the "dodgy dossier" was released on the day of a crucial parliamentary debate on the war, giving no time for sceptical Labour MPs to check it through before the debate.

Furthermore, all these considerations would have to be re-evaluated in the broader context of the Iraq war itself—the reasons for the war, the conduct of the war and its aftermath—and in the context of a thorough investigation of what the whole episode has to tell us about the political landscape in Britain in general, and about the evolution of the Labour Party and the future of labour movement politics in particular.

With these issues in mind, then, our own opinion of the document is that it was a piece of crude, shoddy, and mendacious propaganda whose immediate aim was to influence—through the party apparatus and the media—the crucial debates and votes in the UK Parliament in order to stave off what the government saw as a major political catastrophe over the war, and to continue to deliver the necessary political and constitutional authority to the (long) planned imperialist war of conquest of Iraq. The hysterical clamour about "WMD" provided a pretext but not the reason for the war. The document itself, the fruit of an unprecedented level of political collaboration between Blair's ruling circle and the secret service bosses, was a novel indication of the further degeneration of British social democracy. It demonstrated the complete political putrefaction of the higher echelons of the Labour Party, and as such, should have given a clear signal to the labour movement in Britain (and the world)—if indeed it were still needed—that 'New Labour' was not their ally in the pursuit of social advancement, but their enemy, and that the process of political renewal would have to be pursued in earnest.

Now, this is, certainly, an analysis of the document, and one in which we focus our attention very closely on *the language*, but it is not 'discourse analysis' in the usual linguistic sense. When we ask ourselves the kind of questions that we posed to the reader above—and these are, by the way, the kind of questions that people usually ask themselves about what politicians say—we immediately adopt an attitude towards the language of the text which is at odds with the approach taken by CDA. In asking and trying to answer these questions we engage in a process of enquiry which does not work at all in terms of the constructs of orthodox linguistic theory. We are not trying to identify, classify and trace the words and phrases of the document in terms of their lexical, grammatical or generic relations to other words and phrases in the same or other documents; constructs of this kind are simply not the stuff of critical interrogation and evaluation. And this is because, when we are reading the words of this document, we are *engaging with its author over some matter; we are evaluating and responding to the author's position both with regard to the relevant facts of the matter and towards us as participants in the action*. And this process of engaged critical enquiry and response with respect to a particular matter, a process basic to all communication, is something that the linguistic procedures on which discourse analysis rests have signally failed to deal with.

Our position, then, is that the political significance and ideological orientation of the document in political terms cannot be established by looking for "relations between the discourse moments of different practices and different orders of discourse" (Chouliaraki and Fairclough 1999, 63), but is something that emerges as we work out how the document is contributing to political events at a particular conjuncture and, in so doing, penetrate ever more deeply to the heart of the relevant problem.[10] Without reconstructing the whole field of political practice in which the document is placed, we have no chance of a realistic and accurate political and ideological evaluation of it. The ability to make such an evaluation, therefore, depends on what and how much we know and understand about the factual events and circumstances making up particular political conjunctures.

At the same time, such an analysis presupposes the requisite theoretical understanding of the relevant phenomena—surplus value, the capital-labour relationship, the capitalist state and, not least, social democracy in Britain—but exactly how the bodies of theory we may draw on relate to newly unfolding events or conjunctures is an open question which requires difficult intellectual work in the course of which the theories themselves may be revised or modified.[11] In sum, our interpretation of the document is political; it is the result of informed political analysis and it stands or falls by the cogency and coherence (or otherwise) of its overall interpretation of the role and contribution of this particular piece of communication within the political processes to which it belongs.

Consequently, when it comes to trying to interpret a novel piece of communication in the political sphere there is no guarantee either that we will have all the relevant facts at our disposal or, even if do, that we will know straightaway what to make of it and, still less, how to respond. Generally speaking, acts of communication do not nail their political or ideological colours to the mast, as we know from the history of debates, splits and conflicts within

20th century revolutionary movements or, indeed, from the history of the British Labour Party. Even the examples of Blair's "WMD" assessment or the 'dodgy dossier' show in a rather straightforward way that a concrete analysis of a political communication involves preliminary investigation and detective work in order to establish what the relevant facts are in the first place.[12]

Because ideology, then, is in fact a dimension or aspect of practice, it cannot be apprehended, identified, evaluated or responded to as a communicative phenomenon other than through an informed critical interrogation of that practice as a whole in its relevant empirical circumstances and conditions, its factual implications and consequences. Our general conclusion, then, is that the premise of CDA, namely that one can identify ideology in discourse independently of discovery and consideration of the facts of the matter (and, therefore, of the veracity of claims and proposals) is false; the "pejorative view" of ideology is simply incoherent.

Let us illustrate the point with an example of the CDA approach in action.

CDA AND IDEOLOGY IN "REPRESENTATIONS OF GLOBAL ECONOMY"

In Fairclough's (2001b) discussion of a text attributed to Tony Blair in which "dominant", i.e., neo-liberal, "representations of change in the 'global economy'" are being presented, Fairclough focuses on "one social problem manifested in the text" which is that:

> Feasible alternative ways of organizing international economic relations which might not have the detrimental effects of the current way (for instance, in increasing the gap between rich and poor within and between states) are excluded from the political agenda by these representations (2001b, 127 & 129).[13]

Fairclough is interested in "linguistic features of the text in its representation of economic change" on the grounds that "dominant representations of 'the new global order' have certain predictable linguistic characteristics". One such is that "processes in the new economy are represented without responsible social agents" (2001b, 131). His point is that if global economic change just "happens", rather than being brought about as a result of particular decisions and actions, then there is nothing that can be done about it: there are no alternatives and resistance is futile. This is the ideological significance that Fairclough claims can be carried by particular linguistic features and which he claims to find in passages like the following: "The modern world is swept by change. New technologies emerge constantly; new markets are opening up. There are new competitors but also great new opportunities". Fairclough makes the following observations:

Agents of material processes are abstract or inanimate. . . . "change" is the agent in the first (passive) sentence, and "new technologies" and "new markets" are agents in the second—agents, notice, of intransitive processes ("emerge", "open up") which represent change as happenings, processes without agents. The third sentence is existential—"new competitors" and "new opportunities" are merely claimed to exist, not located within processes of change (2001b, 131).

The procedure of CDA, then amounts to making claims about correspondences between aspects of sentence structure (described using Hallidayan systemic functional grammar) and the alleged ideological orientation of the relevant text. The whole procedure, in other words, is based on the premise that we can draw reliable conclusions about how particular events or processes are conceptualised from a linguistic description of the sentence.

But this premise is decidedly fragile, to say the least. For one thing, it simply does not follow that Blair, whatever else he may be guilty of, is representing "agents of material processes" as "abstract or inanimate" by writing a sentence like "the modern world is swept by change". Nor is it necessarily the case that "new competitors" in the second sentence are "merely claimed to exist, not located within processes of change". Suppose someone says, 'the entrance to the stadium was blocked by traffic', are they representing traffic as a phenomenon without an origin or source in the driving activities of particular people? Or if somebody suddenly says, 'there is a goat in the garden', are they claiming that the goat 'merely exists' and has not trotted in from anywhere? And what if Blair had followed the above pair of sentences with a further sentence that actually spelled out who was responsible for the changes in question, such as: 'All these changes are the fruits of the drive, enterprise and determination of millions of people around the world'?

We are not suggesting that Fairclough is wrong in attributing neo-liberal ideology to Blair or that he is necessarily wrong about his interpretation of these sentences. But we are suggesting that his interpretation is informed rather more by what he knows about Blair's politics than by 'grammar'. The difficulty that Fairclough has got himself into with this kind of 'analysis' is only too clear, in fact, from his own writing, as Jones (2007) demonstrates. Below, for example, are three passages from Chouliaraki and Fairclough showing how the authors themselves "represent" the social changes of "late modernity":

(a). "The past two decades or so have been a period of profound economic and social transformation on a global scale. Economically, there has been a relative shift from 'Fordist' mass production and consumption of goods to 'flexible accumulation'".
(b) "Advances in information technology, mainly communications media, underlie both economic and cultural transformations, opening up new forms of experience and knowledge and new possibilities of relationships with faraway others via television or the internet".

(c) "These social changes create new possibilities and opportunities for many people" (1999, 3).

The reader will note that the sentences display the "predictable linguistic characteristics" of neo-liberal ideology. In (a) economic and social changes are presented as "happenings, processes without agents". As Jones (2007) observes, in (b) the "advances in information technology" referred to are "agent-less" and these agent-less processes are themselves the "agent" of "opening up". In (c) it is the impersonal and agent-less "social changes" which are the "agent" responsible for "creating" possibilities and opportunities.

The most charitable interpretation of this episode is that CDA's "checklists of linguistic features which tend to be particularly worth attending to in critical analysis" and which are offered to those "who are not specialists in linguistics" (Fairclough 2001b, 126), are a most unreliable tool for ideological critique. But we are inclined to the more general conclusion that the formal constructs of grammatical description are altogether unsuitable vehicles for the difficult intellectual labour of meaningful political critique. As we have attempted to demonstrate elsewhere, through an analysis of a document claiming to offer a 'socialist' housing policy for the city of Glasgow in the mid-1980s (Collins and Jones 2006), from the point of view of linguistic analysis, what appear to be the same or similar words or phrases in different texts, or even in the same text, may not be the same thing at all from the point of view of the informed reader.[14] The process of understanding what the words are and what meaning they have involves making a *decision* about a particular bit of communicative *behaviour on someone's part.*[15] And, as we must do for any bit of behaviour, we interpret it in the light of what we know or can find out about all the relevant facts and circumstances, including, of course, what has been said and done before on that subject by this person or others.

If 'discourse analysis' of this kind is a rather peculiar way of arriving at a political evaluation of a text, it is also a method which has serious implications for the theorizing of the social process as a whole. The tendency in CDA is simply to conflate the processes of *thinking* with the *properties of verbal forms and meanings* as identified by orthodox linguistic description, and to equate *the critical interrogation of communicative acts* with a *linguistically based 'discourse analysis'*. This, unfortunately, distorts the real processes of social and political action. Rendering the living properties of communicative practices down into the stable and repeatable forms and figures, detectable on the linguistic radar, introduces a "fictional stasis" (Thompson 1978, 262) into the dialectically developing system of transitions between thinking, communication and action. And since, as a purely linguistic methodology, it cannot provide a concrete picture of the actual role of communication in social changes, it must, then, posit an imaginary picture in which the social changes taking place today are "constituted to a significant extent by changes in language practices" (Fairclough 1992, 6; see Jones, 2004 for a more detailed discussion).

OUR OBJECTIONS TO CDA

The arguments we have presented lead us to the simple conclusion that there is no such thing as 'Critical Discourse Analysis' because discourse in the linguistic and, therefore, CDA sense does not actually exist. While there can be no objection to using such general notions as 'communication', 'discourse', 'language', or 'genre' to refer to and talk about particular communicative phenomena, we reject the CDA *understanding and treatment of these phenomena*. Our position, in contrast with the practice of CDA, is that the identification of the communicational processes and strategies relevant to particular engagements, the understanding and interpretation of what the relevant or significant communicational forms, meanings and patterns are in a particular situation or event is something that emerges in the course of detailed empirical investigation of the relevant event in all its complexity. There is simply no method or procedure of discourse analysis to be applied short of this process of deciding what words mean in the course of interpretatively reconstructing an entire action or event to which the words contribute. Within the event itself there is no level or dimension of 'discourse' as a self-contained, stable and iterable system of forms and meanings.

From that point of view, lay parlance is more accurate than the terminology of discourse analysis. In everyday life we do not write, speak, see or hear 'discourse'. Rather, we engage with and react to a particular political speech, and to the proposals and arguments made in that speech, a bus timetable, a memo from our superiors, an advertising campaign, an unsightly piece of graffiti, a racist comment, a proposed change to our contract of employment, a confidential report, a theoretical account of communication processes, a set of instructions for using a DVD player, a statistical table, a bit of friendly banter, and so on. Communicative practices and their products are identified and handled according to their factual linkage or *integration* (Harris 1996) within particular types of on-going activity. This does not mean that when we come to interpret these practices and products we do so without any expectations or preconceptions at all to do with what might be communicated or how. It is just that our judgements about what is being said and meant in context, and, in particular, our decisions about what to count as 'the same thing' in different communicative encounters, are not made in accordance with orthodox linguistic methodology, in which the 'tokens' of particular communicative acts are assigned to 'types' in the 'system' or 'code' (cf Hutton 1990), but on the basis of what we take to be actually going on in the situation and what role the communicative conduct of those we are engaging with might be playing.[16] Vološinov puts it well:

> The basic task of understanding does not at all amount to recognizing the linguistic form used by the speaker as the familiar, 'that very same', form ... No, the task of understanding does not basically amount to

recognizing the form used, but rather to understanding it in a particular, concrete context, to understanding its meaning in a particular utterance, i.e., it amounts to understanding its novelty and not to recognizing its identity (1973, 68).

The lexicographer, the linguist, the stylistician or language teacher have terms to describe functionally different 'styles', 'registers', 'genres', 'speech genres' and so on, and these classificatory notions have their practical and descriptive value.[17] But the tasks and problems which face communicators in everyday life have a logic to them which subverts any systematising tendencies which might be implied by an overly formalistic application of such descriptive classifications. While it does not take much communicative gumption to tell the difference between a legal contract and the instruction manual for a DVD player, whether we should sign up to the contract or how we get the DVD player to do what it says in the manual are communicative tasks of a quite different order, to do with the practical integration of particular communicative practices into our lives and on-going activity, tasks which require us to relate to and evaluate the texts from this practical point of view.

Everyday communicative activity, then, involves exactly the kinds of thing that linguists usually regard as the business of other professionals or disciplines, such as telling the difference between a fair and an unfair legal contract, between a clear and a completely hopeless set of instructions, between a true statement and a false one, between a profound and a simplistic argument, between a viable plan and an unrealistic one, a beautiful or banal account, an inspiring or boring appeal, a betrayal and a loyal commitment to the cause, a reliable or unreliable bus timetable. And, as we have shown elsewhere, we need much more than the techniques of 'linguistic analysis' to tell the difference between a 'socialist' strategy for public housing and a reactionary one (Collins and Jones 2006), a sincere or manipulative attempt to secure local community participation in urban 'regeneration' (Collins 2008), or a well-intentioned or malign government appeal for 'co-operation' and 'negotiation' with a workforce over the future of their industry (Collins 2000). Even such a basic, but communicationally essential, fact as whether a bus timetable is current or out of date would not usually, as we know, be considered a linguistic or discursive fact, since it involves the practices of establishing and constantly re-establishing a factual link between the document and the world. As Harris puts it:

> Even the use of ordinary grading words, like *heavy, good, unusual*, typically involves a simultaneous assessment of facts and terminological appropriateness, correlated in such a way that when doubts arise it often makes little sense to ask whether they are factual doubts or linguistic doubts. They may in one sense be a mixture of both, but not necessarily a mixture that could even in principle be sorted out into two separate components (1981, 180–181).

This is not to deny that the drafting and interpreting of the terms and conditions of a legal contract or treaty, for example, require special knowledge and expertise, and the more the better, in handling legal discourse, in understanding legal terms and concepts and the system of law to which these belong. But it is to emphasize that such communicative expertise in the handling of the language is acquired and exercised only through a simultaneous apprehension of the whole legal system and framework, in theoretical and institutional terms, along with the factual basis on which legal judgements are made, to which legal distinctions relate, and the specific implications of such judgements for particular cases.[18] As the storm over the designation of individuals captured during the US invasions of Afghanistan as "enemy combatants" by the US government shows, the application of the law and the appropriateness or otherwise of legal terms is a matter not only of interpretation and decision in relation to the relevant factual details but also, of course, political expediency.

The process in which we come to such judgements and decisions about the meaning, value and implications of communicative phenomena on the basis of the situated links between communicative and other practices is not something extraneous to language and communication but is the very heart and soul, the be-all and end-all, of communicative behaviour. This process, when examined carefully, teaches us that when we approach particular communicative acts we should reject any assumptions, based on the abstract procedures of linguistic analysis, about what the communicationally significant properties of such acts will be. All the myriad practices of actual, historical individuals present circumstantially unique meaning-making activities which are adapted and integrated into the overall course of these practices. How communication takes place in these circumstances, what is being communicated and what the relationship is between the communication processes taking place within different practices and different circumstances are all, then, open questions to be decided by informed, concrete examination and analysis of the relevant practices and circumstances themselves.[19]

COMMUNICATIONAL IMPLICATIONS: "INTEGRATION" OR "SEGREGATION"?

We hope it is clear that our objection to CDA is not an objection to the study of language, nor, more to the point, to the close study and analysis of discourse. On the contrary, we accept that the study of communicational processes and practices is, and always has been, an integral and necessary part of any attempt to understand and critically respond to what is going on in the world. Communicative practices can be as decisive in their contribution to the success or failure of a project and, by the same token, as objectionable on ethical or political grounds as any other aspect of conduct.

Our objection, rather, is an objection to the conception of language and discourse on which CDA is founded; it is an objection to the turn to a certain school of thought in contemporary linguistics for weapons of political and social critique. It is also, most emphatically, an objection to what this procedure entails, namely an effort to take the communicative dimensions of the living processes of social action, conflict and change and reduce them down to the meagre and abstract fodder of linguistic analysis.

To be more exact, we have in our sights those linguistic approaches which Harris (1996) calls "segregational". The essence of segregationalism lies in its initial assumption that a clear, generally valid line of demarcation can be drawn between linguistic and non-linguistic phenomena and in the consequent attempt to identify and systematise a realm of properly and purely linguistic structures and meanings independently of the actual situated practices of communicative interchange in their empirical complexity. The result is a conception of linguistic communication as a process which presupposes and expresses an already established and more or less self-contained, more or less stable, intersubjectively shared and recognisable 'code' or system of form-meaning correlations (or 'signs'), a conception which Harris (1981) dubs the "language myth".

As Harris (1980) argues, the segregational conception is based not so much on a careful exploration of situated communicative practices as on the theoretical glorification and elaboration of a preconception about communication – and one, moreover, which already embodies a certain view of social relations and processes. Saussure's linguistic theory, for example, in "its quasi-mystic appeal to the absolute sovereignty of the community, its deliberate subordination of the linguistic role of the individual, and its presentation of *la langue* as a kind of psychological manifestation of collective uniformity" offers us "a theory of languages which explicitly mirrored the ideally integrated, stable community which the nation-state would have liked to be" (Harris 1980, 157). In other words, the "language myth" which is at the heart of orthodox linguistic theory—including the Hallidayan "systemic functional" approach on which CDA so relies—has its roots in a particular ideological conception, which now comes back to haunt us in the guise of the "structuralist-constructivist" view of discourse.

We do not wish to deny the practical usefulness, within certain limits, of methods and insights from "segregational" linguistics. But to take the assumptions and results of such practices as a general model or theory of communication is to put ourselves at some distance from the sources, springs and dynamic of communicative activity. In particular, the segregational approach forces the analyst to foreclose on the novelty of actual, conscious communicative behaviour by forcing what is being said and done *now* into categories derived from a certain way of looking at what was said and done *previously*.[20]

The only alternative to the segregational account of language is, as Harris argues, an "integrational" one whose main principles are as follows:

First and foremost, an integrational linguistics must recognise that human beings inhabit a communicational space which is not neatly compartmentalised into language and non-language ... It renounces in advance the possibility of setting up systems of forms and meanings which will "account for" a central core of linguistic behaviour irrespective of the situational and communicational purposes involved (1981, 165).

The point of departure for such an integrational approach to communication is not, then, the mythical 'linguistic system' in the shape of a 'code', a 'language', a 'discourse type' or 'genre', but rather "the individual linguistic act in its communicational setting".[21] It is not 'the language' or 'linguistic system' which determines the possibilities of linguistic expression on the part of the communicators, rather:

language is continuously created by the interaction of individuals in specific communicational situations. It is this interaction which confers relevance upon the participants' past experience with words, and not, as orthodox linguistics would have us believe, past experience (that is to say, mastery of "the language") which determines the communicational possibilities of their present interaction (1981, 166).

Of course, there exists "a fund of past linguistic experience" on which participants may, or must, draw, but "from an integrational perspective" the key thing is not this fund as such but "the individual's adaptive use of it to meet the communicational requirements of the present", a use which "is—and can only be—manifest in the communication situation itself" (1981, 86, 187).

This integrationist's focus on "the individual linguistic act in its communicational setting" is not, however, an empiricist's paradise; it does not at all negate the social character of communicative acts, but it makes us think about their sociality in different terms. To start with, it makes us look for and try to understand communication there where it is actually taking place, where individuals are not social ciphers, sociological variables or "mere figureheads" (Harris 1996, 62) whose utterances display and combine elements of the 'code' or 'discourse type', but are real historical individuals going about some business. It makes us realise that communication is conscious human conduct taking place in definite circumstances for which the participants are responsible and, in varying degrees, accountable. It also makes us realise that making sense of the communicative conduct of a particular individual involves nothing less than trying to figure out 'what they are up to', what the real and potential impact of their conduct on us and others might be, and what their motives and purposes are in relation to whatever is at stake in the business at hand. And, after all, it is only when we look at things this way that we are able to pass judgement on what they say, sometimes hastily, sometimes carefully, but always fallibly, as 'stupid', 'irrelevant', 'truthful', 'insulting', 'banal' or 'inspiring', etc. The theoretical elucidation of communication seen from this perspective is not about boiling particular utterances, texts and documents down to some mythical residue of stable and constantly reproducible forms and meanings, but about finding and understanding the distinctive contribution that the relevant parties make by their situated communicative conduct to a developing sphere of activity or engagement. This means finding ways to discover the relevant factual relations—the interconnections, transitions and contradictions—between the communicative conduct of the communicators and everything else that is going on in the developing and changing "integrated continuum" of practices "which is itself the sole source of signification" (Harris 1996, 164). If, therefore, the identification and interpretation of communicatively significant behaviour is dependent on factual questions about the people communicating, 'what they are up to', and what they believe, then we cannot draw a principled, generally valid dividing between linguistic form and meaning on the one hand and context on the other. In that case the theoretical rationale for segregational linguistics, with its systems of codes and rules, disappears. And from that point of view it is simply a mistake to think that we can do justice to the sociality of communicative processes and practices—including their role in "the reproduction of relations of power" (Fairclough) more specifically—by reducing them to the elements of an already given 'code'.

It might be objected that modern linguistic theory has shown itself more than willing to take into account the role of what is referred to as 'context' as a factor in communication. However, more often than not, context and language are seen as two separately identifiable spheres which then 'interact' in some way so that the 'code' is more or less determinable in isolation and is then put to use in context.[22] "What these models need to safeguard at all costs", as Harris puts it, "is the proposition that the same sign can appear in indefinitely many different contexts without losing its identity" (1996, 156). The integrational position, by contrast, is that "there is no sign without a context, and contexts are not given in advance. Signs, in short, are not waiting to be 'used': they are created in and by the act of communication" (Harris 1996, 6).

CONCLUSION

We have argued that there are flaws in CDA's conception of discourse and its social role which result from adopting the abstract and one-sided account of linguistic communication offered by "segregational" linguistics and, in particular, the Hallidayan "systemic functional" paradigm. But our quarrel with Fairclough and CDA over what discourse is and how to give an account of it has implications beyond the realm of linguistic description and methodology. While Harris has clearly brought out the negative influence of segregational assumptions on the development of linguistic science, we have been concerned here with the damage these assumptions cause to our understanding of social action and the possibilities for social change when they are converted into a way of tackling ideology. If communicative processes are a dialectically integrated and differentiated dimension of social practice as a whole, then adopting a segregational approach to discourse necessarily entails a view of the dynamic of the social process which is distorted beyond recognition by the need to make that process fit with the properties of 'discourse' as that approach sees them. The CDA position that language is "perhaps the primary medium of social control and power" (Fairclough 1989, 3) is more a reading back of its own ideological orientation, imported from linguistics, into the social process than the result of careful exploration of communicative processes in today's world.

In one sense, CDA damns itself in two ways: firstly, by the abyss between its conception of language and power and the violent reality of the exercise of power in the world today, and, secondly, by its manifest irrelevance to the actual practices of political criticism and oppositional action which spring up, irrepressible, in every corner of that world. The devastating critiques of the political process, of corporate power, of military action, and of the workings of ideology to be found in a Chomsky, Pilger, Monbiot, Klein, Said, or even a Michael Moore, to mention only those writers who have some success in the mainstream, owe nothing to the methods of CDA. Here there is no "linguistic analysis", nor any preconception about the "constitutive role of discourse". Instead, there is a passionately engaged process of discovery and exposure of the workings of power based on diligent exploration and informed piecing together and analysis of the facts and circumstances, making sense of the significance and distinctive contributions of documents, speeches and other records of communicative practices in the light of their emerging insights into the sequence, causes, logic and meaning of a series of events. Here there is no 'discourse analysis' in the CDA sense but there is plenty of careful, informed and critical examination of the communicative activities and conduct of those whose job it is to "manufacture consent" or to organise a war in secret. There is more to be learnt from their work about the ideological role of communicative practices, as well as about the practices of opposition, critique and resistance, than in all the works of the CDA tradition.

And yet, as academics, we cannot afford to ignore the role of the 'linguistic turn' in influencing, to one degree or another, the intellectual climate and research culture within the academy and beyond. The impression one can get from CDA that the pressing issues, problems and crises we face in the world today do not require detailed and conscientious empirical investigation or knowledge and expertise in the relevant spheres, but can be understood and addressed using a toolkit taken from segregational linguistics, is an impression that we wish to vigorously contest.

NOTES

1. The document can be found on the Number10.gov.uk website.
2. Previous discussions can be found in Jones (2004, 2007) and Collins (1999, 2000 and 2008).
3. One of the most recent being the application of "Cognitive Linguistics" to ideological matters (cf Jones 2001). Others include that of Habermas which is based on the theory of "speech acts" (cf Gunson & Collins 1997).
4. This is essentially the criticism of CDA that has been systematically levelled by Widdowson (eg 1998).
5. So-called "intertextuality" (1999, 118–9).
6. Useful critical discussion of these problems can also be found in, for example, Abercrombie et al (1980, 1990) Thompson (1984, 1990), Eagleton (1991) and Scott (1990).
7. The term "constructivist-structuralist" combines the sense of linguistic structuralism with that of "constructivism" which means "the assumption that language in interaction is constitutive of the social world and of the self". Chouliaraki and Fairclough claim that their view of discourse "as a moment in social practices and as a form of social production ("joint action") in practices entails a constructivist focus on social life as produced in discourse, as well as a structuralist focus on the semiotic (including linguistic) and non-semiotic structures, which are both conditions of possibility of discourse and products of social (including discursive) production" (Chouliaraki and Fairclough 1999, 48).
8. The authors add that "the comparative strengths and limitations of different discourses are constantly being judged in the course of practice" (1999, 136) but how this could be accounted for in "structuralist-constructivist" terms is not explained and, in practice, CDA avoids examination of the empirical links between discourse and social events.
9. The document can be found on the Number10.gov.uk website.
10. Ilyenkov sharply distinguishes between "categories"—forms of critical thinking necessary to the cognition of the different spheres of being – from verbal forms and meanings which, in contrast with categories, express superficial commonalities between different phenomena (1997, 64).
11. Ilyenkov: "It goes without saying that the assimilation of the results of previous theoretical development is not a matter of simply inheriting ready-made formulas but rather a complex process of their critical reinterpretation with reference to their correspondence to facts, life, practice. A new theory, however revolutionary it might be in its content and significance, is always born in the course of critical reassessment of previous theoretical development" (1982, 159).
12. We should add that the transparent lies and fabrications of the dismal Blair dossier are not even worthy of the epithet "ideological", although there are obviously ideological issues at stake in the continuing influence of the Labour Party on the British labor movement.
13. The same example is discussed at length in Jones (2007).
14. Collins and Jones (2006) offer a detailed example in support of this argument. See also Collins (2008).
15. Harris (1981, 193) argues that the "resolution of semantic uncertainties" involves "decision rather than discovery; and it is indefinitely revisable".
16. "The claim is not that speakers cannot produce or recognise instantiations of the same expressions on different occasions, but rather that this ability does

not yield a criterion of demarcation between the linguistic and the non-linguistic, nor imply that whatever we say is decontextualisable" (Harris 1981, 155).
17. And see Collins (1999, 2008) for a use of the Bakhtinian notion of "speech genre" in the analysis of communicative acts at particular political conjunctures.
18. Cf Harris (1981, 187–193) on legal decisions.
19. Cf Marx on the term "Caeserism": "I hope that my work will contribute towards eliminating the school-taught phrase now current ... of so-called Caeserism. In this superficial historical analogy the main point is forgotten, namely that in ancient Rome the class struggle took place only within a privileged minority, between the free rich and the free poor, while the great productive mass of the population, the slaves, formed the purely passive pedestal for these combatants" (Marx and Engels 1969, 395).
20. In this context we note Vološinov's critique of the "abstract objectivism" of structuralist linguistics: "Language as a stable system of normatively identical forms is merely a scientific abstraction, productive only in connection with certain particular practical and theoretical goals". To which he added: "This abstraction is not adequate to the concrete reality of language" (1973, 98). Unfortunately, linguists who have appealed to Vološinov (including, ironically, the pioneers of Critical Linguistics and CDA) have unfortunately ignored the overall thrust of his critique, in particular his appeal for a "re-examination ... of language forms in their usual linguistic presentation" (1973, 96).
21. Again, we note a parallel with Vološinov's own position that "the actual reality of language-speech" is "the social event of verbal interaction implemented in an utterance or utterances" (1973, 94).
22. Furthermore, see Harris on the "insurmountable" difficulties posed by what he calls "weak segregationism", that is the view that "the relevant communicational unit is not the sign as defined by the linguistic code but, in practice, the sign-in-its-context" (1996, 147).

REFERENCES

Abercrombie, Nicholas, Stephen Hill and Bryan S. Turner. 1980. *The dominant ideology thesis*. London: Allen and Unwin.
———. 1990. *Dominant Ideologies*. London: Unwin and Hyman.
Anderson, Perry. 1976. *Considerations on Western Marxism*. London: New Left Books.
———. 1983. *In the tracks of historical materialism*. London: Verso.
Bennett, Tony. 2003. *Formalism and Marxism*. London: Routledge.
Chouliaraki, Lilie and Norman Fairclough. 1999. *Discourse in late modernity: Rethinking critical discourse analysis*. Edinburgh: Edinburgh University Press.
Collins, Chik. 1999. *Language, ideology and social consciousness: Developing a sociohistorical approach*. Aldershot: Ashgate.
———. 2000. Developing the linguistic turn in urban studies: Language, context and political economy. *Urban Studies* 37: 2027–2043.
———. 2008. Discourse in cultural-historical perspective: Critical discourse analysis, CHAT and the study of social change. In *The transformation of learning: Advances in cultural-historical activity theory*, ed. Bert Van Oers, Ed Elbers, Wim Wardekker and René Van der Veer, 242–272. Cambridge: Cambridge University Press.

Collins, Chik and Jones, Peter E. 2006. The hidden connections of critical discourse analysis: a critique and an alternative. *Atlantic Journal of Communication* 14: 51–69.
Eagleton, Terry. 1991. *Ideology: An introduction.* London: Verso.
Fairclough, Norman. 1989. *Language and power.* London: Longman.
———. 1992. *Discourse and social change.* Oxford: Polity Press.
———. 1995. *Critical discourse analysis: The critical study of language.* London: Longman.
———. 2000. *New Labour, new language?* London: Routledge.
———. 2001a. *Language and power.* Second edition. London: Longman/Pearson
———. 2001b. Critical discourse analysis as a method in social scientific research. In *Methods of Critical Discourse Analysis*, ed. Ruth Wodak and Michael Meyer, 121–138. London: Sage.
———. 2003. *Analysing discourse: Textual analysis for social research.* London: Routledge.
Fairclough, Norman and Phil Graham. 2002. Marx and discourse analysis: Genesis of a critical method. *Estudios de Sociolinguistica* 3: 185–230
Fowler, Roger and Gunther Kress. 1979. Critical linguistics. In *Language and control*, ed. Roger Fowler, Bob Hodge, Gunther Kress and Tony Trew, 185–213. London: Routledge and Kegan Paul.
Gunson, Darryl and Chik Collins. 1997. From the "I" to the "we": Discourse ethics, identity and the pragmatics of partnership in the west of Scotland. *Communication Theory* 7: 277–300.
Harris, Roy.1980. *The language-makers.* London: Duckworth.
———. 1981. *The language myth.* London: Duckworth.
———. 1996. *Signs, language and communication.* London: Routledge.
Hodge, Robert. and Gunther Kress. 1979. *Language as ideology.* London: Routledge and Kegan Paul.
Hutton, Christopher M. 1990. *Abstraction and instance.* Oxford: Pergamon.
Ilyenkov, Evald V. 1982. *The dialectics of the abstract and the concrete in Marx's 'Capital'.* Moscow: Progress Publishers.
———. 1997. *The dialectics of the abstract and the concrete in theoretical- scientific thinking* [in Russian]. Moscow: Rosspen.
Jones, Peter E. 2001 Cognitive linguistics and the Marxist approach to ideology. In *Language and Ideology. Volume 1: Theoretical Cognitive Approaches*, ed. René Dirven, Bruce Hawkins and Esra Sandikcioglu, 227–251. Amsterdam: Benjamins.
———. 2004. Discourse and the materialist conception of history: Critical comments on critical discourse analysis. *Historical Materialism* 12, 1: 97–125.
———. 2007. Why there is no such thing as 'critical discourse analysis'. *Language & Communication* 27: 337–368.
Marx, Karl & Frederick Engels. 1969. *Selected works in three volumes: Volume 1.* Moscow: Progress.
Scott, James. C. 1990. *Domination and the arts of resistance.* London: Yale University Press.
Thompson, Edward P. 1978. *The poverty of theory and other essays.* London: Merlin.
Thompson, John B. 1984. *Studies in the theory of ideology.* Oxford: Polity Press.
———. 1990. *Ideology and modern culture.* Oxford: Polity Press.
Trew, Tony. 1979. "What the papers say": linguistic variation and ideological difference. In *Language and control*, ed. Roger Fowler, Bob Hodge, Gunther Kress and Tony Trew, 94–116. London: Routledge and Kegan Paul.
Van Dijk, Teun A. 1993. Principles of critical discourse analysis. *Discourse and Society* 4: 249–283.

Vološinov, Valentin N. 1973. *Marxism and the philosophy of language.* New York: Seminar Press.
Widdowson, H. G. 1998. The theory and practice of critical discourse analysis. *Applied Linguistics* 19: 136–151.

2 Ideology, Discourse and Moral Economy
Consulting the People of North Manchester
Colin Barker

"I don't know what you mean by 'glory'," Alice said.
Humpty Dumpty smiled contemptuously. "Of course you don't—till I tell you. I meant 'there's a nice knock-down argument for you!'"
"But 'glory' doesn't' mean 'a nice knock-down argument'," Alice objected.
"When I use a word," Humpty Dumpty said, in rather a scornful tone, "it means just what I choose it to mean—neither more nor less."
"The question is," said Alice, "whether you can make words mean so many different things."
"The question is," said Humpty Dumpty, "which is to be master—that's all."

(Carroll: 196)

When we seek to understand a word, what matters is not the direct meaning the word gives to objects and emotions—this is the false front of the word; what matters is rather the actual and always self-interested use to which this meaning is put and the way it is expressed by the speaker, a use determined by the speaker's position (profession, social class, etc.) and by the concrete situation. Who speaks and under what conditions he speaks: this is what determines the word's actual meaning.

(Bakhtin, 1981, 401)

IDEOLOGY AND STRUGGLE

Thinking about oppositional speech and ideas necessarily implicates a number of classic issues in social theory, concerning *ideology* and *discourse*. A single article cannot aspire to explore all these matters adequately. But we can, at least, search for an approach which avoids some obvious pitfalls.

Theorizing about ideology has two faces. The first looks at how ('dominant') ideologies contribute to stability, with ideology appearing as system, as 'second nature', as *habitus* and *hexis* (Bourdieu 1990). The second, perhaps less familiar, views ideology as a zone of disturbance, of conflict and contest, marked not only by ruling hegemony but equally by creative impulse, innovation, doubt, ambiguity. What makes the second more promising is that, while not doubting the existence of apparent continuities and permanences in thought and speech, it can explore them as 'constituted out of flows, processes and relations operating within bounded fields', posing questions about how such processes are constituted and sustained, and about their inner tensions and contradictions (Harvey 1996: 50; see also Abbott 2001).

Accounts of ideology as a means of social regulation from above, where elites mystify the masses by shaping popular perceptions through discourse and ritual, assume unwarranted coherence within ruling classes and allow no room for meanings and symbols to be contested. Ideologies are rarely homogeneous but, rather, are 'usually internally complex, differentiated formations, with conflicts between their various elements which need to be continually negotiated and resolved'; in any case, they exist only in relation to *other* ideologies, and must *negotiate* with these, producing an 'essential open-endedness' (Eagleton 1991: 45). Scott (1985, 1990) suggests we look, within hegemonic 'public transcripts', for the 'loopholes' that provide subordinates with justification for criticism and resistance, even if this achieves no more than covert expression. 'Any ruling group, in the course of justifying the principles of social inequality on which it bases its claims to power, makes itself vulnerable to a particular line of criticism' (Scott, 1990: 102–3). 'Hegemony' is never complete, for the many-voiced nature of speech always creates some room for alternative meanings to be asserted and explored. And there are motives to search for such alternative standpoints: power breeds humiliation, wealth breeds poverty, exclusion breeds longing. Hence, as Williams (1977: 112) remarks, hegemony has 'continually to be renewed, recreated, defended, and modified'.

Inattention to subordinates' concrete speech and practice appears, multiplied, in those (structuralist and post-structuralist) accounts of ideology as something going on behind people's backs, 'interpellating subjects' so that they cannot avoid colluding in their own domination. The ideological appears somehow quite independent of social action and organization, and often far too holistically, as if it were a coherently structured body of ideas imprisoning popular thought and speech.

We can't consider ideologies without considering their key constituent, language; ideology is 'discursive'. 'The word,' declared Volosinov (1986: 13), 'is the ideological phenomenon par excellence'. Ideology is 'a process of producing shared meanings of social relations . . . it and discourse are inseparably tied' (Steinberg 1994: 507). In this view, discourse is not a 'text', as in post-modernism, but is a process of social interaction. It lives, as Bakhtin put it, 'only in the dialogic interaction of those who use it' (1984: 143). Contrary to the provocative post-structuralist assumption, that 'meaning makes subjects and not subjects meaning' (Joyce 1994:13), it is indeed people who create, and modify, meanings in the course of their interactions. Speakers and listeners are active, purposive 'agentic' beings using language to achieve ends. Language, being inter-subjective, is inherently dynamic. The meanings it imparts are never fixed by the socially shared signs that compose it, for part of the meaning of human utterances is conveyed by their 'evaluative accent' or 'tone' (Volosinov 1986; Rochberg-Halton 1982). Meaning is constrained and expressed by the context of ongoing dialogue. The meanings of words, indeed, are often contested. As, in the course of social relations, groups and classes of people struggle with each other, they establish shared and 'partisan meanings' in language (Steinberg 1997), contesting the 'tenure' of specific terms, indeed 'poaching' words from the discourse of other groups to make them their own. This is not deny that such contests are conducted on uneven ground, that there are dominant ways of saying and meaning, or that categories and frameworks of understanding are often difficult to occupy and invest with our own meanings (Collins 1999). Yet there is always a potential for subversion within language—by jokes, parody and all means to actual capture and conversion—and commandering words for purposes opposed to those whose 'property' they might seem. By challenging meanings, those below can begin to develop outlines of alternative conceptions of the world, of their own worth and possibilities, even if often in patchwork form, as emergent oppositional languages for struggle.

The ideological is an inherent aspect of larger ongoing struggles between rulers and ruled for hegemony, involving local battles to invest particular words and phrases with preferred meanings. Rather than pitting one discursive construction against a completely different alternative, challengers engage in more piecemeal processes of questioning particular meanings in given social settings. In so doing, they can draw on 'discursive repertoires' (Steinberg 1999a) which reveal their understandings of wider issues of equity, justice and order. Often their successes are no more than partial, for challengers often lack other resources (institutional bases, adequate sanctions) to impose and articulate their own understandings.

ARGUMENTS IN TWO PUBLIC MEETINGS

In the light of the above, this article considers a specific case of oppositional speech, drawn from a study in North Manchester in the mid-1990s of people campaigning to save a local children's hospital from closure. Booth Hall Children's Hospital was a long-established facility, held in considerable esteem in a predominantly working-class area. The threat of closure by the Manchester Health Authority initiated local protest campaigns. These attracted tens of thousands of petition-signatures, organized street stalls, meetings and marches, and a brief sit-in within an unoccupied ward at the hospital. The local town councils in the affected area passed unanimous

Ideology, Discourse, and Moral Economy 43

resolutions opposing the closure, and a readers' poll by a local newspaper recorded a vote of 1,004 to 3 against closure.[1] 'Public opinion' could hardly have been more unanimous.

Existing administrative regulations required the Health Authority to engage in 'public consultation' about their plans. To meet this requirement, they booked several local halls and invited the public to meet them. Transcripts of recordings at two of these meetings, at Moston and Middleton, provide the basis for what follows.

These attending these 'public consultations' were already active campaigners against hospital closure. The meetings were thus pre-defined as arenas of combat. While the audiences did not know who would speak for the Health Authority, or what precisely they would say, they were primed to listen carefully for any weak points in the Authority's arguments, and oppose them.

The ways the audiences responded to the Health Authority's arguments depended on what the Authority's spokespeople—mostly paediatricians and health service managers—argued, and how they argued it. Some of their case for closure was listened to in silence, while other parts were sharply questioned, and others again met with noisy interruptions, laughter and abuse.

The Authority spokespeople argued their case predominantly on 'medical' grounds. Firstly, they suggested, the existence of two children's hospitals in Manchester, involving division of their specialist staff over two separate sites, made for medical inefficiency. Secondly, less children's beds were needed across the area, because of changes in medical technology: the advent of personal nebulizers, for example, meant asthma sufferers no longer need spend long periods in hospital. The Health Authority proposed to replace Booth Hall with a new children's ward at the local general hospital, and to expand the range of community-based medical services available to children and their parents in their own homes.

At first, the audiences seemed to have no answer to these arguments, though they were quick to catch at apparent contradictions in the Authority's presentation. They had fun with one consultant, who claimed both that his work was interrupted by having to move a few miles from one local children's hospital to another, and that he regularly traveled some eighty miles to another hospital in Barrow-in-Furness. 'Barrow!' was a popular heckle during that meeting.

However, such victories were small. Speakers from the floor lacked access to the kind of knowledge with which to undermine the 'medical' case. Although, in a poll, most local GPs had opposed the hospital's closure, none of these doctors, who might have questioned the official spokespeople's expertise, attended the meeting.

In that sense, the medical arguments became what Bakhtin terms an 'authoritative word', not really open to discussion or modification.[2] Except, that is, for one question: what would replace the existing hospital facilities? At the first meeting, the Authority offered plans for a new set of community-based services for children. The chief executive explained:

> Chief Executive: Children, by and large, are well. It's a minority of children that are unwell. And a minority of that minority that do have to go to hospital. The technology of health care is changing and we can treat more children in a community setting. Keep them in their home if at all possible in a safe environment.

At first these ideas were not challenged. But then a woman in the audience (a local Labour councillor) rose to say, in a speech interrupted by general applause:

> Woman: And now the lady on the end—the consultant, whatever she is, about this er. I get the feeling that we're going to get a 'Care in the Community' for children now, which we've got for the old people. Which we all know has not been working for the last twelve months. This is what it comes to me . . . *(Cries of* Hear hear, *and clapping)* . . . So if you can't do it for the pensioners of the country you're certainly not going to do it for the children of the country.

Once that theme had been enunciated, others picked it up:

> Woman: I'd like to say to Dr Ferguson that what you're describing is absolutely wonderful and if you could guarantee that then fine. But we've seen Care in the Community, we've seen the mentally ill and how they're cared in the community. We've seen the geriatric patients and how they're cared for in the community, and we don't trust what you're saying because it doesn't work.
> Dr Ferguson: But it's beginning to happen all the time while you watch. There are more and more children . . .
> Woman: How many have to die . . . ?
> Dr Ferguson: Nobody's died.
> Woman: . . . before. People are dying. People are being killed by the mentally ill because they haven't got a hospital bed. Now you're saying that's your dream for the future.

With each new development of this theme, the antagonism grew more confident. The final speaker from the floor at Moston added a significant social generalization:

> Woman: Can I just say that I I er although part of me agrees with er Care in the Community I'm also very very worried about it and I'm very worried about the pressure that that puts on working class people. Because to me Care in the Community is a middle class theory and to nurse at home lots of women in working class areas, and in middle class er societies, have to nurse elderly relatives, sick husbands and they have other children and now what we're talking about is bringing other

sick children with nurses popping in and out and everybody else in to your home and I just find
Chair: Okay.
Woman: absolutely appalling and
Chair: Care in the Community
Woman: and I'd like to know when are you consult with people like me on this stupid idea of Care in the Community with our children.

Reviewing the evening's proceedings afterwards, like sports fans after a game, protestors recalled the speeches on 'community care' with especial relish.

STRUGGLING OVER WORDS

The arguments about 'community care' in North Manchester exemplify what Volosinov termed a struggle over 'the tenancy of a sign'. The word 'community', Williams suggests, is always a 'warm' term, which 'seems never to be used unfavourably, and never to be given any positive opposing or distinguishing term' (1988: 74). In similar vein, Muncie and Wetherell argue that 'community'—along with other terms like 'family' and 'neighbourhood'—forms part of a signification system, or chain of concepts and associations, which includes other key terms like 'natural', 'harmonious', 'organic', 'healthy', 'warm', 'evolving', 'personal', etc. Governments, they contend, attempted to deploy the term 'community' to justify what turned out to be cuts in public welfare spending. The term's connotations, they suggest, can inhibit or confuse opposition: 'The argument against community care is rendered more difficult by the reassuring humanistic imagery of neighbourliness, close ties, social support and a lifestyle more akin to a mythical image of village life than the urban housing estate' (1995: 56). By 1994, however, the North Manchester audience's speeches indicate that 'community' could be used—especially linked to that other warm word 'care'—as a term of *suspicion*. It had become associated with privatizing and closing public services, in both the mental health and geriatric fields. When the first woman speaker invoked that sense of suspicion, provoking rapid applause from other protestors, she opening the way to a cascading series of criticisms. The second speaker amplified the opening theme by connecting 'community care' with killings by mental patients, while the third went on to critique the whole idea of 'community care' as a 'middle-class' imposition on working-class families. She challenged sentimental accounts of both 'community and 'family' by referring to the toil and trouble of managing a household with a sick child.

In the course of the meeting, speakers creatively picked up these variable associations, turning the Authority's own words into weapons against them. As Bakhtin insisted, words are 'multi-accentual': they do not relate to things in singular ways, but are regularly re-made in use within the 'elastic environment of other, alien words about the same object, the same theme' (1981: 276). The protestors did not challenge the single word alone, but its location within a whole 'interpretative repertoire', its practical theorization. Their struggle was not merely linguistic, but over the social practice the word represented and threatened.[3]

The most promising theoretical framework for discussing these interchanges is provided by the 'dialogical school' initiated in post-revolutionary Russia by such figures as V. N. Volosinov, M. M. Bakhtin, and P. N. Medvedev, along with Lev Vygotsky. For these thinkers, the study of speech should not be left to linguistics. Human discourse must always be considered in the context of speakers' and auditors' ongoing social relations. Language is an entirely social phenomenon, which must be studied in action, as people use it in social life.

The fundamental unit of study, the 'cell form' of dialogue, is not the word, sign or sentence, but the *utterance* given by a speaker to a listener (or 'addressee'), in a definite context. Every utterance involves this person addressing that person, in a particular manner and for a specific purpose. Utterances are pregnant with social life and intentions. We should think of speakers and audiences alike as if on springs, coiled for interaction, actively engaged in mutual communication. Speaking—as the cognate school of rhetorical social psychologists argues—is not distinct from acting, but is itself a form of action, a social practice with its own 'action orientation'. Most discourse, writes Eagleton (1991)—borrowing from J.L.Austin—is 'performative' rather than 'constative', aiming not merely to provide information, models, rules, directions, but to influence the practical and ideological orientation of those who hear it. Speakers' social purposes shape the rhetorical devices and evaluative tones they deploy.

Dialogical theory is distinctive in its attention not only to the producers of discourse but also to their audiences. Far from treating addressees as passive receptors, Bakhtin (1986) insists on their *active* and *responsive* stance; they are beings 'full of words', with all their own experiences and 'apperceptive background' encoded in inner speech, critically appraising what they hear.[4] Any single utterance is but one event in a chain of dialogical exchanges, itself constructed as an active response to what has been said before. Listeners, attending to other persons' utterances, are already preparing their answers.

Speakers and listeners share a common language with shared meanings, else there could be no communication between them. But within that shared language they impart their own 'senses' to words. Individuals 'individualize' and 'subjectivize' word-meanings, in line with their own social locations, particular experiences and perspectives.[5] They thus both reproduce and modify, share and contest the significance of language. All manner of politically sensitive terms have this conflict of meaning and sense running through them: think only of such terms as 'socialism' and 'capitalism,' 'management' and 'workers,' 'democracy,' 'freedom,' 'market,' 'equality,' 'racism' and 'justice' and so on and on. The class struggle runs through the language, about the language, for control of the language.

The protestors who claimed 'tenure' of the word 'community' largely succeeded. Summing up at the end of that meeting, the Health Authority chairman acknowledged the point:

> I think fourthly we're agreed erm on er the importance of developing, I'm not sure we are agreed on this, but I think the support for the delivery of community services if we could get past the skepticism that it's let down the public in other areas like old age and mental illness, there's a lot of skepticism about it
> (*comments from floor*)
> but but supported it could be done right.

By the time of the next meeting, a few days later, the Health Authority dropped all mention of its 'community medicine' proposals. It was the protestors' opening speaker who offered this theme, now in an offensive vein. Holding up the Authority's document he declared:

> This booklet is riddled with one central concept, and that is Community Care . . . That rhetoric, that theme, is actually masking the real central core, the objective is to close Booth Hall

The Health Authority, once burned by 'community care', declined to play with that fire again.

'IT'S ALL ABOUT MONEY'

Active listeners evaluate the status of what is said but also, simultaneously, of the person speaking. Orienting themselves towards others in dialogue, speakers and listeners 'place' their interlocutors, forming pictures of who those others are and what they might want (Hall 1995). In the consultation meetings, such evaluations proved damaging to the Authority's cause. For the protestors questioned not simply the Authority's *arguments*, but their *motives* and their *trustworthiness*.

The audiences granted some legitimacy to medical personnel, so long as they were discussing strictly 'medical' matters. However, they strictly de-limited this legitimation. They rapidly challenged the consultants if they strayed from their medical expertise into other matters—and notably into issues concerning *money*. This happened at both meetings. At the first meeting, a woman paediatrician was heard in silence as she presented the Authority's case for unifying specialist services, until she began to talk about financial advantages. Here the audience became restive. She worsened matters worse for herself by offering an analogy:

> Suppose you had half your family in one house and half your family in another house and you've got to run the rates and the rent and poll-tax and God know what else they sting you for . . .

Here audience interruptions compelled her to halt. A speaker from the floor told her:

> Woman: Can I just say to Doctor Phillips, I understand you trying to draw analogies, but the analogy you're doing is basically very much the Mrs. Thatcher patronizing housekeeper's basket . . . (*applause*) . . . I think we do understand that analogy. It's extremely patronizing to think that we that is the level you have to come to try and explain budgets to the community.

Here, that multi-accented word, 'community', performed a new duty. Re-populated with new meanings, it now referred to people hostile to patronizing by doctors. The doctor's 'medical' persona was discounted as she was re-identified as moving in the same linguistic universe as an immensely disliked politician, whose 'economics' were deeply mistrusted.[6]

At the second meeting, a male consultant spoke without interruption for several minutes, but then strayed into urging the financial benefits of merging specialist services:

> Consultant neurologist: . . . for every pound you pull out of your pocket to buy that sort of thing it's a pound less to hire a nurse or a scientist in the laboratory or a . . .
> (*shouts from floor*): Rubbish
> Now why is that rubbish? If you. If you at home are given a fixed budget you have a choice on what to spend it on. The reality . . .
> (*shouts from floor, the chairman intervenes to restore order, but the doctor has temporarily lost his speaker's authority*)
> A pensioner from the floor: It's all about money all the time.
> Chair: The whole world's about money, love.
> (*shouts from the floor*)
> Chair: Dr. Newton may we progress please, if we could progress . . .

Later, when Dr Newton referred in positive terms to the 'purchaser/provider split' in the Health Service, he was heckled. He ploughed on through interruptions:

> Now in the new system everything that happens a bill is raised for it, but the money from the purchasers instead of coming to Pendlebury will go to Hope and the status quo is maintained. So there's no actual change it's just erm a financial arrangement.
> (*sarcastic laughter*)

> Man from floor: Sack the managers.

The Booth Hall Campaign secretary told him, to applause:

> I want doctors who are doctors, I don't want doctors who are frigging accountants. I want. I don't want purchasers and providers, I want doctors and nurses in our hospitals running it and I don't appreciate hearing consultants, paediatricians or whatever adopting this terminology which is totally bogus. If the man could concentrate on the job for which I hope, I'm sure he's very good at it, but if he would concentrate on that.

When the doctors raised questions about money, the audience opposed them, and in so doing called their social roles into question. Wandering into the contested sphere of 'political economy', they faced audiences who recognized immediately what kinds of language to mistrust and to challenge. What you're actually doing, the audiences charged, is pursuing an alien 'monetarist' philosophy, seeking to *cut* the health services we enjoy —and when you deny it we simply don't believe you.

Audience members repeatedly asserted that, behind their claims, the Authority possessed a covert agenda they dare not assert in public. The Authority's Chief Executive opened the Middleton meeting with the words:

> Let me make two very clear unequivocal points by way of introduction. The first is that this not about saving money on Children's Services . . . '
> (*sarcastic laughter and comments from floor*)
> Man's voice from the floor: Big joke.
> (*comments from floor*)
> Chief Executive: I I'm sure you'll disagree with me later . . .

And when he repeated the point at the end of his opening address, a woman near the front inquired, 'Do you mind if we laugh again?' and a man in the audience called out: 'Rubbish. Tell the truth.' At the Moston meeting, a pensioner asked, rhetorically: 'What is your real reason for wanting to close Booth Hall? What is it? Money to balance the books. ' (*applause*) The chairman noted that the question had been asked 'almost with venom'.

Again and again the same charges flowed freely. Bigger hospitals, said one activist, 'mean more money for the bureaucrats who manage them.' One floor speaker described the officials on the platform:

> They don't deserve to be on there because they're just money grabbers, put there and paid by the Tory government.

And one woman told them:

> Woman at Middleton: You're not willing to put your money where your mouth is and that's why we don't believe a single word that you say. And if the money's gone down from forty million six years ago that it would have cost to provide a hospital down to fifteen or twenty million I bet you any money that you could improve Booth Hall site and provide all those services on that site well for that price. Or has somebody like Eddie Shah already offered you the money for that site? (*applause*)[7]

The theme of 'money' kept coming up in different ways. The platform were accused of attending the meeting only because they were *paid*, while the audience was there because they *cared*. The Authority wanted, speakers alleged, to close Booth Hall in order to sell off the land to private developers. Our scale of values is different, the Authority was told: we pay happily for Booth Hall, but should we be paying for you?[8]

> Man at Middleton: We were clearly told that the Health Trust could not afford two children's hospitals. This town has never decided that it cannot afford to save children's lives. We don't want some sycophants coming in telling us that we have. If it takes more money, then we have to go back to government and say that we want more money. I'll leave you with a question. How much does it cost to employ a nurse and how much does it cost to employ you lot sat on that table coming here to tell us something we don't want to hear? (*applause*)

Running through a whole series of contributions, interruptions and heckles at the meetings was an effort to 'de-credential' the Authority's speakers, by challenging their personal or social character.[9] The Authority's spokespeople were accused of bad faith, of being 'minions' of the Tory minister of Health, of changing their story from meeting to meeting, and of attempting to run down the hospital secretly even before the consultation period was over. The officials were called 'unelected men in their grey suits and plush offices', who never stayed long in their jobs and thus had no loyalty to the people they were supposed to serve. 'You are,' one woman told them, 'liars and hypocrites'. Every remark and gesture by the Health Authority representatives was liable to be taken suspiciously, sometimes with ribald amusement.

The mistrust was amplified by a further theme. Officials had no right to decide the future of the hospital. The protestors knew they had 'public opinion' on their side, reminding the platform of how unpopular their plans were, and of how unrepresentative they were of local opinion.

Thus the question arose, what weight did the Health Authority give to local opinion, and to the views of local elected bodies? There was no escape from this. Asked directly what credence he gave to local views, the Health Authority Chairman attempted to divert the question to a competitive theme:

> Health Authority Chairman: A lot of credence but I'm not going to advise or my authority will not er in trying to devise the best services for your children and grand-children be just taken over by views that want to defend one hospital. I mean the very remark we had earlier: 'Why not move Pendlebury to Booth Hall?'—erm you know, if that was the right solution we'd have a meeting like this round Pendlebury.

But at both meetings he was compelled to acknowledge that he and his colleagues were in the difficult position of saying that they knew better than the people what was in their best interests.

> Chair: Again I like to get answers and boil them down. If I can boil that answer down you seem to be saying the hundred percent of public opinion which is against it, apart from the two people you spoke to, are against it because they are ill informed. Is that what you're saying?
> Health Authority Chairman: Yes.
> *(comments from floor)*
> Chair: Okay, well...
> Save Booth Hall Campaign Secretary *(from the platform)*: There. There. There's. There's a democrat. There's a democrat.

A MORAL ECONOMY?

As Michael Billig (1995, 1996) notes, thinking and talking involves a complex dialectic of both generalization and singularization. Generalization involves placing an item of experience within a larger category, while singularization involves determining which of several potential categories is appropriate, thus introducing a 'dilemmatic' quality to discourse and thought. Two features make this more possible. Firstly, the world of 'public discourse' or everyday 'ideology' is itself a world of argument containing contradictory potentials and oppositions, where 'there is no theme without a counter-theme' (Gamson and Modigliani 1989: 6). Secondly and consequently, people are already 'familiar' with idea-sets that they do not themselves necessarily hold all the time, so that their adoption of 'new' ideas or their summoning up of 'submerged' themes is not a very difficult process, involving merely a shift in rhetorical stance.

Ideological themes persist across time and across populations, their persistence reflecting continuities in social relations and antagonisms. These represent forms of ideological 'resource' on which speakers can draw in a variety of situations, as 'ways of seeing' (Berger 1972) which they can assume listeners will recognize and share, providing common 'vocabularies of motive' (Mills 1940). Such persistent themes, however, don't exist in monological or monotonic form, but always in complex dialogical interdiscursive relations with other possible persistent counter-themes (e.g.

'class' vs 'nation', 'cooperation' vs 'conflict' etc), Further, the importing of such themes into concrete speech always requires attention to the actual setting or situation, including the speech or actions of others.

In a specific interaction like the 'consultation meetings' in Manchester, there developed a kind of interpretative contest as to what the meetings were actually about. The Health Authority spokespeople sought to shape the dialogue at the meetings so that, in a sense, it would extend the doctor-patient relationship into the reorganization of the health service itself. They would appear as disinterested professionals, deploying their technical expertise to benefit the population and their children, offering an 'education' in the changing realities of medical practice to their client-consumers. The changes we are proposing, they suggested, are in your own best interest, adding that we understand and sympathize with your 'feelings'. As the Authority chairman summed up at the Moston meeting, in a final effort to re-credential his side:

> What I hear is that there is a lot of feeling of anger, there's a lot of feeling of distress and worry, and there's a lot of feeling that we're not truthful and there's a lot of feeling that it's finance driven. And I hear those remarks ... We've got to persuade you with more facts and figures that what we're doing is actually to your kids' benefit and is not just to save Mrs Bottomley, or whatever she's called.

But their audiences responded by invoking a different, and antagonistic, 'social or evaluative purview' (Volosinov 1986: 21, 106; 1976: 101; Bakhtin 1981: 401) to account for what was going on.[10] One term that might usefully describe their particular purview is 'moral economy'. E. P. Thompson developed this term as a means to make sense of the specific 'rationality' of 18th century food rioters.[11] It refers to the set of ethical assumptions underpinning resistance to top-down social reorganizations, which were 'experienced by the plebs in the form of exploitation, or the expropriation of customary use-rights, or the violent disruption of valued patterns of work and leisure' (Thompson 1991: 9).

A 'moral economy' is marked by several characteristics. First, working people identify the cause of some breach in their lives as what Thompson called 'the innovation of capitalist process', where wealthy or powerful figures propose changes at odds with people's needs. The origins of a moral economy are to be found *within* a capitalist economy.[12] Second, a moral economy affirms a positive counter-ethic, a vision of the common good entailing *non-monetary values*. Third, that vision contains elements of 'tradition' or 'custom', affirming something already practiced and valued; it is 'conservative' in seeking to protect a humanly valuable pattern of social activity, rights and obligations. Fourth, the enunciation of a moral economy is a kind of battle-cry, or at least a justification for action; and its defence licenses forms of action and speech (for example, physical confrontations

Ideology, Discourse, and Moral Economy   53

with authority, 'imprecations against the rich') which, in other circumstances, might be adjudged inappropriate.

A moral economy, in this conception, is negotiated, relational, dialogical, constructed and reconstructed as part of an ongoing interaction between power and powerlessness. Far from being fixed, its precise terms, boundaries and extent are open to reshaping, challenge and modification. A moral economy (or almost any other ideological form) should not be viewed as a carefully articulated theoretical system. Rather, it has the character of a loosely coupled and dynamic *ensemble* (Steinberg 1999:20) of ideas and evocative symbols, developed in opposition to ruling ideas (which are themselves commonly similar 'assemblages' of signs and notions). A moral economy is developed and shared through conversations among its adherents within a local environment of speech or 'community of response'.[13] Its tenets may be only partially self-conscious, becoming so only when the 'tissue of customs and usages' it articulates is threatened by 'monetary rationalization' (Thompson 1991: 340).[14]

Noting the role of 'rumours'—and the rulers' dismissive view of them—in generating 18th century popular rebellion, Thompson remarked that the people had direct information sources which could not be easily discounted. In the arguments over Booth Hall, too, 'rumours' were significant. Speakers quoted concrete facts. This ward was closed, that section was being moved. In one ward the window frames were rotten, but new carpet was being laid for offices. Surely, closing a newly refurbished accident and emergency suite was pure wastefulness? Protestors remembered that this child died when no intensive care bed was available. Those parents with a sick child had difficulty getting to the hospital, that child should not have been sent home without an x-ray. The audiences' knowledge might be as piecemeal as many oppositional ideologies, and might often be anecdotal, but it was also concrete. From their social location an overall picture was hard to form, and they were prepared to listen to those with information they lacked and who offered a general perspective. But they listened with suspicion, for that other perspective was 'from above', and was always liable to contamination from its contact with others 'above', who were known to put their own class interests first.

Given Thompson's (1991:340) own cautions about over-extending his concept, is it appropriate to apply the notion of a moral economy to the views of the North Manchester protestors? Cautiously, I think it is. The sense the protestors enunciated was indeed that the Health Authority's proposals represented 'innovation of capitalist process'. What was going on, they insisted, was exploitation, the expropriation of existing use-rights. For them, the very use of the language of 'cost' and 'economy' in relation to the Health Service was quite as contentious as the abolition of regulation in the corn trade in the 18th century. The audiences at the meetings were deeply sceptical that the Authority could, in the 'monetarist' climate of the time, be proposing anything good; rather, they interpreted the proposals as an attack on established and valued rights. As for *children's healthcare*, that was sacred ground.

The audiences expressed a view about what is legitimate and illegitimate in the running of a valued public service, linking this to views of social norms and obligations, and of the proper functions of the several parties in medicine. Doctors and nurses should concern themselves with patients' welfare, and not mix in management politics or start talking managerial jargon. If 'management' within the Health Service was permitted any legitimacy, its role was to facilitate the provision of good services for the community, and not to line its members' own pockets or impose alien 'market' values. Whatever privileges the rich and powerful might have won in other spheres of social life, health care should be exempt from these. The audiences expressed passionately held views of the common weal, along with a claim that these were indeed the shared notions of the whole people. By contrast, they represented the Authority as embodying an opposed, alien and vicious agenda.

AUDIENCE ORGANIZATION

The audiences at the Manchester 'consultation' meetings revealed a powerful capacity to interrogate the Health Authority's proposals, along with a strongly held set of antagonistic beliefs. They could draw on months and years of everyday talk across North Manchester, and assume a 'community of response' for the ideas they expressed. While each speaker and heckler spoke with his or own individual 'accent', speakers were mostly willing to support and encourage each other, and to share and develop common themes in their criticism of the Authority's plans. In the consultation meetings, successful speeches from the floor evoked certain themes—about 'community care', about 'money', about 'democracy' and so on—that other participants could recognize because the currency of those themes in North Manchester made them rapidly familiar. If there was a 'moral economy' at work, this is how it was drawn on and recognized. Speakers summoned up a existing stock of ideological resources they could assume others shared, revealing how they fitted this occasion.

The more effective speakers were those who, in a sense, 'spoke for the community' through this process of evocation. Their success was marked by responsive markers: they won audience applause, later speakers either referred back with approbation to what they said, or picked up a theme they had opened and developed it further. Those who were especially appreciated were those who found 'loopholes' in the Authority's statements through which their own 'counter-themes' could be developed.

In the very process of arguing with the Health Authority the audiences were also evaluating and organizing their own forces. They were not the structureless 'crowds' assumed by Le Bon, Freud and others. They listened, judged, evaluated, discovered—and organized. They rewarded approved speakers with applause, laughter, supportive remarks, waves, smiles and pats on the back. By such means, they awarded 'leadership' status to some speakers. However, they also withdrew or limited that status. At the first meeting, the Campaign Secretary told the Health Authority they were not 'wedded to the bricks and mortar actually on the particular site', and that they welcomed the idea of an expanded community service for children. An Authority manager immediately embraced this remark—for it seemed to suggest they could discount attachment to the physical fabric of Booth Hall Hospital. But the very next speaker from the audience made a point of disagreeing with the Campaign Secretary on the matter of 'bricks and mortar', while, as we have seen, other speakers went on to question the 'community care' notion. Some speakers from the floor did not attract applause, even though they spoke passionately: they failed to enthuse the audience, to make telling points, to enunciate shared themes in convincing ways. Their contributions were awarded no prizes of recognition. By interactively 'accrediting' and 'discrediting' their own members, the audiences at both meetings gave themselves an emergent shape and direction, thereby recognizing and developing their own ideas.

LIMITS OF DISCOURSE

The North Manchester campaigners could enunciate a powerful 'moral economy'; they forced the Health Authority to abandon one of its main justificatory claims; they demonstrated the unpopularity of the hospital closure plan. If anyone could claim 'victory' at the consultation meetings, it was the protestors. But that victory had limits. Steinberg remarks of ideological conflict that, while it can map a terrain of legitimate action and validate contention, it can't organize networks, can't garner resources, and can't take action: 'People do that' (Steinberg 1994: 515). Realities 'beyond discourse' conditioned the passionate speech of the North Manchester protestors. True, they could claim to speak for hundreds of thousands of local people, but only small numbers turned out for a November evening meeting. Angry dissatisfaction at the Authority's proposals was widespread, yet few people were mobilized into more than signing petitions and displaying posters. No campaign demonstration exceeded a few hundred participants. Also, a voice was missing from their own ranks—that of organized hospital workers whose jobs were threatened by the closure. For the most effective of the demonstrations, two hospital porters made their own banner. Carried at the front of a march through Manchester city centre in the summer of 1993, it declared, 'Jesus Said "SUFFER Little Children" SO DO THE TORIES'. Such voices were not heard again within the campaigns. No appeals were therefore made to other workplaces for action in solidarity with the hospital workers.

The potential *practical* sanctions the protestors could bring to bear on the Health Authority were weak. They could speak woundingly, but lacked the capacity to inflict more deadly blows. In interviews, one campaigner described his modest hopes for success: 'If we achieve nothing else, at least we will have made them limp.' Another reported her own feelings of frustration during the meeting:

> I went to one of those consultation meetings, at Moston Brook, and there people were attacking people on the top table, considerably, very much so... They were talking very Left. I had the feeling, What could we say? And the thing was, there wasn't anything at that point, because of the way the campaign had gone... Unless we'd organized people walking out, or storming the platform or doing something that. I remember discussing it afterwards and feeling dissatisfied with that meeting and the contribution that we'd made. Maybe we should have —but that would have just been a stunt saying, 'We're disgusted'—somehow done something along... In a sense we'd lost the argument by then with the people that mattered, that could turn it round.... And we did try to build that meeting. I remember doing a lot of going round a lot of people trying to get people to come to that meeting.... Mostly they didn't come.

The audiences had openly expressed the view that the Authority were knaves or fools, or both. The officials and doctors, more circumspectly, had articulated a view that the people were ill-informed, characterized more by emotional reactions than a rational appreciation of circumstances. Yet, in a sense, the Authority never needed to win the argument, even if they might have preferred doing so. For, as one floor speaker alleged, the meetings involved 'pseudo-consultation'. The Authority was bound to *listen to* but not to follow local opinion.[15] It retained the power of decision.

And it would demonstrate this. In January 1995, the Authority held a final meeting in Manchester Town Hall. It was, the chair explained to a sizable crowd, a 'private meeting being held in public.' At that meeting, in an extraordinary piece of unpopular theatre, the members of the Health Authority voted through every point in the original proposals. Their hands went up and down some twenty times, in front of an audience that heckled and insulted them as 'puppets'. At the end, the Authority members departed rather quickly, leaving a room full of rather stunned and angrily subdued people. The power of argument, it seemed, gave way ultimately to a slightly shamefaced argument of power.

NOTES

1. *Moston Express*, 11 August 1994, 'Your Verdict: Keep Open 1,004, Close it 3'

Ideology, Discourse, and Moral Economy   57

2. Bakhtin 1981: 341–6 discusses the distinction between 'authoritative' and 'internally persuasive' words. Elsewhere he uses such terms as 'inert' and 'sacred' words for the former idea.
3. There is an account of a not dissimilar battle over the words 'negotiate' and 'cooperate' during the 1971 work-in at Upper Clyde Shipbuilders in Collins 1996, 1999.
4. The American pragmatist Charles S Peirce's account of language use has many resonances with the Russian dialogician. He distinguishes between two kinds of 'sign'—that provided by the speaker as against the 'interpretant' sign of the listener—stressing the difference between these two forms in conversation and life. There is a valuable account of Peirce's views in Rochberg-Halton 1982.
5. The 'meaning/ sense' distinction is drawn most sharply by A N. Leontyev (1978), a pupil of Vygotsky.
6. Hill has summarized the evidence on 'how restricted a purchase Thatcherism [had] on the lower classes and that it was contested by significant numbers even among the service class'. Most people, he notes, 'still subscribe to the welfare compromise and a "dependency" culture' (Hill 1990, 21). We might contest his language, but not the content of his argument.
7. Again, context is relevant. Eddie Shah had recently attempted to purchase a large piece of public park-land to develop a private golf course, a project defeated in part by another local campaign.
8. The 'money' theme had another side. The audience made its own positive claims to determine the hospital's future. We pay your wages, they told the platform. But also, we have raised large sums of money to buy a scanner for Booth Hall. Over the years, North Manchester clubs, churches, unions and the like would always give a good hearing to fund-raising efforts for 'our children's hospital.' 'Charity' here meant something different from images of 'Lady Bountiful'. Embedded in, not imposed on, local working-class life, their own fund-raising founded claims to moral ownership of the hospital.
9. See Billig (1996) on speakers' 'credentialing' work.
10. Volosinov insists that for an item to enter the social purview of a group and 'elicit ideological semiotic reaction,' it must be associated with the vital socio-economic prerequisites of the particular group's existence, making contact, even if obliquely, with the bases of the group's material life (1986: 22).
11. Thompson first used the expression 'moral economy' in *The Making of the English Working Class* (1963), developing it in 1971 and further exploring and refining it in 1991.
12. Moral economy takes on its meaning in 'dialectic tension' with *market economy* (Randall and Charlesworth 2000:2). Randall (1991:255, cit Steinberg 1995: 80) remarks, on the moral economy of trade relations among woollen workers, 'The origins of the moral economy therefore have to be found within a capitalist economy, not outside or in opposition to one'. This seems slightly mistaken: a moral economy emerges *within and against* a capitalist economy. Otherwise there is no sense in Thompson's suggestion that moral economy can be seen 'constantly regenerating itself as anti-capitalist critique, as a resistance movement' (1991:341).
13. The term *community of response* was developed in cultural studies by Martin Barker (2000), who identifies it as an 'essential circulatory medium' for shared evaluations and stances.
14. In becoming self-conscious, a moral economy may provide materials for some degree of systematization. However, it can be invoked for different sociopolitical purposes. A moral economy may provide underpinnings to a socialist critique of capitalism, for example, but may equally be limited to

demands for a capitalist economy modified by a stronger 'public service' element (Davies and Flett 2002).
15. Molotch (1990, cited in Staggenborg 1993), drawing on studies of ecological protests, suggests that elites have the capacity, after periods of 'vulnerability,' to recoup their positions. They can organize public meetings as 'pseudo-events'—'strictly planned and ceremonious encounters'—where the *illusion* of popular participation is maintained, while simultaneously 'creeping events' (real events 'arranged to occur at an inconspicuously gradual and piecemeal pace') actually determine the outcome.

REFERENCES

Abbott, Andrew (2001), *Time Matters: On Theory and Method*. Chicago: Chicago University Press

Bakhtin, M.M. (1981), *The Dialogic Imagination: Four Essays*. Translated by Caryl Emerson and Michael Holquist. Edited by Michael Holquist. Austin: University of Texas Press

Bakhtin, M.M. (1984) *Problems of Dostoevsky's Poetics*, edited and translated by Caryl Emerson, Manchester: Manchester University Press

Bakhtin, M.M. (1986), *Speech Genres and Other Late Essas*. Translated by Vern W McGee. Edited by Caryl Emerson and Michael Holquist. Austin: University of Texas Press

Barker, Martin (2000), *From Antz to Titanic: Reinventing Film Analysis*. London: Pluto

Berger, John (1972), *Ways of Seeing*. Harmondsworth: Penguin

Billig, Michael (1995), Rhetorical Psychology, Ideological Thinking, and Imagining Nationhood. In Hank Johnston and Bert Klandermans (Eds.), *Social Movements and Culture* (pp. 64–81). London: UCL Press

———. (1996), *Arguing and thinking: a rhetorical approach to social psychology*. Cambridge: Cambridge University Press, 2nd edition

Bourdieu, Pierre (1990), *The Logic of Practice*, translated by Richard Nice, Stanford: Stanford University Press

Carroll, Lewis 1939), *Through the Looking Glass and what Alice found there*. In *The Complete Works of Lewis Carroll*, London: Nonesuch Press

Collins, Chik (1996), To concede or to contest? Language and class struggle. In Colin Barker and Paul Kennedy, (Eds.), *To Make Another World: Studies in protest and collective action* (pp. 69–90). Aldershot: Avebury

———. (1999), *Language, Ideology and Social Consciousness: Developing a sociohistorical approach*. Aldershot: Ashgate

Davies, Megan and Flett, Keith (2002), So bloody much to oppose: the moral economy of privatisation. In Colin Barker and Mike Tyldesley (Eds.), *Eighth International Conference on Alternative Futures and Popular Protest* (Vol 1). Manchester: Manchester Metropolitan University,

Eagleton, Terry (1991), *Ideology: An Introduction*. London:Verso

Gamson William A. and Modigliani, Andre (1989), Media discourse and public opinion on nuclear power. *American Journal of Sociology* 95, 1–38

Hall, Joan Kelly (1995), (Re)creating our Worlds with Words: A Sociohistorical Perspective of Face-to-Face Interaction. *Applied Linguistics*, 16, 1995, 206–232

Harvey, David (1996), *Justice, Nature & the Geography of Difference*. Oxford: Blackwell

Hill, Stephen (1990), Britain: The Dominant Ideology Thesis after a decade. In Nicholas Abercrombie, Stephen Hill, Bryan Turner (Eds.), *Dominant Ideologies*. London: Unwin Hyman

Joyce, Patrick 1994, *Democratic Subjects: The Self and the Social in Nineteenth Century England*. Cambridge: Cambridge University Press

Leontyev, A.N. (1978), *Activity, Consciousness, and Personality*. Englewood Cliffs: Prentice Hall

Mills, C. Wright (1940), Situated Actions and Vocabularies of Motive. *American Sociological Review*, 5, 904–913

Molotch, H. (1970), Oil in Santa Barbara and power in America. *Sociological Inquiry*, 40, 131–144

Muncie, John and Wetherell, Margaret (1995), Family policy and political discourse. In John Muncie, Margaret Wetherell, Rudi Dallos and Allan Cochrane, eds, *Understanding the Family* (pp. 39–80). London: Sage

Randall, Adrian (1991), *Before the Luddites: Custom, Community and Machinery in the English Woollen Industry, 1776–1809*. Cambridge: Cambridge University Press

Randall, Adrian and Charlesworth, Andrew (2000), The moral economy: riot, markets and social conflict. in Adrian Randall and Andrew Charlesworth, eds, *Moral Economy and Popular Protest: Crowds, Conflict and Authority* (pp. 1–32). London: Macmillan

Rochberg-Halton, Eugene (1982), Situation, structure, and the context of meaning. *The Sociological Quarterly* 2, 455–476

Scott, James C. (1985). *Weapons of the weak : everyday forms of peasant resistance*. New Haven : Yale University Press

———. (1990), *Domination and the Arts of Resistance. Hidden Transcripts*. New Haven: Yale University Press

Staggenborg, Suzanne (1993), Critical events and the mobilizations of the pro-choice movement. *Research in Political Sociology*, 6, 319–345

Steinberg, Marc W. (1994), The Dialogue of Struggle: The contest over ideological boundaries in the case of the London silk weavers in the early nineteenth century. *Social Science History*, 18, 505–541

———. (1997), 'A Way of struggle': reformations and affirmations of E.P. Thompson's class analysis in the light of postmodern theories of language. *British Journal of Sociology*, 48, 471–492

———. (1999), *Fighting Words: Working-Class Formation, Collective Action, and Discourse in Early Nineteenth Century England*. Ithaca: Cornell University Press

Thompson, E.P. (1963), *The Making of the English Working Class*. London: Gollancz

———. (1971), The moral economy of the English crowd in the 18th century. *Past and Present*, 50, 76–136

———. (1991), *Customs in Common*. London: Merlin

Volosinov, V.N. (1976), Discourse in life and discourse in art (concerning sociological poetics). In *Freudianism: A Marxist Critique*. Translated by I.R. Titunik. New York: Academic Press, 1976

———. (1986), *Marxism and the Theory of Language*. Translated by Ladislav Matejka and I.R.Titunik. Cambridge, Mass.: Harvard University Press

Vygotsky, Lev (1986), *Thought and Language*. Translated and edited by Alex Kozulin. Cambridge, Mass.: MIT Press

Williams, Raymond. (1977), *Marxism and Literature*. Oxford: Oxford University Press.

Williams, Raymond. (1988), *Keywords*. London: Fontana

3 Where State Power and Opposition Collide

Discourses of Labor Protest in a New Market Economy

Charles Woolfson

This chapter explores the emergent discourses of labor protest that have accompanied the transition process from socialism to the market economies of the former Soviet Union. It is a first preliminary attempt, based on admittedly fragmentary samples of discourse, to provide a basis for future more extensive analysis. Even these limited snatches of discourse, however, provide a condensed telegraphy of protest revealing the potential emergence of more challenging "emancipatory" discourses (Huspek 1991). The discourses are comprised of spoken utterances of participants in labor protests captured in news reports, slogans on banners and placards, protest manifestos, and declarations. These are "dialogic" statements of discontent "from below," addressed to new ruling authorities and posing uncomfortable, even potentially incompatible questions about the new social order of postcommunism. Very often such dialog takes a moralistic accusatory tone, addressing issues of fairness in society, more particularly, of the perceived betrayal of expectations and promises in what a "free" democratic post-Soviet Lithuania should offer to its citizens.

Theoretically, this chapter draws on the work of V. N. Vološinov, a scholar who laid the basis for a Marxist school of social dialogics during the first phase of socialist transformation in Russia. Vološinov's theoretical work has been in English translation for some three decades but, although increasingly recognized for its profoundly innovative character, has been largely unapplied empirically (Vološinov 1973; Woolfson 1976, 1977). The approach outlined by Vološinov has, however, been developed in the active critique of both structuralist and Habermasian approaches to social discourse analysis (Brandist 2000; Collins 1999; Foster and Woolfson 1999; Gardiner 1992; Holborow 2007; Jones 2004; McNally 2001; Welty 1989). In contrast to structuralist analyses, here priority is given to the linguistic sign in the realized and contested spoken utterance as the vehicle of ideological social consciousness. Distinct from, although not necessarily in opposition to cognitive cultural theory (Ignatow 2004), the analysis presented here remains on the terrain of collective group identities, formed in specific social and historical circumstances. The dialogic realization of utterances is conceptualized in this chapter as contingent upon the underlying and unfolding processes of the new forms of labor's collective solidarity and alienation in the sphere of production, the systemic relocation of labor within emergent capitalist relations of production. Empirically, postcommunist transition society offers a unique window into these changing forms of consciousness in a changed world, one in which labor's alienation is taking radically new appearances.

Within this altered world, the specific refraction of reality which each ideological sphere attains through the semiotic materiality of signs achieves particular clarity in the dialogic discourses of labor protest. As Vološinov (1973, 15) put it:

> Every ideological refraction of existence in the process of generation, no matter what the nature of its significant material, is accompanied by ideological refraction in word as an obligatory concomitant phenomenon.

However, language is no mere mechanistic reflection of the struggle of base with superstructure. Vološinov identified not simply the reflection of reality in signs, but its ideologized refraction, infusing an "inner dialectical quality" in word meaning (Vološinov 1973, 23). This dialectical tension creates a clash of "differently oriented social interests within one and the same sign community" (Vološinov 1973, 41). The refraction of class struggle is registered in what Vološinov (1973, 23) termed, the "social multiaccentuality" of the ideological sign, in which theme and form of sign are inextricably interconnected and ultimately determined by these sets of contested forces:

> Indeed, the economic conditions that inaugurate a new element of reality into the social purview, that make it socially meaningful and "interesting," are exactly the same conditions that create the forms of ideological communication (the cognitive, the artistic, the religious and so on), which in turn shape the forms of semiotic expression. (Vološinov, 22–23)

For these purposes, the "new element of reality" is the complex unfolding of class identities in the newly emergent market economies of postcommunism. This process is conditioned by the legacies and inhibitions of the previous era, but it is also sensitive to the impacts of economic and political change of unprecedented scope and rapidity, no less than the establishment of a new order of the market economy. Dialogic discourse allows us to begin to analyze these impacts within changing forms of social consciousness. As Vološinov (1973, 23) suggested:

> The word is the most sensitive index of social changes, and what is more, of changes still in the process of growth, still without definitive shape and not as yet accommodated into already regularized and fully

defined ideological systems. The word has the capacity to register all the transitory, delicate, momentary phases of social change.

But the "indexical" potential of words, in providing a window into changing social consciousness, is conditioned by contemporary ideological interventions which are themselves politically and socially "motivated" by the need to secure the hegemony of new market forces. Over the period of more than a decade and a half since the collapse of the Soviet Union, an attempt has been made to impose forms of social dialog based on non-class "shared" assumptions of "social partnership" between labor and capital, "united" in the common project of transition. This has been an acutely "necessary" form of intervention, given the fraught social tensions created by the spiraling inequalities of postcommunist society, and the supplanting of collectivist outlooks and supports with those based on forms of radical individualism. Like all ruling classes, the new elites of postcommunism have attempted to give a supra-class, or eternal and "immutable," quality to word meaning in language, and therefore, to perceived reality. Above all, it has been necessary to forestall any return to previous "alternative" discourses of socialism, creating a radical rupture in social consciousness, by superimposing a new unified national identity in order to carry through the awkward business of postcommunist transition. The search for new common unifying ideology was well articulated by one spokesperson for the nascent Lithuanian independence movement of the early 1990s: "It is necessary for us to become citizens of Lithuania. It would be our common joy . . . we would have common duties and common concerns" (Juozaitis 1990).

Crucial to the consolidation of this constructed unified national identity of "common duties" and "common concerns" was the resurrection or reinvention of symbols of nationhood. This required the negotiation of an uncomfortable authoritarian (largely proto-fascist) legacy from the interwar era of Lithuanian national independence. The resurrection of Lithuanian national identity also entailed the contemporary reinstatement of the primacy of the Lithuanian language over Russian, now the rejected language of the Soviet "occupier," although still the first language of a significant minority, especially of the older working population. Largely deprived of the legitimizing resources of past history, and consumed with the expurgation of its more contemporary Soviet history, the nascent independence movement in Lithuania resorted to the creation of a sometimes spurious vocabulary of symbolic unity. Such conscious deployments of meanings and language, however, are always liable to contestation, creating what Vološinov called semiotic "flux" within language. It is this continuing potential for flux, which potentially poses socially disruptive challenges to the increasingly fragile assumptions underlying the new social order, that is examined here. It is the privileged site within which a more or less fierce and ongoing "socially interested" interrogation of signs between labor and capital takes place.

The study of contemporary labor protests accompanying the class reformation of Lithuanian society provides an empirical field for the application of these theoretical insights, and in the real world, for a contest around the newly constructed "unity" of the Lithuanian nation. The analysis this chapter seeks to develop is predicated, therefore, on understanding the preeminent arena of contested dialogic utterances, the actively embodied language of labor protest, viewed in the developing context of rising class tensions. The approach is concrete and historical, and is applied to a specific body of empirical circumstances. Following a brief political and economic analysis of postcommunist Lithuania, emergent discourses of labor protest accompanying "new elements of reality" in postcommunist labor relations are then examined.

LITHUANIA: UNITY AND DEMOCRACY IN A POSTCOMMUNIST SOCIETY

In the Central and Eastern Europe of the late twentieth and early twenty-first centuries a double transformation has occurred, first from planned socialist economies to the free market, and second, from protective economic integration into a politico-economic bloc to sudden exposure to the raw forces of globalization. In the most recent period, a third transformation has been inaugurated, the wider integration of major parts of the former communist world of Central and Eastern Europe into the European Union project of eastwards enlargement. The massive economic changes that have taken place in Central and Eastern Europe since the early 1990s have been well rehearsed many times. These have included the dissolution of state enterprises, emergent foreign and joint ownership, as well as the massive growth of domestic small and medium entrepreneurial concerns. The transition process to market economies has been accompanied by privatization, bankruptcies, restructuring, and the growth of unemployment, underemployment, and a radical "flexibilization" of the workforce (Rainnie, Smith, and Swain 2002). All of these factors have created a sharp imbalance in power between employers and employees at the workplace and the marginalization of labor rights.

Typical here is the ex-Soviet republic of Lithuania, a small Baltic nation close to Scandinavia with a population of some 3.3 million. Although one of the smallest countries in the Soviet Union, Lithuania played a pivotal role in its final breakup. Most memorably on August 23, 1989, the formation of a 370-mile human chain stretching from Lithuania in the south, through Latvia to Estonia in the north, linked anywhere from 1 to 3 million "Balts" in a unified popular protest against Soviet rule. The demonstration climaxed a series of denunciations of Soviet occupation, marking the fiftieth anniversary of the Nazi-Soviet Non-Aggression (Molotov-Ribbentrop) pact, the "secret protocols" of which assigned the Baltic States to the Soviet sphere of influence. These actions, meant to highlight the "illegitimate" character of the subsequent nearly fifty years of Soviet rule, symbolized a newly found Baltic unity and a common striving to "restore" their independence. The Lithuanian Reform Movement (the *Sajūdis* movement for *perestroika*), under its astute leader Vytautas Landsbergis, sustained the ongoing struggle for national independence in the 1980s through the continued mobilization of anti-Soviet sentiment (Lane 2002). The declaration of the *Sajūdis* showed their close sensitivity to the power of language in legitimizing political struggles:

> Today all the people of Lithuania know that there is a word in the Lithuanian language which is pronounced with hope. The word is *Sajūdis* (movement). For the first time, the word attained new meaning in the Great Hall of the Lithuanian Academy of Sciences in the late evening of June 3, 1989. Later the word became known to everybody and it came to mean what we call "The Lithuanian Reform Movement." (*Lituanus* 1990)

Landsbergis, throughout his long political career thereafter, retained an almost paranoid hatred of all the symbolic manifestations of socialism, the Soviet regime, and its "totalitarian" symbols, equated with those of Nazi Germany. Today, both swastika and hammer and sickle are banned from public display in Lithuania (*The Baltic Times* 2004).

While *Sajūdis* movement won parliamentary elections in 1990, its continuing reliance on the mobilization of symbolic anti-Soviet sentiment was insufficient to sustain its electoral base (Lane 2002, 141). Divisions within its own ranks over major issues like de-collectivization of farmlands alienated key sections of its rural support. By 1992, in the face of sharply deteriorating economic conditions, growing unemployment, and hyperinflation reaching 1,000 percent per annum, the urban working class electorate also rejected the *Sajūdis*.

In what appeared a surprising result, the electorate voted the tried and tested leadership of the now reformed communists of the Lithuanian Democratic Labor Party (LDDP) into office on a program promising greater social protection against the shocks of transition. However, such protective assurances could not be realized within the policy constraints imposed by international financial institutions and, in turn, they too were to lose popular support and power. Moreover, in this unstable political process, the notion of "democracy" as such was increasingly discredited as a result of its perceived association with gross abuses accompanying the restructuring process of the economy. The rejection of the LDDP was the result of "widespread belief in the corruption of its leading politicians, and the cynical way in which it feathered the nests of the old communist *nomenklatura* at a time when standards of living for ordinary people were in rapid decline" (Lane 2002, 134). In 1996, elections resulted in the formation of a coalition government led by the right-wing Homeland Union (TS) party, a successor to *Sajūdis* movement. Since then, various coalitions of right wing parties led by Conservative and Liberal parties, and of centrist parties led by the Social Democratic Labor Party (now Social Democratic Party), have held power in Lithuania although with increasing popular alienation from the political process as corruption and insider dealing in the process of privatizations have continued apace.

The political and business elites have embraced neoliberal ideology fostering the myth of a stable prospering Lithuania, with few social and economic problems. The January 2001 edition of *EuroBusiness* (2001, 69) contained a special Baltic states supplement entitled "New Breeds of Tiger." Among the specific virtues of Baltic Lithuania, *EuroBusiness* noted "aggressive economic liberalization, privatizations, wily courtship of foreign capital, and the painful reorientation of trade away from volatile Russia." All of these factors were said to "have underpinned a truly remarkable flourishing of prospects, generating year upon year of high yet sustainable growth." The report went on to record that, according to the *Wall Street Journal*, Lithuania, and its next-door neighbor Latvia, superseded only by Estonia, outranked Denmark, Finland, and Germany in the "league table of economic freedom." The reality of the privatization of the Lithuanian economy and the drive for foreign investment have been rather more problematic.

The form of privatization did much to undermine the attempt to establish a supra-class "unity" of Lithuanian society. The rapid expropriation of state assets in the process of transition to capitalism was effected, in the main, via emerging business criminality. Privatization, the economic engine of the transition process, according to its most enthusiastic proponents, was supposed to make workers "co-owners" and fulfill egalitarian "social justice" and equity objectives (Lithuanian Free Market Institute 2000). Yet within a matter of a few years, sometimes even within months, the majority of privatization vouchers handed out to workers in former state enterprises were sold on the black market for cash. They ended up in the pockets of enterprise managers on extremely favorable discounted terms, jarring with "public expectations . . . strengthened by propaganda, promising high dividend rates, high profitability of the shares and higher living standards" (Maldeikis 1996, 3). So great was public disaffection and unrest concerning "corruption and the influence of organized criminal groups" over the process of privatization that it was temporarily halted (Maldeikis 1996, 16). The distribution of assets before auctions, via "payments to organized criminal groups for the right to acquire particular assets, the selling of "insider" information by officials, and their participation in privatization process" produced a negative popular view of the whole process of privatization, akin perhaps to a sense of collective victimization (Maldeikis 1996, 16). This appraisal is no mere academic commentary. As minister of economics, Maldeikis later resigned from a Conservative-led coalition government over shady privatization deals.

In sum, since its exit from the Soviet sphere of influence, Lithuania's path of transition to the market economy has been guided by an aggressive neoliberal program. Despite local disputes over the pace and spoils of privatization, this project has been largely uncontested among the political classes. Pressures, in particular from the International Monetary Fund and the European Bank for Reconstruction and Development, have left successive governments little room for maneuver. Although increasingly viewed with suspicion and disillusionment at a mass level, 80 percent of enterprises were rapidly privatized. Today, only a few significant enterprises remain in state control.

The deep-seated degree of disenchantment with the political process in the new "democracy" continues to be a major issue as corruption and gain-seeking by the new elites erode whatever little legitimacy the new system might have attained. So much so, that it has required the importation of an "outsider," a Lithuanian émigré, Valdas Adamkus, to act as a unifying presidential figurehead in an attempt to restore the moral authority of the state. As one contemporary observer has put it, aptly capturing the linguistic "flux" of the word "democracy" in the context of postcommunist Lithuania:

> The political class mouthed the vocabulary of democracy but sometimes their actions showed either that they did not understand the meaning of the term, or cynically ignored it. The election of President Adamkus in 1997, in a sense an outsider who had spent most of his adult life in the United States, epitomized the contrast between two political cultures, each using the same vocabulary but differing radically in their understanding of the words. (Lane 2002, 131)

Significantly, Adamkus, on the right of the political spectrum, embarked on his presidential electoral campaign by offering himself as the embodiment of nonparty unity under the supra-class slogan "Accord of the nation."

EMBRYONIC LABOR PROTEST

The darker side of the transition process has been evident in the sheer scale of impact of economic reforms on the workforce. The first decade and a half of transition was marked by a massive deterioration in the wages and working conditions of labor, and the growth of high levels of unemployment. However, mass hardship was not simply a passing feature of the early turbulent years of transition. In two years, between 1997 and 1999, as a result of ongoing privatizations in Vilnius, the capital city of Lithuania, nearly one-quarter of job positions disappeared in the largest five factories. In the Kaunas industrial region, where the largest number of factories are located, the number of jobs in large enterprises decreased by about

40 percent (UN Human Development Report 1999, 64). According to one analysis, these job losses have disproportionately affected older workers, the unskilled, and women, whose workforce participation declined from 56 percent to 50 percent (Dovydenienė 2000). The process of marginalization of a large group of workers has been accompanied, as elsewhere in Eastern Europe, by a sharp growth in income differentials. By the year 2000, approximately a decade after the transition process had begun, one third of families with three or more children, representing 16 percent of the population, were estimated to live below the official poverty line of 50 percent of the average wage (Republic of Lithuania 2001). Estimates of Lithuania's "informal" economy suggest that this sector employs some three hundred thousand workers, or more than 20 percent of the total working population (Bagdzevičienė and Belazrienė 2001, 25–28). All of these workers, by definition, are excluded from protection with regard to secure and safe employment conditions.

The levers of economic and political power, both at national level and in the workplace, have been firmly gripped by the new employer class. So far, however, organized trade union resistance has failed to emerge to match the scale of the assault on labor. The classical expression of a labor dispute, an official strike, has been a rarity in Lithuania, especially in recent years. When it has occurred, it has experienced significant legal as well as organizational impediments. The U.S. Embassy has noted reassuringly that "labor unions are relatively uninfluential" and that the country "has not seen any major industrial strikes since regaining independence" (US Embassy 1998). In fact, in 1992, public-sector workers took industrial action, as well as hairdressers, photo studio operators, and transport drivers. However, "strikes and other confrontations between labor and management . . . are limited by the nascent free-enterprise system and the perception that employment alternatives are limited" (US Department of the Army nd). Systematic collection of statistical data about the strikes in Lithuania only started in the year 2000. According to these statistics, in the year 2000, there were fifty-six strikes (including twenty-one warning strikes), and during 2001, there were thirty-four strikes (of which twenty-nine were warning strikes). Most of these strikes were organized in educational institutions of the state sector, although there were also strikes in transport and manufacturing sectors. The main reasons for striking were conflicts concerning late or nonpayment of wages (European Foundation for the Improvement of Living and Working Conditions 2002). In the more recent period, the lack of registered strikes does not mean that labor conflicts have been entirely extinguished, however. While major union-led industrial disputes have been the exception, it is precisely these "unregistered protest actions," or embryonic collective actions by labor, that are significant indicators of continuing underlying and often suppressed forms of conflict. It is just such protest actions which comprise the main body of material analyzed here.

For the new elites of postcommunism, any collective assertion of labor rights and identities, outside of strictly bounded limits, has been viewed as a potential impediment to their economic survival (Woolfson and Beck 2002). In essence, free-market philosophy remained largely uncontested by any significant countermovement in the first phase of transition. Yet the transition process has been accompanied by a sharp polarization of society, as previously described, in terms of the growth of inequality. With this has come the emergence of the objective basis for class-based discourses of labor protest. However, the articulation of such discourses has been far from straightforward. A legacy of anti-Sovietism has meant that any collective class-based expressions of discontent, for example, through the organized trade union movement, have been largely discredited. In the emerging pro-independence movement in Lithuania in the late 1980s and early 1990s, unlike the campaign for independence in neighboring Poland, there was no involvement of collective labor through industrial actions such as strikes. This was probably because of the integration of the Lithuanian trade unions in the all-Soviet trade union structures of the USSR, and the significant ethnic Russian component of the Lithuanian industrial working class, which was somewhat ambivalent about the burgeoning independence movement. Indeed, a sporadic though largely unsuccessful attempt was made to organize factory strikes against the *Sajūdis* by the pro-Moscow anti-independence *Yedinstvo* (Unified) movement, especially in the later phases of the independence campaign. In general, however, the Russian-speaking section of the working class remained essentially a passive spectator throughout these protracted struggles. Thereafter, the formerly unified Soviet -led union trade union confederation divided into four separate federations aligned with various political groupings across the politically tolerated spectrum, from centrist Social Democratic to rightist Christian Democratic (Dovydenienė 2000)

At a mass level, the trade unions, until now, have not been "trusted" institutions of the "reconstituted civil society," primarily through their association with the previous regime. Thus, trade union membership in Lithuania, as elsewhere in Central and Eastern Europe, has plunged to catastrophically low levels in recent years and is about 14 percent of the workforce, mainly concentrated in the public sector, with collective bargaining agreement coverage levels being even lower (EIROnline 2005). Moreover, a particularly restrictive set of antistrike laws was in place, with an extensive list of "essential services" in which the right to strike is either removed or severely limited (Woolfson and Beck 2003). With elaborate mandatory prestrike procedures for conciliation, and a requirement for at least a two-thirds majority of workers to vote in favor of industrial action, these made collective action difficult to organize, and indeed were the cause of continuing concern by international human rights bodies (Office of the United Nations High Commissioner for Human Rights 2004). Thus, in the first phase of transition, legitimized oppositional collective discourses have struggled to emerge in any defined "class" sense. The fragmentary discourses of labor protest chart the difficult road that Lithuanian labor has traveled in the last decade and a half.

At workplace level, a new dynamic was beginning to assert itself, as workers responded to the imposition of a significantly more stringent labor regime than anything previously experienced under the former system. This new labor discipline was commonly described in the ironic observation "At least under Communism we only had to work 8 hours a day. Now we have to work all the hours of the day." Yet, the response to this process has been typically individualistic in nature rather than collective. Some measure of this can be gauged from the following incident. In its review for the year 2000, Lithuanian state television included brief news footage of a distraught middle-aged man being wrestled to the ground by three police officers, before being bundled into the back of a police *Lada* (originally a Soviet-built passenger car). The man, who had doused himself in petrol and was about to set himself on fire in front of the presidential palace in the capital city of Vilnius, was shouting "let me die—I have nothing left to lose." In this one single utterance, the despair of the postcommunist dispossessed is articulated. The incident was a solitary act of desperation by one of several dozens of workers who had been on hunger strike in protest against the nonpayment of wages by defaulting employers of bankrupt enterprises. The newsreel summed up much about the state of Lithuania's economy and labor relations. The industrial enterprise from which this particular worker had come, *Litoda*, was located in a town in the west of the country and formerly produced synthetic leather. In the new Lithuania, in which Mafia men and imitators strut in regulation black leather, the demand for its synthetic imitation has slumped, while export of this product had proven almost impossible. Hunger strikes by employees cheated of wages, in some cases, lasted for six weeks and saw their participants removed to hospital with probable permanent physical damage.

This brief and desperate cameo of individualized public protest action is remarkable only in the sense that it was captured on camera. Most such acts of attempted self-destruction are entirely "voiceless" and take place in private hidden corners. Lithuania currently has the highest official rate of suicide in Europe, and possibly one of the highest in the world. Moreover, these rates have been rising in recent years since the mid-1990s. In 2001, the Department of Statistics recorded that 1,533 Lithuanians committed suicide, something like 4 percent of deaths overall, or 44 deaths per 100,000 of population (compared to U.S. and UK rates of about 11 per 100,000) (Republic of Lithuania 2001). This rate is more than twice the average for the candidate countries and more than four times the average for the European Union, according to the World Health Organization (WHO 2001, 15). The extraordinarily high rates of suicide are mirrored in another remarkable phenomenon, the numbers of employees who kill themselves in the workplace. Recorded workplace suicides more than doubled from fourteen (for the years 1995 to 1997) to thirty-seven (for the years 1998 to 2000; personal communication 2001 from State Labor Inspectorate). The National Health Council Report of Lithuania, for year 2000, comments that "suicides at work may be linked with work strain, inability to adjust . . . to new, more complex working conditions, delayed payment, threat of unemployment, (abusive) behavior of employers or authorized persons" (National Health Council 2000). While it is impossible to gauge how many of the total of suicides are the result of work-related stress or other pressures of occupational origin, it would seem that the new disciplinarian workplace environment of postcommunism plays a significant role.

LABOR MARKET LIBERALIZATION

A second contemporary labor protest in Lithuania reveals a shift from largely individualized forms of protest, although not as yet a full collective resistance of labor. It was a substitute symbolical protest performed on behalf of workers by their organized union leadership, such as existed. After a period of center left–led government in the earlier part of the 1990s, a Conservative government took power in the late 1990s. This Conservative government was routed at the polls in October 2000, in the backwash of renewed disillusion with privatization and falling living standards. However, even though the Social Democrats won the largest number of seats in the *Seimas* (parliament), a coalition of Liberals and the New Union (Social Liberals) assumed office with a radical program of antilabor "business-friendly" proposals, and within weeks of gaining office, the new government published a resolution spelling out its intentions (*Seimas* of the Republic of Lithuania 2000). Under the heading of "Liberalization of Labor Relations," this resolution proposed a raft of changes to trade union and employment laws including: the removal of the approved typical form of an employment contract; removal of all restrictions in concluding any type of civil contracts between natural persons, as well as between natural and legal persons; phasing out of restrictions on temporary employment contracts; mandatory working time records no longer to be kept; the requirement that employees have employment identification documents waived; compensation for public servants and other employees made unemployed reduced in amount; employers no longer required to consult trade unions before making workers redundant; increased employer rights to redeploy workers at one-third of the minimum wage rate instead of the full statutory minimum rate; a requirement that workers who receive training at the employer's expense compensate the employer if changing employment.

The proposed measures, officially aimed at "reducing unemployment in Lithuania," were part of a concerted attempt to create labor market "flexibility." They appeared as a major threat to the trade unions. The four trade union confederations, united for the first time since independence, threatened nationwide industrial action. Articles on employee rights and conditions appearing in the Lithuanian press exposed "routine slavery" conditions (see Laima Žiūkienė-Lavaste, *Lietuvos Rytas* February 23, 2002. In the kingdom of women—slavery is routine). By the early Spring of 2001, the trade union opposition led to a postponement of the planned liberalization package. On March 23, nonetheless, the *Seimas* (parliament) passed new liberalization legislation that amended, inter alia, the *Law on Employment Contracts*, the *Law on Wages*, the *Law on Holidays*, and the *Law on Trade Unions*.

In response to these proposed measures, labor protests took place outside the homes of members of parliament from the Liberal party, while over a hundred trade unionists from throughout Lithuania attended as "silent witness" at the plenary debate on the new legislation in the *Seimas*. Opposition Social Democratic coalition members of parliament, who had sponsored the trade unions' "silent witness" in parliament, called on the president not to ratify the new law. Presidential ratification, however, duly followed. During this dispute, overt protest on the part of the trade unions created public relations risks for them. In most instances, these protests involved small quiet pickets of perhaps a dozen or so smartly dressed men and women, standing with placards in dignified order outside MPs' homes. Some newspapers claimed the protesters had caused a fatal heart attack to one member of parliament's mother and denounced the "intimidation" of families and innocent children. The wife of another was seen on the television news arriving home in a *Mitsubishi* 4-wheel-drive vehicle unmolested by the "pickets." The direct "personalization" of the protest against the liberalization measures was easily misconstrued by a hostile media. The linguistic "flux" of social opinion, to return to Vološinov's perspectives, was captured in television broadcasts. These broadcasts provided pictures, remarkable in the context of media representations of postcommunist society, of the condensed and semantically loaded telegraphy of protest. One placard read almost cozily, only to end with stinging rebuke: *Dear Neighbors—We elected your neighbor Rolanda Pavilionis but he voted in the Seimas for measures that will make you a slave without rights*. On other placards there was an even more bald accusatory tone: *We did not elect you to vote for our enslavement*, and *We did not elect you to vote to remove our rights and jobs*. One protest placard displayed a message asking a member of parliament, *Do you know what an autocracy at work means G. Dalinkevicius?* Another banner contained a cartoon representation in one corner of a boss aggressively pointing a finger down at a worker on his bended knees. The personalization of *you* in the slogans implied a real human identity as its referent. The *you* is named; it is someone known to and present in the community, albeit that s/he is a member of parliament. Such keywords as *autocracy* (*savivale*) and *slave* (*vergas*) may seem quaint to outsiders, but they are imbued with accusatory, potentially explosive, meaning. Lithuania was meant to have emerged democratically reborn, but now the forces of free market capitalism seemed to undermine that common interest. It is perhaps not going too far to suggest that the use of these terms was an implicit riposte to the language of the post-1991 order, in terms of its self-justification as one of "freedom" and in contrast to the "autocracy" of the previous regime. The "one-nation" ideology, which was an important political lever in the dislocation of Soviet power, now had ironic resonance in the post-Soviet period. In the new democracy, where politicians are supposed to represent the "unified" interests of the people, the sense of betrayal was palpably conveyed by such personalized admonishments.

Given the magnitude of the threat posed to basic labor rights by the new liberalization legislation, it can be argued that the trade unions acted with "restraint." Most likely, this restraint was a mark of their overall weakness and, perhaps, a recognition that, in Lithuania, concerted worker protests could be not yet be fully legitimized. On a more positive note, the scale of the assault on labor rights provoked united trade union opposition for the first time since independence, and in 2002, the two major trade union centers amalgamated into one body.

"MUTED" COLLECTIVIST DISCOURSE

In this section, "muted" collectivist discourse is analyzed. It concerns a group of workers not normally associated with public protest actions, the police. The Constitution of the Republic of Lithuania and the 1991 Law on Trade Unions recognize the right of workers and employees to form and join trade unions (Republic of Lithuania 1991a). The Law on Trade Unions Article 1 extends this right to employees of the police and the armed forces via statutes regulating their activities. In the case of police officers, this is the Law on Police (Republic of Lithuania 1991b). Article 8 of this law allows for the "Realization of Professional Interests" and states: "Police officers may establish societies, clubs, professional unions, and other associations in order to meet their professional, cultural, and social needs" (Republic of Lithuania 1991b, Article 8). However, the Law on the Regulation of Collective Disputes of 1992 does not allow withdrawal of labor by employees involved in law enforcement and state security:

> It shall be prohibited to call a strike within the structures of internal affairs, national defense and national security ... The demands of the employees of such services ... shall be considered by the Government of the Republic of Lithuania. (Republic of Lithuania 1992, Article 10)

This prohibition on the right to strike has had particular effects on the police as an occupational group in Lithuania. In the early period of independence during the 1990s, there were few attempts to raise their status and effectiveness as professional law enforcement officers. The origins of labor unrest date back to 1997 when government promises of higher wages for senior police officers were not matched by an appropriate budgetary allocation while rank-and-file police officers complained of low wages as well as lack of funds for basic equipment such as replacement uniforms. Even petrol for police vehicles was in short supply. At that time, more than half the police vehicle fleet were still the Soviet-era *Ladas* with a tendency to self-immolate, and no match for the new BMW-driving criminal classes. Even in the capital city officers were on occasion without facilities for long-distance telephone connections, due to unpaid bills, while some six thousand employees had been laid off. It was against the background of rising frustration that the police officers' trade union, the Union of Police Constables and Police Employees, was established.

By December 2000, the police trade union was sufficiently well organized in the Vilnius region to mount a public protest. This consisted of a "lunchtime walk through Gedimino Prospect," the main thoroughfare of the capital, by around four hundred policemen and women in full uniform, supported by fire-brigade colleagues. The "walk" culminated in the handing over of a petition listing their grievances to the *Seimas* (see *Lietuvos Rytas* 2002, 16 December. Dignified walk of police). The leader of the police trade union commented, "We have no money for lunch, so at least we will have some fresh air to breath." A simultaneous demonstration was held in Klaipėda, the port city of northern Lithuania. Two further mass demonstrations of this nature were held (June 2001 and May 2003), involving police trade unionists from the increasingly well-organized outlying regions of Lithuania, as well as at least one spontaneous sit-in at the end of shift over delayed payment of wages, a fairly remarkable occurrence in view of the strict police discipline code. In the case of the public demonstrations, the Lithuanian police trade unionists were latterly able to call on the support of Italian and German police union colleagues who marched side by side with Lithuanians as fellow members of the European Police Trade Union Confederation, CESP. This is the first recorded example of international trade union solidarity at European level in a dispute involving any section of the Lithuanian workforce.

Senior police officers, who had been publicly hostile to the first protest action, now supported the demands of their lower ranking officers. A measure perhaps of their growing strength as a union was the absence of reported victimization of activists, a commonplace in Lithuanian labor relations. The police trade union now claimed to have recruited about 1,000 of the capital's 2,500 police and some 5,000 out of the 11,000 for the whole of Lithuania (Interview by author 2004). If correct, these figures represent the highest trade union density of any sector of the workforce. The public impact of these demonstrations, especially of the first, was sufficiently great to produce a substantial new budgetary allocation. It also brought to a halt the ongoing redundancies of police officers. Nevertheless, some important grievances remained unresolved and the language of incorporation has only partially met its goal of dampening labor protest among Lithuanian police.

The promised increase in salaries for lower ranking police did not emerge. Moreover, a new statute governing police work stipulated shift work in excess of the forty-eight hours allowable maximum working week, according to ILO's Convention. This adversely affects more than half of the police officer workforce and resulted in formal complaint to the ILO Committee of Experts on the Application of Conventions and Recommendations (ILO 2004). Besides unwelcome exposure to international scrutiny with respect to labor standards in Lithuania, the police trade unionists' protests have had a singular significance: nationwide collective labor protest appears to be emerging, even in sectors of the workforce that are legally precluded from taking part in withdrawal of their labor. Meanwhile, in an extraordinary Congress of Lithuanian Trade Union Confederation, the former chairperson of the Lithuanian Trade Union of Constables and Police Employees, Artūras Černiauskas, was elected as a new chairperson of Lithuanian Trade Union Confederation (LPSK), perhaps the first of a new generation of more combative labor leaders to emerge in postcommunist Lithuania.

The response of the Lithuanian authorities to labor unrest among the police has been predictable: the incorporation of the new police trade union into a framework of social dialog and the recognition of the union as a "social partner." Yet how far this "incorporation" represents an enduring "restabilization" is a more open issue, as the conclusion section suggests. Police officers in their thousands subsequently successfully undertook legal action against the state to recover lost wages, although so far further threats of (illegal) strike action have not materialized. Meanwhile, as unrest among police officers has intensified, presidential intervention has urged "dialogue" and "compromise" on both sides (Seputyte 2005).

EUROPEAN PROTEST

One of the most important inhibitions on the growth of organized labor in postindependence Lithuania has been sustained antiunion harassment. In Lithuania today, in common with many other new democracies in Central and Eastern Europe, there is widespread ongoing victimization and intimidation of trade union activists. For example, among supermarket employees, where trade unions were beginning to make some inroads, fixed-term contracts of trade union members in some large retail stores were not renewed on expiry (ICFTU 2006). The International Helsinki Federation for Human Rights (2003) country analysis for Lithuania has noted:

> In 2003 a new Code on Civil Procedure will come into force, which, in specifying that trade union lawyers are no longer allowed to represent and defend their union members on appeal to the Supreme Court,

effectively violates provisions of the European Social Charter. In 2002 Lithuanian law guaranteed certain rights for Lithuanian workers, however the practical and economic mechanisms necessary for the effective protection of these rights were not established . . . Lithuanian employers were effectively able to dictate working conditions. Employers worded employment contracts with terms favorable to them, leaving the worker with no employment guarantees.

In a further report, the Helsinki Committee on Economic, Social and Cultural Rights (2004, 274) noted regarding "labor rights" in Lithuania that "The authorities continued to tolerate gross violations of employees' rights: individuals were illegally fired after fictitious liquidation claims and rehired as new workers with fewer rights."

Following privatization of the railroads, antiunion activities on the part of management were experienced by members of the Lithuanian Railway Workers' Trade Union. The deputy chairperson of the union was dismissed three times, although on each occasion ordered to be reinstated following a court ruling. However, no sanctions were imposed on the managers concerned for noncompliance with the court. A locomotive driver, who had given twenty-five years' satisfactory service, was dismissed after taking an active role in the union. (ICFTU 2004a, 2004b). In only a few cases, however, has employment reinstatement followed a ruling of unfair dismissal. To draw attention to these and other abuses, the Railway Workers Union decided to take their grievances to Brussels, headquarter city of the European Union, on the very eve of Lithuania becoming a full member. In late March 2004, two Lithuanian railway trade unionists began a pavement hunger strike opposite the entry to the European Commission building, near the Schuman metro station in Brussels. Their sleeping bags and umbrellas were framed by a placard which announced in English: "Lithuanian hired workers' hunger action." Before starting the hunger strike, the union had sent a "petition" to the president of European Parliament, to the European Commission chairman, and to the European commissioner responsible for European Union enlargement. The trade unionists drew attention to the "horrible situation of hired workers and cynical violation of independent organizations' labor rights, and pitiable social security in candidate countries." The commencement of the hunger strike was accompanied by a declaration in which the new point of reference for the remedy of labor injustices in Lithuania was clearly identified. Union chairperson Vladimiras Troschchenka (Socialist Party of Lithuania 2004) put it as follows:

> Although politicians of Lithuania and other countries joining the EU fulfill all the requirements of European Union Commissioners, the EU Parliament and the Commission are *straightforwardly responsible for the situation of hired citizens in our states, which today is tragic.*

The declaration continued with a seemingly reasonable, but politically "impossible," demand—that Lithuania should conform to EU labor standards, or its membership should be renegotiated.

> Breach of labor rights of hired workers and their organisations is an everyday reality in the candidate-states, and nobody is going to solve that. Therefore we request that the enrolment of the new States in the European Union be suspended and new talks on the enrolment's conditions take place. During the talks, there should be a discussion and adjustment of the protection of labor rights and social environment to present EU-standards, orders and terms.

The other Brussels hunger striker was Leonidas Malomuzhas, the dismissed locomotive driver referred to earlier, who at this point had already experienced seven months without salary. Malomuzhas's comments were aimed at the "citizens of Europe":

> It is not important for me if I go to hunger strike, either in my homeland Lithuania, or here, in the capital of Europe. The difference is that here I can *draw the attention of Europe's citizens to the appalling situation* in the labor market of the Candidate States. (Socialist Party of Lithuania 2004, emphasis added)

Within a week, after a period of "administrative custody" during which they were fingerprinted by the Belgian police, the two Lithuanian trade unionists were summarily deported in handcuffs. Accompanied by a three-car high-speed police escort, with full sirens blaring, the two hunger strikers were bundled onto a plane to Lithuania without explanation, or a reasonable opportunity to seek legal assistance. Troschchenka put it as follows: "Workers fighting for their rights have been treated as gangsters! This is the reality of European Union" (Socialist Party of Lithuania 2004). The next day a declaration detailed at length their summary treatment and harassment at the hands of the Belgian authorities. Their disturbing account of these events asked the following: "Is the Convention on Europe's human rights and main freedoms valid in Brussels [also] for East Europe's inhabitants?" (Troschchenka 2004).

THE FUTURE OF LABOR DISCOURSE

The question that remains is whether the emerging discourses of protest may be assuming more clearly defined oppositional collective and class-based articulation, more in keeping with commonly understood expressions of labor protest in established Western democracies. On May 1, 2004, Lithuania, together with seven other Central and East European states, joined the enlarged European Union. The choice of "Labor Day" as the date of accession of the former communist states was an act of inspired symbolic theft. However, it may yet come back to haunt the masters of the new Europe. With entry into the European Union, latent dissatisfaction with the consequences of the pursuit of neoliberal economic policy among the workers in postcommunist countries such as Lithuania may acquire a new dynamism. The European social model is meant to balance the market and social priorities. European Union directives address many aspects of working environment, including health and safety conditions, hours of work, consultation and information rights, and so forth, while the accompanying European Charter of Fundamental Rights legitimates the basic right to collective forms of protection through trade unions, up to and including the right to strike. Thus with European Union membership, a new assertive impetus may be given to the discourses of collective labor rights, resonating with underlying accumulated grievances of the workforces. Whether such impetus will be realized depends, to some extent, on the trade unions' organizational capacities, which, as noted, are currently depleted, as well as the commitment of the European Union itself to preserve workers' rights in the enlarged union.

Until now, the discourses of labor discontent in postcommunist Lithuania have mainly expressed themselves through individual and symbolic acts of resistance. In part, the lack of strike action is also the result of two generations during the Soviet era in which there would have been little collective labor action, and possibly a decline of class consciousness. In part also, the undeveloped nature of this discourse is the result of the breakup of collective class confidence—and of the explicit ideological marginalization/suppression of the language of class action, through concepts of "common interests," "unity of the nation," and institutional structures of "social partnership." Emergent labor protests, therefore, have taken both a personalized and a political form—rather than immediate resort to the use of "traditional" collective strike action. Protests have included hunger strikes and public demonstrations by placard-bearing "victims" of injustice. These have occurred outside the employer factory gate or residence, as well as outside the symbolic site of the new state, be it the presidential palace and parliamentary building, or even outside the offices of the European superstate. Occasionally and, most dramatically, protest actions have entailed huge personal sacrifices, setting up the dialogic tension between accusatory symbolic gestures and the self-harm resulting to those making them.

The future may be rather different. Following the expansion of class horizons accompanying membership of the wider enlarged European Union, the potential for larger scale, more organized strikes in postcommunist societies can now be recognized. The predominantly neoliberal approach of ruling elites in the new EU member postcommunist states, and their one-sidedly class-based nature, is becoming increasingly transparent. The legitimizing potential of demands for labor rights may reinfuse the trade union movement with combative vigor. With that, the temporary national unity of the early postcommunist years may finally be dissipated. The first significant blows in the coming battles have already been struck, in terms of an employers' offensive, through the imposition of labor market liberalization measures in new labor codes throughout Central and Eastern Europe (See Republic of Lithuania 2002). The reactions of labor can only grow more defined, especially as the established European trade unions extend their solidarity actions and assistance to the new member states. Thus, it can be argued that there will be an inevitable shift from more individualized and muted acts of protest to more open collective forms of labor struggle as the process of European integration proceeds, and as links between organized workers are solidified and capacities strengthened on a pan-European basis.

Paradoxically, the accession to the EU of former communist countries now brings the uncomfortable requirement for the re-legalization of Communist parties. The prospects for mass influence of Marxist ideas in Eastern Europe are remote at this time. Nevertheless, the class-fracturing of the language of "social partnership" has begun. The failure of social democracy to protect workers rights in both the older and newer member states of the European Union may in the future become subject to renewed critique and development in a more explicitly class-based direction. The accession of Lithuania, along with seven other Central and East European countries to the enlarged European Union, may mark a turning point in the dynamics of labor protest. Its accompanying discourses, while not in any sense determinative, may undergo significant change. The compass of ideological reference is pointing away from the past negative associations towards trade unions and collectivism and the Soviet system is now a fading memory of nearly two decades ago. A new reference point is emerging, where trade unions are increasingly to be seen as necessary active defenders of legitimate labor rights, in the face of continuing employer abuse. Moreover, the right to the collective withdrawal of labor, and to free association and collective bargaining, are both endorsed as democratic rights at European and international levels in conventions to which Lithuania is a signatory. This new reference point provides a discourse of democratic rights legitimizing independent collective trade union action. A free society is, by definition, a society of "free" collective bargaining. It suggests that the (re)legitimization of collectivist labor discourses may be one of the most significant, although unintended, consequences of the eastwards expansion of the European Union. The gathering prospect of an end to postcommunist "labor quiescence" brings with it potentially incompatible challenges to the current order of neoliberal "truths", a development which, in itself, seems likely to be increasingly reflected in the discourses of labor protest.

ACKNOWLEDGMENTS

John Foster and Chik Collins provided valuable comments on earlier drafts of this chapter. All errors and omissions remain the responsibility of the author.

REFERENCES

Bagdzevičienė, Rita, and Giedrė Belazrienė. 2001. Shadow economy in Lithuania. *Lithuanian Business Review* 8:25–28.
Brandist, Craig. 2000. Bakhtin, Marxism and Russian populism. In *Materializing Bakhtin: The Bakhtin Circle and social theory*, eds. Craig Brandist and Galin Tihanov, 70–93. London: Macmillan.
Collins, Chik. 1999. *Language, ideology and social consciousness—developing a sociohistorical approach*. Aldershot, UK: Ashgate.
Dovydenienė, Roma. 2000. *Trade union responses to globalization in Lithuania*. Geneva: International Labor Organisation, Institute for Labor Studies, Labor and Society Programme, http://www.ilo.org/public/english/bureau/inst/download/dp11199.pdf (accessed October 6, 2008).
EIROnline. 2005. Lithuania—trade unions in focus. Dublin: European Foundation for the Improvement of Living and Working Conditions, http://www.eurofound.europa.eu/eiro/2004/12/feature/lt0412102f.htm (accessed October 6, 2008).
EuroBusiness Magazine. 2001. Special report, Baltic States. January edition, 2, 8.
European Foundation for the Improvement of Living and Working Conditions. 2002. *Social dialogue and conflict resolution in Lithuania*, http://www.uni-mannheim.de/edz/pdf/ef/04/ef0451en.pdf (accessed October 6, 2008).
Foster, John, and Charles Woolfson. 1999. How workers on the Clyde gained the capacity for class struggle: The Upper Clyde shipbuilders' work-in, 1971–72. In *British trade unions and industrial politics, Volume 2: The high tide of trade unionism, 1964–79*, eds. John McIlroy, Nina Fishman, and Alan. B. Campbell, 297–325. Aldershot, UK: Ashgate.
Gardiner, Michael. 1992. *The dialogics of critique*. London: Routledge.
Helsinki Committee on Economic, Social and Cultural Rights. 2004. Concluding observations on the implementation of the International Covenant on Economic, Social and Cultural Rights (E/1990/5/Add.55), 27, 28 April 2004.
Holborow, Marnie. 2007. Putting the social back into language: Marx, Vološinov and Vygotsky re-examined. *Studies in Language and Capitalism* 1:1–28, http://www.languageandcapitalism.info/ (accessed October 6, 2008).
Huspek, Michael. 1991. Language and power. *Language and Society* 20, 1:131–37.
ICFTU (International Confederation of Free Trade Unions). 2004a. *Annual survey 2004 violations of trade union rights*, http://www.icftu.org/survey2004.asp?language=EN (accessed October 6, 2008).
———. 2004b. Europe: alarming trend in anti-union measures in Eastern Europe. 7/6/2004, http://www.icftu.org/displaydocument.asp?Index=991219351&Language=EN (accessed October 6, 2008).
———. 2006. *Annual survey 2006 violations of trade union rights*, http://www.icftu.org/displaydocument.asp?Index=991223916&Language=EN (accessed October 6, 2008).
Ignatow, Gabriel. 2004. Speaking together, thinking together? Exploring metaphor and cognition in a shipyard union dispute. *Sociological Forum* 19, 3:405–33.

ILO (International Labor Organization). 2004. Letter from director of International Labor Standards Department to Lithuanian Trade Union of Constables and Police Employees (received 16 January) (author's possession).
International Helsinki Federation for Human Rights. 2003. *Human rights in the OSCE region: Europe, Central Asia and North America, Report 2003* (Events of 2002), Lithuania Report, June 24, http://www.ihf-hr.org/documents/doc_summary.php?sec_id=3&d_id=3938 (accessed October 6, 2008).
Interview by Charles Woolfson with Artūras Černiauskas, head of the Union of Police Constables and Police Employees, Vilnius, 4 February 2004.
Jones, Peter E. 2004. Discourse and the materialist conception of history: Critical comments on critical discourse analysis. *Historical Materialism* 12, 1:97–125.
Juozaitis, Arvydas. 1990. Lithuania: Love and justice. Statement of member of the *Sajūdis* initiative group, *Lituanus, Lithuanian Quarterly Journal of Arts and Sciences*_36:1, http://www.lituanus.org/1990_1/90_1_06.htm (accessed October 6, 2008).
Lane, Thomas. 2002. *Lithuania stepping westward.* London: Routledge.
Lithuanian Free Market Institute. 2000. *Privatization in Lithuania, analysis,* http://www.freema.org/Research/Privatisation.phtml (accessed October 6, 2008).
Lituanus, Lithuanian Quarterly Journal of Arts and Sciences. 1990. 36:1, http://www.lituanus.org/1990_1/90_1_06.htm (accessed October 6, 2008).
Maldeikis, Eugenijus. 1996. *Privatisation in Lithuania: Expectations, process, consequences.* CERT discussion papers, 96/3. Edinburgh: Herriot-Watt University, http://www.som.hw.ac.uk/cert/wpa/1996/dp9603.pdf (accessed October 6, 2008).
McNally, David. 2001. *Bodies of meaning: Studies on language, labor and liberation.* Albany: State University of New York Press.
National Health Council. 2000. *Occupational health and safety at work* (Annual Report, Part 4.10). Vilnius, Lithuania: Occupational Medicine Center.
Office of the United Nations High Commissioner for Human Rights. 2004. *Concluding observations of the Committee on Economic, Social and Cultural Rights: Lithuania.* 07/06/2004. E/C.12/1/Add.96. Thirty-second session, 26 April–14 May. Principal subjects of concern, Point 15. Geneva, Switzerland, http://www.unhchr.ch/tbs/doc.nsf/898586b1dc7b4043c1256a450044f331/8380bf7f0e0c7388c1256f4300596af4/$FILE/LithuaniaEng.Published.pdf (accessed October 6, 2008).
Personal Communication. 2001. Figures supplied by Lithuanian State Labor Inspectorate, via Violeta Michelkeviciute.
Rainnie, Al, Adrian Smith, and Adam Swain, eds. 2002. *Work, employment and transition: Restructuring livelihoods in post-communism.* London: Routledge.
Republic of Lithuania. 1991a. On Trade Unions, Article 3. Freedom of Activities of Trade Unions. Article 4, The Legal Basis of Trade Unions, Law No. I-2019, 21 November.

———. 1991b. On Police, Article 8. Realization of Professional Interests, Law No. 1-851, 11 December.

———. 1992. On the Regulation of Collective Disputes, Law No. 12386, 17 March.

———. 2001. *Statistical yearbook of Lithuania 2000.* Vilnius, Lithuania: Department of Statistics.

———. 2002. Labor Code Part II, Collective Labor Relations, Chapter VII, General Provisions, Articles 40–47.

———. 2003. On Internal Services, Law No 1X-1538, 1 May.
Seimas of the Republic of Lithuania. 2000. *Resolution on the Program of the Government of the Republic of Lithuania for 2000–2004,* 9 November, No. IX-20, Vilnius, Lithuania: Republic of Lithuania.

Seputyte, Milda. 2005. Adamkus mediates police, government discord. *The Baltic Times* 10, 456, 1:5.
Socialist Party of Lithuania. 2004. Hunger strike Lithuanian railway trade-unionists in Brussels, Brussels, 29 March (author's possession).
The Baltic Times. 2004. MEPs: Ban hammer, sickle and swastika. 10, 443, February 3–9, 1:5.
Troschchenka, Vladimir. 2004. *Declaration of Lithuanian railway trade-unions' chairman, Vladimir Troschchenka. Is convention on Europe's human rights and main freedoms valid in Brussels for East Europe's inhabitants?* April 2, Vilnius (author's possession).
United Nations. 1999. *United Nations Lithuanian human development report, 1999*. Vilnius: Lithuania.
U.S. Embassy. 1998. *Country commercial guide: Lithuania*. Vilnius: U.S. Embassy.
U.S. Department of the Army. (nd). *Country studies/area handbook series, Lithuania*, http://countrystudies.us/lithuania/17.htm (accessed October 6, 2008).
Vološinov, Valentin. N. 1973. *Marxism and the philosophy of language*. New York: Seminar Press.
Welty, Gordon. 1989. *A critique of Habermas' proposed reconstruction of historical materialism presented to the Czechoslovak Academy of Sciences*, http://www.wright.edu/~gordon.welty/Habermas_89.htm (accessed October 6, 2008).
WHO (World Health Organization). 2001. September 12. *Accession—is it healthy? Health prospects in countries that are candidates for accession to membership of the European Union*, http://www.euro.who.int/mediacentre/PressBackgrounders/2001/20010927_5 (accessed October 6, 2008).
Woolfson, Charles. 1976. 2007. The semiotics of working-class speech. *Working Papers in Cultural Studies* 9:163–97. Centre for Contemporary Cultural Studies, Birmingham, UK: University of Birmingham. Reprinted in *CCCS Selected Working Papers: Volume 1*, eds. Anne Gray, Jan Campbell, Mark Erickson, Stuart Hanson, and Helen Wood, 504–35. London: Routledge.
———. 1977. Culture, language and the human personality. *Marxism Today* 21, 8:229–40.
Woolfson, Charles, and Matthias Beck. 2002. Re-mapping labor's rights: The case of transitional Lithuania. *Europe-Asia Studies* 54:749–69.
———. 2003. The right to strike, labor market liberalisation and the new labor code in pre-accession Lithuania. *Review of Central and East European Law* 28:77–102.

PART II
State Responses to Oppositional Discourses and Democratization from Below

4 Challenging New Laws with Old Values
Indigenous Resistance to State "Enforcement" of Children's Rights in Ghana

Janice Windborne

In the debate over human rights, there is a theoretical split in perspective that falls largely along geographical lines. Those from the industrialized West have generally argued that human rights are universal; they belong to every individual, beyond culture and history. Those from the developing world have taken a cultural relativity perspective, claiming that no individual can be separated from his or her culture, and that one's understanding of human rights should be defined according to and within one's culture. Fields and Narr argue further that human rights cannot be separated from the "specific historical and geographical contexts" of any given setting (1992, 3). Further complicating the discussion is the status of the child. Does the child have human rights independent of the needs, desires and values of the parent? Or, does the child belong first to the community and the family with rights flowing only through those relationships?

In 1990, under pressure from the United Nations, its western lenders, and domestic interest groups, Ghana became the first nation to sign the UN Convention on the Rights of the Child (CRC). The government went on to pass its own laws designed to reinforce those rights. However, almost two decades later, many Ghanaian children have not realized the human rights promised by the CRC. Children from this segment of the population remain unpaid workers in the informal economy. Many do not go to school, nor do they receive adequate food or shelter. Few of them have any leisure time at all. Based on conversations with children for this research, it is evident that many are aware that they should be entitled to certain rights, particularly the right to education, but they also are resigned to their powerlessness before the will of adults. It is facile in any impoverished setting to base one's analysis solely on economics. In this case, one might say that poverty forces parents to depend upon their children as wage-earners, therefore, until living standards are raised to a certain level, the rights of individual children must come second to the needs of the family. While it is true that economics play an important role in determining whether children are granted specific rights, there are other social and historical factors—including tradition and gender roles—that lead parents to resist granting their children the rights specified under the CRC. The State contributes to that resistance with conflicting messages that challenge the familiar, traditional and gender roles but do not offer parents viable options. Such policies make compliance with the CRC more difficult for parents.

RIGHTS VERSUS DEVELOPMENT

Within the discourse over human rights are the issues surrounding economic development. Mbaye introduced these concepts to the United Nations in the early 1970s arguing that the right to development belongs to a group and it is unnecessary to speculate "whether the right to development is really a collective right or an individual right" (M'baye and Ndiaye 1982). While M'baye places the individual squarely within community, Fields and Narr attach the individual to historical moment:

> Human rights constitute a historical phenomenon . . . People may be born with the potential for rights; they may long for them consciously or unconsciously; and they may struggle for them. But human rights are norms and practices which can be achieved only if proper historical circumstances are created (1992, 5).

In the early 1990s, Ghana was undergoing a complete remake of its government. The new constitution, drafted in 1992, included an independent Commission on Human Rights and Administrative Justice (CHRAJ). Along with the National Commission on Children, formed after the CRC was signed in February 1990, CHRAJ was charged with protecting the rights of children. At the same time, Ghana was in process of complying with the mandates of World Bank and International Monetary Fund to restructure its economy. Structural adjustment included privatization of state-owned industries, cutbacks on social services, lay-offs for government employees and a devaluation of currency. The consequent impacts of structural adjustment on the population were increased migration from rural areas into cities in search of work, increased pressure on families (Cornia, Jolly, and Stewart 1987), particularly on women who could no longer afford medical care and other basic necessities for children and elderly relatives (Brydon and Legge 1996), and an increase in the cost of living because of currency devaluation (Siddiqui 1997; Walle 2001). Economic reforms of the early twenty-first century have left structural adjustment policies behind, but Ghana remains caught in a complicated push and pull between powerful forces, that of official public policy supporting human and children's rights, and that of economic policies that make life difficult for the average person. Within such circumstances, parents are forced to choose which rights are more important for their children. To grant one right, for example, the right to adequate shelter, would force parents to compromise another right, for example, the right to education. This complication, manifest through the intrusion of the State into the intimacy of the family, continues to collide with the attitudes, practices and priorities of a significant portion of the public even as structural adjustment policies have been abandoned. More than fifteen years after the Convention on the Rights of the Child was ratified, many Ghanaian children have not realized their rights.

Foucault recognized that "State and familial forms of power have each retained their specificity and have only been able to interlock so long as the specific ways in which they each operate have been respected" (1977, 189). The State's attempt to change past and present practices of families toward their children crosses the lines of specificity to which Foucault refers. Material conditions combine with traditional roles for children to create circumstances in which families cannot or will not comply with the tenets of the CRC or the national laws designed to reinforce those tenets.

When the family is seen as a collective unit, the economic hardships it faces appear uniform among family members. On closer examination, one finds that within families, the weight of economic hardship falls more heavily on certain individuals than on others. Furthermore, families also choose to foster certain rights for individual children while ignoring or taking away the same rights for other children within the same family unit. I am calling those choices resistance, borrowing from Foucault the idea that

> [T]here are no relations of power without resistances . . . resistance to power does not have to come from elsewhere to be real, nor is it inexorably frustrated through being the compatriot of power. It exists all the more by being in the same place as power; hence, like power, resistance is multiple (1977, 142).

In any analysis of social change, it is productive to solicit the population's perspective on the proposed changes (Servaes 1996). Thus, resistance within Ghana's population to the concepts and implications of children's rights and the reasons for this resistance are an important part of the discussion. This study is offered as an exploration of some of the attitudes and practical realities that might influence the discourse inherent in grass roots acceptance—or not--of the goals of the CRC and parallel domestic laws by people in the Ashanti Region of Ghana. Specifically, the research asks: what kinds of social, personal and economic factors might influence a significant portion of the population in Ashanti Region to resist the rights of their own children to education, health care, shelter and security, adequate nutrition and leisure? This research was conducted with technical assistance from Ghana's National Commission on Children, but was initiated, funded and designed independent of any government agency.

HUMAN RIGHTS DISCORD

Nagengast describes the period leading up to the ratification of the Universal Declaration of Human Rights (UDHR) as "one of the earliest global discourses." Coming on the heels of the Nazi Holocaust, the agreement assumes that all individuals have a right to be protected from more powerful groups and from the State. Although all of the UN member states in 1948 endorsed the UDHR, as "the common standard of decency" (1997, 269), the dialogue has continued. At issue are the values proposed by the UDHR and consequent international agreements that specify rights assumed to be inalienable for all human beings by birth. Many of the voices of disagreement have come from countries in Africa and Asia that, by circumstances of their colonial history, were not represented in the original discourse. In 1948, when the UDHR was ratified, the members of the United Nations included only two sub-Saharan countries, South Africa and Liberia.

While each country, as it became a member of the United Nations, signed the UDHR, a number of countries have challenged the focus on the individual that is inherent in the human rights discourse. Western philosophy assumes the individual to be the core unit of society, as evidenced by the English Magna Carta (1215), the US Bill of Rights (1774), and the French Declaration of the Rights of Man and the Citizens (1789), as well as Greek, Roman and Judeo-Christian tradition (Messer 1997). Inherent in those documents is a history of feudalism, the rise of the bourgeois class, and centuries of struggle between "the ruler and the ruled." The UDHR, born during the Nuremburg trials, continues in the same tradition, with a defense of the individual against unwarranted aggression, either from the state or from other groups.

Legesse argues that putting the individual in a "sacralized position" is anathema to African social values (1980, 124):

> No aspect of Western civilization makes an African more uncomfortable than the concept of the sacralized individual whose private wars against society are celebrated (124) . . . If Africans were the sole authors of the Universal Declaration of Human Rights, they might have ranked the rights of communities above those of individuals (128).

Challenging New Laws with Old Values 89

Aké positions the individual interests of the rural African outside Western concepts of liberal democracy and freedom. "Freedom is embedded in the realities of communal life; people worry less about their rights and how to secure them than finding their station and its duties and they see no freedom in mere individualism." Rather than autonomy, Aké says, rural Africans seek "embeddedness . . . in an organic whole" (1994, 5).

Aké's position is consistent with that of many African political, religious and cultural leaders who argue that the rights of the individual should be subsumed beneath the needs of the community. Nagengast makes the point, however, that tyrannical leaders often use cultural relativity as a convenient justification of their own oppressive acts.

> Human rights-violating countries often defend their actions in the global arena by invoking national sovereignty and by drawing on . . . cultural relativity. Spokespersons claim that certain methods of social control (e.g., flogging and amputation) and practices associated with marriage, the family, or sexuality (e.g., female genital surgeries, violence against women, and differential access to food, education, and health care) are traditional and therefore not subject to criticism from abroad (1997, 270).

Any criticism of human rights violations, Nagengast says, is likely to bring charges of Eurocentrism or "the glorification of the individual at the expense of the community" (270).

Some African scholars have realized the importance of taking an integrated approach to both classes of rights (Shivji 1989) such as that found in the African Charter on Human and People's Rights (Nguema 1990). While the beginning of the Charter spells out individual rights similar to those of the UDHR, Chapter II speaks of the duties of the individual toward family, community and nation.

The problem is that individuals within groups are often sacrificed for the supposed good of the larger whole. As Zechenter (1997) argues, such sacrifices are consistently made by the least powerful for the benefit of the most powerful members of the group. Using the examples of the Indian custom of sati, or bride-burning, and of the rape and murder of two Algerian teenagers at the behest of an Islamic ruler, Zechenter shows that the logic of cultural tradition actually hides more venal interests by others.

African feminists often find themselves caught between their desire to support African self-determination and cultural relativism on the one hand, and their support of the liberation of women and children from oppressive politics and cultural traditions on the other (see, e.g., Nfah-Abbenyi 1997). In the 1980s and 1990s, African feminists pushed for political protections for themselves and their children with considerable success across the continent. In Ghana, the State passed several laws that are consistent with the UDHR, including the Intestate Succession Act, which challenges customary inheritance law by "abolish(ing) for all practical purposes the stigma of illegitimacy" for both women and children (Manuh 1997). Ghana, as the first signatory on the UN Convention on the Rights of the Child, (1990) added to its Constitution (Ghana Constitution 1992) specified rights and freedoms for children. Among those rights is "the right to be protected from engaging in work that constitutes a threat to his (sic) health, education or development" (Article 28, Section 2). This section would imply protections for the child as an individual; however, in the same Article are two other rights that reflect the interest of the family and community, and the consequent oppositional discourses involved in children's rights. Section 1(a) states:

> Every child has the right to the same measure of special care, assistance and maintenance as is necessary for its development from its natural parents, except where those parents have effectively surrendered their rights and responsibilities in respect of the child in accordance with the law.

Likewise, Section 1(e) states:

> The protection and advancement of the family as the unit of society are safeguarded in promotion of the interest of children.

The protection of the family unit is consistent with the African customary respect for community, however, the traditions of many Ghanaian ethnic groups include various systems where children, particularly young girls, are separated from the family unit and any protections that might come from being in close proximity to one's family. For example, many girls, and some boys, are given to relatives or friends for training in a skill or craft. While the tradition of such training is ancient, the remnants of colonial laws and structures that favor boys over girls, along with economic difficulties, particularly in rural areas, have changed the conditions under which such children are given to adults. Impoverished parents often send their children away because they can no longer afford to feed, clothe and shelter them. In the ideal situation, the child is protected, cared for and trained in a skill that will be useful in his or her adult life. Often, however, the ideal situation does not exist and the child becomes the victim of a bad economy and exploitative adults. A study of street children sponsored by UNICEF found that many rural parents give their children to market traders (women who sell in the informal markets) believing they are helping the child. Instead, the child becomes an unpaid worker:

> The madams convince parents who cannot put their offspring through school that they can offer their children a better future. They promise

to employ the children for a certain period, generally two years, and then provide them a sewing machine and vocational training or send them to school. But they rarely keep this promise (Beauchemin 1999).

One of those children, Ama, spoke with me about her life. The following is from my field notes:

> Ama is 13 ... She sleeps at a place where she is a virtual slave to a friend of her mother. She spends every day in the heavily trafficked streets of Kumasi's Obuasi District balancing on her head a large pan of plastic baggies filled with ice water chilled in her guardian's refrigerator. She and hundreds of young children spend their days on the congested urban roads, darting into traffic at every red light trying to sell bread, fish, candy, and newspapers to impatient drivers and their passengers.
>
> When the pan is empty, Ama goes back to the house, gives her guardian the money, and begins the process all over again until the sun goes down. Then, she carries water for the household and does laundry for her guardian's family.
>
> In the morning, Ama says, "I am given 500 cedis (about 14 cents US) to go out and find food ... We do not eat in the afternoon ... I only receive very little (to eat) in the evening. I would wish to go back to my mother because the woman beats me always."

If the Convention on the Rights of the Child was enforced on the streets of Kumasi, children like Ama might have very different lives. Article 19 states that children should be protected from "all forms of ... physical violence, injury or abuse." Article 28 gives children the right to an education. Article 31 recognizes "the right of the child to rest and leisure, to engage in play and recreational activities," and Article 32 states that children should be "protected from economic exploitation and from performing any work that is likely to be hazardous or to interfere with the child's education, or to be harmful to the child's physical, mental, spiritual, moral or social development."

Arguably, Ama, along with thousands of children like her, is being deprived of her rights. However, a confluence of conflicting interests make it unlikely that Ama's life will change in the foreseeable future. In its report to the United Nations, the government noted that it had empowered the Ghana National Commission on Children (GNCC) to be the main coordinating body for "harmoniz(ing) national law and policy with the provisions of the Convention." GNCC was tasked with publicizing the tenets of the Convention, and with "facilitating the processes needed to give effect to the provisions of the Convention." However, the report stated:

Apart from a small number of juvenile offenders being brought to court the child protection laws are rarely invoked. Culturally it is felt more appropriate for abuse and neglect to be dealt with at a family and community level (Consideration of Reports Submitted by States Parties under Article 44 of the Convention, 1995).

With no access to her family, no financial resources of her own, and no advocate to protect her, to which "community" would Ama turn for help? Under which circumstances would the Convention apply to her? Apart from the hard work and physical abuse, Ama knows she should be in school. Of the eighteen children interviewed for this research, all of them said they would prefer to be in school. Yet, the State mechanism to compel her or the others to attend is inadequate.

CHILDREN AS SITES OF POWER

Foucault traces the influence of State power over the population's personal lives from the 17th Century prison system to a present day where State power is in place, not only in its apparatuses of enforcement, but in the minds and behavior of the population. It is this internal mimicking of State power within individual human relations—even as individuals are resisting the imposition of State power—that maintains the State without violence. The imposition of timetables for activity, of formality of physical actions, and the control of physical spaces for formalized activities, Foucault argued, are part of the State's extension of power over the physical body, which is the site of human activity (1975). Although the history and culture of Ghanaian society have different bases than Foucault's France, some of the efforts of the State to encourage children's rights, particularly to education, parallel those described by Foucault in that they represent the State's attempt to control the daily activities and structure of time use by children, particularly where children are expected to attend school during a significant portion of the daytime hours. Resistance to those efforts comes at least in part from the conflict between parents wanting to control their children, and the State's desire to dictate where children should spend their days (in school) and what they should be doing (getting educated, sheltered, fed and supported). While parents' decisions about which of their children should be educated, which should work at home and which should be sent out to work can in general be traced to traditional roles, it could also be argued that the State and the parents see children as economic units. The conflict comes between the respective visions of how those economic units should be utilized. When the parents send their children to school, they are acting in consonance with the State's vision that children should be a site of investment for the future. From the perspective of the State, the educated child will make a more substantive and valuable contribution to

Challenging New Laws with Old Values 93

the building of the nation and will require fewer state-provided services over time. From the perspective of the parents, the educated child will have more earning power and thus be more quickly independent and take better care of the parents in their older years. However, while the State would claim the right to declare all children as appropriate sites of investment, most parents of limited income see certain of their children, not as sites of investment for the future, but as resources to be exploited for immediate gain. This conflict is both economic and cultural, with historical roots that precede the Convention on the Rights of the Child by hundreds of years (Mikell 1997; Robertson 1984; Robertson and Berger 1986).

THE VALUE OF GIRLS AND THE VALUE OF BOYS

African and Africanist feminists have long debated the status of women and children in traditional culture and the impact of colonialism and the cash economy on women and children of the present day (see, e.g., Manuh 1997; Nfah-Abbenyi 1997). They agree, however, that the dissolution of traditional culture in a changing economy has left women with less social and economic power and more of the burdens of supporting themselves and their children (see, e.g., Mikell 1997; Ardayfio-Schandorf 1994). Ardayfio-Schandorf's examination of "household headship" and women's earnings in Ghana found that women-headed households are increasing while the economic position of women has worsened since the 1970s, especially if they are heads of households. Over 50% of women in urban and rural areas are heads of households. Most married women said they receive no income from their husbands. Most said they needed more than one source of income, and all the women interviewed by Ardayfio-Schandorf said they were looking for another source of income because, with their current finances, they could not make ends meet. In addition to the low income available to women in all job categories, continuous inflation, structural adjustment policies, and a high number of children exacerbated their financial burdens. In addition, colonialism's enforced gender roles privileged men over women and boy children over girls and rigidified the tasks and expectations of women and men (Oduyoye 1995; Roberts 1988; Robertson and Berger 1986). The material results of this imposition of values have been discussed more in depth elsewhere. For the purposes of this discussion, what is important is how those values affect expectations and possibilities for individual children in the same family.

CONFLICTS AMONG RIGHTS

As this and other studies have found, families tend to invest in their children in consistent, predictable patterns. Depending upon the family's income, the eldest boy gets all or most of the resources, especially education, with younger sons getting a chance at school only if family resources allow. Girl children are a distant consideration. Akuffo (1987) found a complex relationship between young girls' childbearing, family expectations of them, and education. Families tended to encourage boys to stay in school while girls' education was seen as a luxury. Far more important was learning to support her children. Girls were expected to help their mothers with care of the home and younger siblings, as well as working in the market or on farms. Such values are reinforced when money is scarce. Ghana's official statistics for 1999 show that girls are sent to primary school less than half as often as boys, with that number decreasing to less than one-third by secondary school, and diminishing even more in higher education (Ahiadeke 2001). However, the official numbers of a government study do not differentiate among economic classes, nor do they include students who are registered but not actually attending school, or those who are enrolled but miss a high proportion of classes. Aisha is a good example of such a child. Aisha is ten years old. Officially, she is a student, but sometimes, as my interview with her shows, her work as a water seller gets in the way of her schooling:

> "I do not go to school regularly, so I cannot speak English." (Many classes are taught in English; almost all books are in English, although there are few books.) "I sell before I go to school, so I am always late. I go out and sell again after school."
> JW: "Are you tired from working?"
> Aisha: "Yes. I sometimes feel pains in my body after doing that job." (Many of the girls I spoke with said they have pain around their waists, a common affliction from carrying heavy loads.)

Aisha wants to go to school, and her mother is attempting to allow her to go. However, for Aisha's mother, her child is, of necessity, also an economic unit. From my fieldnotes:

> Aisha is the youngest child of Maame Salima, who has eight children. M. Salima herself has never been to school. She lives with five of her eight children in a one-room, dirt-floor cottage in the urban neighborhood of Ofirokrom. Her husband is a farmer who lives in the Eastern Region. He comes to see her periodically, but rarely brings any money. At first, she tells me all of her children are in school; then it becomes obvious that school is too much of a financial hardship for her.
> "The daily food and the money to pay the children's school fees and how to get the money to provide for their needs has been my problem. That is why they come from school and sell ice water instead of going to study what they learn in school. They put (their books) down and

come to sell the ice water . . . It is not all days that they go to school. Some of them do stop and later they continue when there is money . . . I am doing my best but the days that I do not have enough money, I stop them from going."

Maame Salima tries to send her children to school, but she runs up against the conflicting discourses created by the State. The Education Act of 1961 made "basic education free and compulsory for children of school age." However, in its report to the United Nations, the government admitted:

> Data . . . reveal a substantial rise in household expenditure on education. Official school fees . . . payments levied on parents to cover building maintenance, parent teacher associations, classroom furniture, sports fees, examination fees, etc. While school enrolment rates have increased . . . cost recovery measures and cuts in government expenditure have worsened the chances of rural children receiving quality education at primary level (Consideration of Reports Submitted by States Parties under Article 44 of the Convention, 1995).

Maame Salima must pay 33,000 cedis ($4.50) for a uniform for each of her five children plus 35,000 cedis ($5.00) per child per year in school fees. The expenses are prohibitive for many parents, forcing them to choose which, if any, among their children should get educated.

Official statistics of school enrollment do not show the problems inherent in the State's approach to education nor the ways parents resist regulations that are impossible for them to follow. In the case of Maame Salima, Ghana's so-called "FCUBE" education system was sabotaged by the State's insistence on school fees and uniforms. The name FCUBE, an acronym for free, compulsory, universal basic education, is misleading. In fact, school in Ghana is neither free nor universal, and plans to increase community support for the schools mean that parents must shoulder an ever larger share of the costs of maintaining the schools. Indeed, in 2008, Ghana's United Youth Movement issued a statement challenging the government to live up to the promises of the FCUBE system (Frciku 2008). Caught in cascading sites of power, children find themselves without a voice, while the discourse from each level claims an interest in their welfare.

There are other, more subtle reasons parents don't send their children to school. Because she has not been to school herself, Maame Salima has little understanding of what children learn in school. Her fondest desire for her children's education is that they learn to sign their names "in case they should ever need to." The reality is, in Maame Salima's world, they may never need to. Even for Ghanaians who can read, unless they are part of the academic system, there is little literature available beyond Christian books (she is a Muslim and the books are prohibitively expensive anyway) and the newspaper, which, for her, is both expensive and irrelevant. Daily business is conducted on an immediate and personal level, using verbal assent without receipts or paper accounting. The utility of school must seem remote indeed. Maame Salima sent her now grown boys to school, but they have not found regular work. "They do not have their own work. They only work as help-mates to others and in the evening they (the employers) give them some little money to go out and eat."

>JW: "So they do not stay with one person where they are doing the same job every day?"
>MS: "No, they do not stay with one person. Wherever there is a job, they try to go and help."

Maame Salima knows that if her sons cannot find work with a bit of education, surely her daughters have less chance of doing so. Ghana's economy is mostly entrepreneurial and it is not possible to start a business without some kind of cash backing. The immediacy of her daughters' ability to bring home cash, however small the amount, is far more real to this mother than the promise of a brighter future if she educates her children. She invests a little in schooling her daughters, but insists that they bring in some level of the family income at the same time. She thus creates a situation that makes it almost impossible for her daughters to succeed in school, but more likely that, with their collective income, the family will survive right now. This kind of resistance is repeated around the nation, as parents are forced to make choices between the present and the future, between the promise of education and the reality they see before them, between their children as individuals and the interest of their family as a whole. Maame Salima and parents like her cannot see education as a right, because it is not even a possibility most of the time. Indeed, the very real need for the children to help her pay the family's living expenses sets up a situation where the children's right to education is in direct conflict with their right to nutrition and shelter, as well as the right of the family as a unit to survive. The right of the child to leisure is not even a consideration.

The government's message that education is invaluable comes to the public through a number of routes, particularly through public pronouncements and the media, with children's rights and national development being emphasized. However, although the aim of such communications is to engender the cooperation of parents, government officials vilify mothers who cannot comply with the government's stated policies. During repeated interviews with Ghana National Commission on Children and school officials, I was told that parents like Maame Salima spend inordinate amounts of money buying new clothes to attend funerals. I also heard such messages on the national radio station. If only those mothers would sacrifice that selfish pleasure, I was told, they could afford to send their children to school. My own eyes told me that this was an unfair argument, but it was a common refrain at all levels of power. The theory on which everyone operates is that it is up to the mother (as opposed to both parents) to send the children to school. Such attitudes conflict with the theoretical premise that the community is the focus of human rights. In this case, mothers are expected to sacrifice for the benefit of the larger community, but they are treated as individuals on whose shoulders fall the responsibilities of educating children, despite their obvious inability to do so.

COMPETING DISCOURSES

While it was traditional within many of Ghana's ethnic groups for women and men to take responsibility for different aspects of child support, (e.g., food and shelter were taken care of by the mother while school fees were paid by the father), economics and a transitional society have confused those traditional roles. For thousands of children, the father is not part of the family unit; for thousands more, the father is no longer present in daily life. Fathers who are part of the home, particularly in the city, often do not make enough money to support their families. Several boys I interviewed made more money running errands for college students than their fathers made. One boy told me his family depended on him to bring in money. When his younger brother got sick, it was the boy's money that paid for the medicine. The boy bought his daily meals with his earnings, and he was trying to save enough money to attend school.

A child's right to be educated is clearly the most vulnerable of the tenets of the CRC in Ghana. As long as parents, particularly mothers, are unable to provide the basics of shelter and food, they will be unable to educate their children. The State has chosen to maintain certain vestiges of colonialism that work against universal education by adding increased and unnecessary demands on parents' incomes, for example, insisting the children wear uniforms, charging school fees, etc. At the same time, the State has created new administrative layers and positions for government officials supposedly to encourage education. Such administrative changes do not materially affect parents, nor do they overcome the parents' personal observations that education does not necessarily pay off. Thus, parents, resisting the individualized identity that separates the child from the family, make choices that oppose the State power structure and its mandate to have an educated populace in favor of actions that make sense to them.

As parents contend with the finances of the household, the child becomes less of an individual and more a member (and economic unit) of the familial community, complete with responsibilities to support the group rather than pursue individual survival. The model of the individual child educated and empowered by a public school education contradicts that of the obedient child doing whatever she must for her family's economic welfare. Ironically, the burden for the family's collective welfare falls most heavily on the weakest of the economic units—the youngest children, particularly the daughters, of large families. In some cases, like that of Ama the water seller, survival of the family means that she must leave the group and work unpaid for someone else.

The government has used its media system, along with the private broadcast entities, newspapers and other communication sources to educate the population about the Convention on the Rights of the Child, and based on responses to this research, the education campaign has been successful, at least in urban areas. Parents and children spoke knowledgeably about the right to education, food and shelter, although the right to leisure was never mentioned. However, while the government responded to pressure to legislate and advertise children's rights, it was also being pressured by the World Bank to cut back on social services including medical care and education subsidies, to make thousands of government workers redundant, and domestic products more expensive than foreign imports (Brydon and Legge 1996). Within those conditions, parents were less able to offer their children the rights specified under the CRC.

Fields and Narr argue that there are certain key values inherent in any definition of human rights: freedom, social recognition, equality relative to the social context in which they live, and integrity (1992). Ghanaian children, while they may long for the "freedom" to go to school or to play, also want social recognition as responsible participants in their own communities. For girls and younger children, social recognition comes only from sacrifice to the greater good. Many of the children I spoke with expressed a deep desire to work less and to go to school, but none showed any resentment toward other siblings who had those advantages. Likewise, if equality is relative, these children are equal to others in their own situation. Street vendors, for example, can see dozens of children just like themselves working. Integrity comes from one's ability to act appropriately within one's station in life.

Fields and Narr argue further that the concept of human rights as the property of the individual arose out of the particular historic moment that marked the rise of capitalist and state interests in the world. With the Hobbesian image of man as an inherently hostile being in need of control, Fields and Narr add Schumpeter's (1947) argument that "liberal democracy has had to pacify those dangerous, self-interested individuals in order to survive" (8). It is unlikely to be a coincidence that Ghana faces these challenges as it enters a period of incipient capitalism and genuine democracy. Before this time, corrupt and authoritative state institutions, along with a state-regulated economy, reinforced inequality and capriciousness from traditional authorities. If the State wishes to legitimize its authority through the democratic process, it must find ways to bring equality to each citizen. Likewise, if the State wishes to become a player in a truly independent, market-based economy, it must maximize the potential of its workforce. However, it cannot do either of these things without meeting the population halfway. As M'baye and Ndiaye might argue, until there is economic development, no country can guarantee individual rights (1982). Still, even with economic development, culture is slow to change. Some children will continue to be favored over others simply because of the structure of society. Conflicting visions of gender and power determine the appropriate roles of family members, with girls and younger boys subsumed beneath the interests of the firstborn. In the competing discourse over children's rights, young children are pitted against their siblings just as their rights are pitted against economics. They are allowed to occupy sites of power only when they give up the very rights that are intended to empower them.

REFERENCES

Ahiadeke, C. 2001. Ghana's Children—2000 Report. Accra: Save the Children, Ghana National Commission on Children.

Akuffo, F. O. 1987. Teenage pregnancies and school drop-outs: The relevance of family life education and vocational training to girls' employment opportunities. In *Sex Roles, Population and Development in West Africa*, edited by C. Oppong. Portsmouth, NH: Heinemann.

Aké, Claude. 1994. Introduction. In *Democratization of disempowerent in Africa*. Lagos, Nigeria: Center for Advanced Social Science, Malthouse Press Ltd.

Ardayfio-Schandorf, Elizabeth, Ed. 1994. *Family and Development in Ghana: Proceedings of the International Training and Research Workshop Held at the University of Ghana, Legon on 14th–18th December 1992*. Accra, Ghana: Universities of Ghana Press.

Beauchemin, Eric. 1999. The Exodus: The growing migration of children from Ghana's rural areas to the urban centres. Accra, Ghana: Catholic Action for Street Children and UNICEF.

Brydon, Lynne, and Karen Legge. 1996. *Adjusting Society: The World Bank, the IMF and Ghana*. Edited by I. B. T. Publishers, *Tauris Academic Series*. London and New York: I.B. Tauris & Co. Ltd.

Consideration of Reports Submitted by States Parties under Article 44 of the Convention. 1995. In *Committee on the Rights of the Child*. Geneva: United Nations. Original edition, Report from Ghanaian government on its adherence to Convention on the Rights of the Child.

Cornia, A., R. Jolly, and F. Stewart, eds. 1987. *Adjustment with a human face*. New York, NY: Oxford University Press.

Fields, A.B., and W.D. Narr. 1992. Human rights as a holistic concept. *Human Rights Quarterly* 14 (1):1–20.

Foucault, Michel. 1975. *Discipline and Punish: The Birth of the Prison*. Translated by A. Sheridan. New York: Pantheon Books.

———. 1977. *Power/knowledge: Selected interviews and other writings 1972–1977*. Translated by L. M. Colin Gordon, John Mepham, Kate Soper. New York: Pantheon Books.

Freiku, Sebastian R. 2008. Ghana: Youth movement wants Fcube implemented to letter. In *Ghanaian Chronicle*: AllAfrica.com.

Ghana Constitution. 1992.

Legesse, A. 1980. Human rights in African political culture. In *The moral imperatives of human rights: A world survey*, edited by K. W. Thompson. Lanham, MD: University Press of America.

M'baye, K., and B. Ndiaye. 1982. The Organization of African Unity. In *The international dimensions of human rights*, edited by P. Alston. Paris: UNESCO.

Manuh, Takyiwaa. 1997. Wives, children, and intestate succession in Ghana. In *African feminism: The politics of survival in Sub-Saharan Africa*, edited by G. Mikell. Philadelphia: University of Pennsylvania Press.
Messer, Ellen. 1997. Pluralist approaches to human rights. *Journal of Anthropological Research* 53 (3):293–317.
Mikell, Gwendolyn. 1997. Pleas for domestic relief: Akan women and family courts. In *African feminism: The politics of survival in Sub-Saharan Africa*, edited by G. Mikell. Philadelphia: University of Pennsylvania Press.
Nagengast, C. 1997. Introduction: Universal human rights versus cultural relativity. *Journal of Anthropological Research* 53 (3):269–272.
Nfah-Abbenyi, Juliana Makuchi. 1997. *Gender in African women's writing: Identity, sexuality, and difference*. Bloomington and Indianapolis: Indiana University Press.
Nguema, Issac. 1990. Introduction. In *The African Charter on Human and People's Rights*: United Nations, New York.
Oduyoye, Mercy Amba. 1995. *Daughters of Anowa: African women and patriarchy*. Maryknoll, NY: Orbis Books.
Roberts, Penelope A. 1988. Rural women's access to labor in West Africa. In *Patriarchy and class: African women in the home and work force*, edited by S. B. Stichter and J. L. Parpart. Boulder, Colorado: Westview Press.
Robertson, C., and I. Berger, eds. 1986. *Women and class in Africa*. New York: Africana Publishing Company.
Robertson, Claire. 1984. *Sharing the same bowl: A socioeconomic history of women and class in Accra, Ghana*. Bloomington, IN: Indiana University Press.
Schumpeter, J. 1947. *Capitalism, socialism, and democracy*. New York: Harper.
Servaes, Jan. 1996. Participatory communication and research in development settings. In *Participatory communication for social change*, edited by J. Servaes, T. L. Jacobson and S. A. White. New Dehli, Thousand Oaks, CA, London: Sage.
Shivji, I. 1989. *The concept of human rights in Africa*. Senegal & London: CODERISA.
Siddiqui, Rukhsana A., ed. 1997. *Subsaharan Africa in the 1990s: Challenges to democracy and development*. Westport, CT: Praeger.
Walle, N. Van der. 2001. *African economies and the politics of permanent crisis, 1979–1999*. Cambridge, UK: Cambridge University Press.
Zechenter, E. 1997. In the name of culture: Cultural relativism and the abuse of the individual. *Journal of Anthropological Research* 53:319–347.

Appendix A: Questions asked of Working Children

1. Basic Information
   (Please give your) name, age, home village or town.
   Tell us about your family: parents' name; are they living? When was the last time you spoke with/saw your mother, your father? What is your position in the family (oldest, middle, youngest, etc.)? Are you in contact with your brothers and sisters?
   How did you come to be working here? How does this compare with other children in your family? (Question format included variations on: What are your other brothers and sisters doing? Did they go to school? etc.)
   Did you come here from elsewhere? Alone or with someone?
2. Working Conditions
   What time do you start work?
   When do you quit for the day?
   About how much money do you make in a day?

Do you have to share that money with anyone? Who? Why?
Do you have to use the money to feed yourself?
3. <u>Shelter and Security</u>
Where do you sleep? Did you have a place to sleep when you came here?
Whom do you sleep with?
Where are your parents? Do you have a guardian here who looks after you?
Did you know anyone here when you came?
Has anyone ever threatened or bothered you? What happened?
Have you ever been robbed? Beaten? What happened?
Have the police ever threatened or bothered you? What happened?
4. <u>Food and Nutrition</u>
When do you eat? (Every day? How many times a day?)
Do you get enough to eat?
What do you eat?
Do you ever feel tired? What do you do then?
5. <u>Medical Care</u>
Have you ever been sick? What did you do?
Have you been injured? What happened?
Have you ever been to a doctor or clinic? (Besides when you were a baby.)
Do you know if you have had any immunizations against disease?
6. <u>Education</u>
Have you ever been to school? (If so, why aren't you in school now?)
If you've never been to school, how did you learn to count money and make change?
If you need to know (to get information about) something, how do you find out? (Whom do you ask?)
Have any of your brothers or sisters gone to school? Did you want to go?
What do you think you will do when you are grown?
7. <u>Awareness of Rights</u>
Do you know that the government passed a law that says all children have the right to education and medical care? What do you think about that?
Do you listen to the radio? If so, what do you listen to?

Appendix B: Ghana Constitution, Section 28

(1) Parliament shall enact such laws as are necessary to ensure that—
 (a) Every child has the right to the same measure of special care, assistance and maintenance as is necessary for its development from its natural parents, except where those parents have effectively surrendered their rights and responsibilities in respect of the child in accordance with law;
 (b) Every child, whether or not born in wedlock, shall be entitled to reasonable provision out of the estate of its parents;
 (c) Parents undertake their natural right and obligation of care, maintenance and upbringing of their children in co-operation with such institutions as Parliament may, by law, prescribe in such manner that in all cases the interest of the children are paramount;
 (d) Children and young persons receive special protection against exposure to physical and moral hazards; and
 (e) The protection and advancement of the family as the unit of society are safeguarded in promotion of the interest of children.
(2) Every child has the right to be protected from engaging in work that constitutes a threat to his health, education or development.
(3) A child shall not be subjected to torture or other cruel, inhuman or degrading treatment or punishment.

(4) No child shall be deprived by any other person of medical treatment, education or any other social or economic benefit by reason only of religious or other beliefs.

(5) For the purposes of this article, "child" means a person below the age of eighteen years.

5 State Power and the Reconstitution of Parental Rights in U.S. Child Custody Mediation

Lynn Comerford

Two of the most serious human relationships are those of parent to child and individual to the state. Embedded in these relationships is the reproduction of gender inequality. Historically, patriarchy's chief institution has been the family. Susan Moller Okin argued "[t]he family is the linchpin of gender, reproducing it from one generation to the next" (1989, 170). Kate Millet stressed how the family mediated between the individual and the social structure, and has acted "as a unit in the government of the patriarchal state which rules its citizens through family heads" (1970, 25). Catherine MacKinnon has emphasized the distinctive abuses of women in the hierarchical family by male householders, including battering, marital rape, and grinding exploitation of unpaid domestic labor and describes the strong combination of social, legal and political institutions that enforce this pattern (2001, 553).

The reproduction of gender inequality in the family is facilitated by law. Men, as a group, have greatly benefited by law which took shape under social conditions of inequality between the sexes. In the case of child custody law, for example, fathers historically had the unqualified right to child custody in the event of a divorce or separation. It was not until 1763, after a series of English custody cases made headlines for the brutality, viciousness, or immorality of the fathers, in which mothers lost custody of their children, that Parliament passed a statute giving courts discretion to order maternal custody and visitation in certain cases, particularly those involving young children (Shanley 1989).

Family law is dynamic and impacts family structure. In the United States, fathers controlled the custody of their children until the mid-nineteenth century. Between the years 1880 and 1925 the presumption that divorced fathers should be granted custody of their children changed. Where once God, Reason, and Nature were invoked to grant fathers automatic custody of their children, within this span of forty-five years, God, Reason, and Nature were invoked to grant mothers automatic custody of children of "tender years" (Mason 1999). The granting of custody to mothers was reinforced by the discourse of Freudian psychoanalytic theory in the 1930s (Donzelot 1979, 188) and by the fact that children were becoming less economically valuable during industrialization (Zelizer 1985). The dynamic aspect of custody law is also evident in the period between 1950 and 1982.

California courts rejected the tender years doctrine as discriminatory in 1950; by 1982, two-thirds of the states in the U.S. had rejected the tender years doctrine as not in the child's best interest.

Family law in the United States has an expressive function, but it is also impacted by strong social forces. During the 1970s and 1980s many laws were changed due to the impact of the second wave of feminism, mothers entering the work force in record numbers, the increase in divorce and single parenthood, domestic violence awareness, the gay rights movement, and the father's rights movement. During this period, most states dropped laws that granted different rights to men and women and replaced them with gender-neutral laws. Family law during this time changed what and who counts as family, where a family exists and ends, and the family's relationship to the state.

With the abolition of gendered custody laws and the "special protection" for mothers in custody cases, the decision about who should receive custody, and at what percentage, became complicated. The abolition of fault-based divorce and the maternal presumption (which made custody decisions fairly routine) led judges to become dependent on mediators for custody recommendations. Since the 1980s, mediation has increasingly become the alternative to the adversarial process due to the high rate of divorce, large court caseloads, recognition of the detrimental effects of parental conflict on children, the vague standards guiding judicial custody determinations, and the increasing privatization of divorce in the United States (see Emery and Wyer 1987, 472). Courts, overwhelmed with the volume and decision-making burden of child custody cases, turned to mediation to substitute for time consuming and costly adversarial court proceedings. Mediation is now mandatory or recommended in child custody and visitation disputes in all states before other adversarial means are employed. There is considerable debate about the practice.

The debate over child custody mediation reflects broader concerns about social justice, marital and parenting roles, and state intervention practices and raises important questions: Are mediation sessions a good place to determine child custody? Do gender-neutral custody determinations break down sex roles, or further entrench male dominance? What is the state's interest in mediation as a practice? In this essay, I provide a brief description of the practice of child custody mediation and then draw from Michel Foucault's (1972, 1978, 1979) work on: 1) power as a productive force, 2) "serious talk," and 3) normalizing judgment, to analyze critical differences in the ways custody mediation impacts women as a group differently than men as a group. The essay concludes with a discussion of the significance of child custody mediation as a social force and site for feminist study.

CHILD CUSTODY MEDIATION

A custody decision must be made when there is an unwed birth or a divorce/separation. Where children end up living, with whom, and at what percentage of time is determined during custody mediation sessions. Custody mediation is an important site to examine because custody decisions impact the majority of U.S. citizens at some point in their lives, form the largest percentage of domestic-relations cases, and account for close to one-quarter of all legal filings making it the largest category of court action. Annually, about 1.1 million children live with a parent who had experienced a divorce in the last year (Kreider 2007, 70). Unwed births constitute 36.9 percent of all annual births (National Center for Health Statistics 2005) and more than half of child support and welfare caseloads (U.S. House of Representatives, Committee on Ways and Means 2000). Since more than fifty percent of all divorces occur by the seventh year of marriage, the majority of child custody cases involve young children (Shiono and Quinn 1994, 8). In the United States, 26 percent of all children live with one parent and the majority (88 percent) of these children live with their mother (Kreider 2007, 70). Children are more than four times as likely to live with a single mother (23 percent) than to live with a single father (5 percent) (Fields 2003, 20).

Although custody mediation policy differs from state to state, generally the purpose of a custody mediation proceeding is to: (a) reduce acrimony that may exist between the parties; (b) develop an agreement assuring the child close and continuing contact with both parents that is in the best interest of the child; (c) create a settlement of the issue of visitation rights of all parties involved that is in the best interest of the child; and, (d) level the playing field and address the gender inequalities associated with the economic costs of the adversarial process where parents who had the most money could "win" custody via expensive lawyers (Chesler 1991, 409).

Kelly (1983, 33) observed that custody mediation is goal focused, task oriented, time limited, and present and future oriented. It is mandatory before the adversarial process can begin. The cooperative model of mediation is viewed as facilitating the ideal of joint custody in a manner that the adversarial trial process does not. Custody mediation tends to be short, informal, private, childless, and the parents represent themselves. Mediation interviews generally last a total of five hours. The mediator first meets with the attorneys and then with the parents together without their attorneys. The mediator may then meet with parents individually if requested or if the mediator thinks it is necessary. Custody mediators describe themselves as neutral third parties who assist disputing parents who are trying to reach agreement. They believe they are facilitating the process of identifying common interests.

According to the rules of custody mediation, it is the disputing parties themselves who have the primary responsibility for making recommendations, determining the final decisions, and finding mutually agreeable solutions (Laue 1987, 17). Custody mediation is a short-term, "solution-oriented" intervention strategy and the characteristics of custody mediation include confidentiality, acceptance, active listening skills, development of rapport and empathy, interpretation of interactive dynamics, role modeling, and an emphasis on the present and future (not the past) (Kelly 1983, 33). Confidentiality is claimed to be essential for effective custody mediation so all written and oral communication that might "emotionally contaminate" the public sessions is protected (Kressel 1985).

The goal of custody mediation is to reach an agreement or solution. Mediators restrict conversation exploration in order to ensure disputants focus on specific goals. To control the intensity of a dispute and encourage politeness, mediators ask disputants to focus on positive aspects of their situation. During custody mediation each party tells his or her story in the presence of the other and the mediator interrupts any communication patterns that prevent dialogue and the opportunity to receive a fair hearing. Mediators monitor the choice of words, the tone of voice, and body language so the parties' involved move away from blaming each other and focus on solutions. Mediators are trained to "empower" disputants and ensure each party has the opportunity to be heard.

Mediators have a lot of power in a mediation session. Mediators encourage disputants to limit their discussion to specific topics, prohibit certain types of comments or behaviors, and redirect conversation when a parent strays from the mediator's task. And, they frequently manage or contain emotions within the parameters of the process. Mediation can proceed when one or both parents working out a custody schedule have charged domestic violence (e.g., California Family Code 3161 and 3181[1]), and mediators have the authority to exclude a domestic violence support person (e.g., California Family Code 3177[2]). Mediators can exclude a person's lawyer from participating in mediation proceedings (e.g., California Family Code 3182[3]), and have the power to proceed with mediation sessions even when restraining orders have been issued against one or both parties engaged in a custody dispute (e.g., California Family Code 3183 and 3900[4,5]).

THE MEDIATION DEBATE

Many researchers find custody mediation to be a proactive and empowering way to manage conflict positively post-relationship. Mediation is thought to be a better alternative to the adversarial approach because it protects "father's rights" (Thompson 1986, 61); it is less costly than court settlements, both to the individuals involved (Kelly 1991, 387) and in terms of the burden placed on the courts; and, it is capable of addressing different types of divorcing couples (Cohen et al 1999, 329). Additionally, mediation is considered to produce greater satisfaction with the divorce process and outcomes (Emery 1994) and claim higher levels of compliance (Kelly 1993, 136; Maxwell 1992, 353) and lower re-litigation rates (Irwin and Benjamin 1992, 35) than litigated or attorney-negotiated settlements.

Some suggest mediation fosters better post-divorce cooperation regarding the children (Kelly et al. 1988, 453; Dillon and Emery 1996, 131) and better school and social adjustment among the children (Stull and Kaplan 1987, 53) than the traditional adversarial divorce. Furthermore, mediation is considered to be a potentially kinder method than adversarial legal proceedings which may greatly exacerbate the enormous stress inherent in the break-up of a marriage (see Hughes and Kirby 2000, 53; Dillon and Emery 1996, 131). Moreover, mediation studies across countries indicate that clients reach agreement in 50% to 85% of cases because it employs principles of cooperation and conflict resolution, unlike the traditional divorce process which turns parents into legal adversaries and reinforces and escalates anger and distrust (Kelly 1996, 373).

However, some researchers worry that because custody mediation sessions are a site where economics, gender, care work, violence against women, and inequality collide, the weaker party may not be fairly represented. Parenting remains gendered, demographers project that more than half of all children born in the 1990s will spend some time in a single-parent household and that five of every six single-parent households are headed by a mother (Demo 2000, 16). Women and children bear the brunt of the economic fallout post-relationship. In 2000, female-headed households with children under 18 comprised 52 percent of all poor households with children under 18 (U.S. Bureau of the Census, 2001). Feminists find custody mediation to be a poor alternative to the adversarial approach and argue that it: harms the weaker party (usually mothers) (Fineman 1988, 727; Featherstone 1999, 43); is a tool of harassment by ex-partners (Chesler 1991, 409; Kurz, 1995); and, an excuse not to address violence against women and children (Edleson 1999, 134; Stark and Flitcraft 1991, 123).

Boyd (2003) is concerned about unfit fathering and questions mediators' desire that children have maximum contact with both parents. Since mothers began gaining custody of children, fathers have tended to be the non-residential parent (Booth and Amato 1994, 21; Ahrons and Tanner 2003, 340; Rowe and Hong 1996, 335) and have not demonstrated large time commitments to their children. Demo (1992, 104) found that in intact families fathers' time with children was two-thirds less then that of mothers and that mothers spend an average of 19.5 hours a week in alone time with their children compared to fathers' 5.5 hours. Fineman (1988, 765) argues that although mediation is described as allowing custody decisions to be made with caring and sharing rather than conflict and contention, "mediation may in fact merely hide rather than eliminate conflict, allowing the stronger of the two parents to dominate and control the weaker."

The debate over mediation has been constructed so that the practice is understood to have either positive or negative impacts on family members. The following analysis draws from the work of Michel Foucault (1978, 1979). Foucault highlights historical rituals of power located in disciplinary mechanisms such as the confessional and panopticon, and provides a methodology which illuminates strategies of domination in child custody mediation practices. In particular, his work on power as a productive force, serious talk, and normalizing judgment provides insight into the practice of mediation, extends the debate on the practice, and highlights the ways in which parents are both subjects and agents of custody mediation.

CUSTODY MEDIATION AS A PRODUCTIVE FORCE

Foucault (1978, 1979) understands power as a productive force and focuses his analysis on cultural practices in which power and knowledge cross, and in which our understanding of the individual, society, and the human sciences is produced. He identifies specific sites in which rituals of power take place—the Panopticon of Bentham and the confessional—to localize and specify how power works. He makes the case that when power is demonstrated in the public realm resistance to power has the opportunity to gather momentum as a social force. The practice of custody mediation can be understood to be a productive force and a site where power and knowledge cross and where our understandings of what it means to be a parent are produced.

Many feminists have drawn on the poststructuralist argument that rather than having a fixed core or essence, subjectivity is constructed through language and is unfixed, contradictory and a historically situated amalgam of different subject positions. The argument that subjectivity is not an innate or natural quality of the body but rather an effect of historically specific power relations provides an analytic framework to examine the economy of power relations found arising from the site of custody mediation. It also helps to overcome tendencies to essentialism and biologism that have dominated theories of motherhood (e.g. Chodorow 1978; Ruddick 1980, 1989). However, the subject positions "mother" and "father," even if understood as outcomes of language and historically situated, still create a dilemma in feminist thinking. This dilemma is evident in the debate over the practice of custody mediation.

Similar to Foucault's (1979) description of the structure of the confessional, the court appointed child custody mediation session is a central component in the disciplining and control of family members. Custody mediation is a site where the ritual of power takes place, where power and knowledge cross and where our understanding of the meaning of custodial parenting is produced. The minutiae of the everyday life of parenting and of individual biography are extracted by mediators. Parents who have gone through custody mediation are known in infinitely more detail than parents who have not, but mediators keep the details private. The privacy of mediation sessions provides mediators, acting on behalf of the state, a site to reconfigure gendered families into "gender-neutral" families relatively quickly, privately, and inexpensively.

During mediation sessions, mediators guide the possibility of conduct, putting in order the possible outcome. They represent the state's interest in knowing, measuring, and regulating family members and participate in the governing of families by structuring the possible field of action for them. While the mediator's role is supposed to be that of facilitator rather than director, the hierarchical gaze and normalizing judgment of mediators can silence parents. The mediator controls and directs the topics of conversation and decides what counts as "a final decision" and "mutually agreeable." This is often problematic for the parent who has done the lion's share of care work. Women still perform the majority of child-raising duties both within relationships and outside of them while the rejection of maternal preference found in the tender years doctrine in family law has taken away the special protection mothers once had. Mediation in many states, including California, dismisses the history of care work that preceded the divorce/separation as having no bearing on the custody decision. Parents who can demonstrate a history of primary care giving during the life of the relationship and who believe they have earned the right to continue to primary parent enter negotiations with mediators who have a preference for equal access.

Mediation is also a forum where parents are informed they have an equal economic responsibility to support their children. The higher-wage earner has child support payments reduced proportionate to the time with the child, which means that if children spend half their time with each parent child support payments are significantly reduced. This law attempts to tie child support to time spent with children, that is, more time with father. Children are often viewed by fathers as their right, their entitlement . . . their purchase. "Pay and play," which makes the child a commodity of exchange, is the method encouraged in mediation for determining child custody.

Child support is often configured for fifty-fifty joint custody in mediation sessions. If it is not, fathers can threaten to contest custody as a strategy to pressure mothers into accepting lower financial settlements, including less child support, even when the men do not actually want the responsibility of the children. Courts routinely offer *de jure* custody to fathers who do not engage in care giving. And because women are often unwilling to accept risking losing custody, this strategy usually works. Joint custody perpetuates male control over children after divorce for what turns out to be a minimal cost. Because the primary cause of poverty for children in single-parent households is women's lack of earning power, the result of many child support orders is increased poverty for women and children.

CUSTODY MEDIATION AS 'SERIOUS TALK'

Foucault's (1972) claim that our culture has a tendency to convert more and more of our everyday speech acts into 'serious' ones, in the sense that a speech act can be serious if there is the necessary validation of procedures and community of experts in place to monitor it, illuminates the state's role in the reconfiguration of the family during custody mediation. Mediators determine what kind of speech counts as valid. What counts as 'serious' talk in mediation sessions for parents is talk that "looks forward, not back," meets the "friendly parent" rule, and takes as a given "equality between parents." Parents in mediation who want to focus on past behavior, criticize the other parent, or discuss inequality between parents are silenced. Parents are forced to embrace the rules of mediation and appropriate a style and moral perspective in accord with these policies. Because mediators reward silent parents and punish critical ones, parents with legitimate complaints that bear on the best interest standard remain silent in order to be seen as "cooperative."

Parents are silenced by the "friendly parent" rule which favors giving primary custody to the parent who behaves in mediation sessions as if they are most likely to allow access to the other parent. Therefore, transfer (or threat of transfer) of custody to the "friendly parent" silences criticism. Mediation has as its goal co-custodial family arrangements and rewards the parent who appears most likely to encourage it. Mediators proceed from the assumption that equal access to biological parents is best for all family members. This can be extremely threatening for parents who do not believe it is in the best interest of their children to have equal contact with both parents. It is overwhelmingly women who have severe grievances to make during a mediation session, such as spousal or child abuse, and as a result may appear as the "unfriendly" parent.

Currently, it is estimated that two million women in the United States are abused by husbands or other male partners who use violence as one way of controlling "their woman" (Johnson and Ferraro 2000). Research indicates that children are abused in up to 70 percent of families in which violence against woman occurs (Edleson 1999, 134; Stark and Flitcraft 1991, 123). Violence against women in domestic settings has serious negative impacts on children, including: substance use; delinquent behavior; mental health disorders and psychiatric diagnoses, including post-traumatic stress disorder, depression, anxiety, sexual disorders, and eating disorders (see Kovrola and Heger 2003, 331; Saunders 2003, 356). Even for women who have not been beaten, forced engagement with their husbands/partners without the protection of a lawyer and the legal process is extremely intimidating and replicates patterns of inequality in the marriage/relationship (Grillo 1991, 1563).

Victims of domestic violence are silenced in mediation. Mediators often consider allegations of domestic violence or child abuse vengeful or manipulative strategies on the part of mothers to withhold access to children and view them with suspicion and mistrust. Child custody mediators failed to recognize and report domestic violence in 56.9 percent of the domestic violence cases, and mediation resulted in poor outcomes for domestic violence victims in terms of protections, such as supervised visitation and protected child exchanges (Johnson et al. 2005, 506). In a study of violence in 8,145 families, researchers found that at least 50 percent of batterers who assault their wives frequently also physically injure their children (Straus and Gelles 1990). A survey of psychologists who serve as child custody evaluators found that 75.6 percent indicated they would recommend against custody to a parent who often attempts to alienate the child from the other parent by negatively interpreting that parent's behavior (Ackerman and Ackerman 1997, 565).

The lack of representation for domestic violence victims during mediation sessions ensures victims of violence are forced to continue a parenting relationship with their victimizers, and the likelihood that children are harmed by this arrangement is ignored in the process of mediation. Batterers meet the standards set up by mediation policy; they are often self-confident and friendly, they are not interested in "looking back," and as a consequence may end up with the lion's share in any divorce or custody agreement (Grillo 1991, 1545).

Opponents of more protective legislation interpret allegations of domestic violence and sexual abuse as weapons of belligerent parents who work out their unresolved conflicts during mediation. Fathers' rights groups have successfully lobbied for laws favoring the "friendly parent" no matter what his or her relationship is to the child, without regard for the record of actual parenting, and without regard to violence against woman. Domestic murder cases illustrate the extreme point that almost no matter what a biological parent does his or her rights are protected against all others. California, as with most states, no longer recognizes a best interests standard in dealing with a biological father's right to custody, on grounds that it must be shown that it would be harmful to the child to live with the biological parent, not merely in that child's best interests. This is extremely difficult to prove unless a parent has past convictions of child (but not spousal) abuse or can be found to be dangerously unstable at the moment of hearing.

Violence against woman and the impact of it on co-custodial family members does not count as "serious talk" during the mediation process. From a Foucauldian perspective, the discursive policy of mediation produces as its effect violent-prone fathers and silent, fearful mothers. Mediators routinely endorse violent men as co-custodial fathers and are likely to favor an award of joint custody to a convicted batterer because custody law favors equal access to both parents following divorce. The "friendly parent" rule assures at least fifty percent physical custody during a mediation session to friendly parents, but does not guarantee "friendliness" after custody decisions are finalized. Acting as a friendly parent during custody mediation can in fact be used as a tool to harass one's former partner. Because domestic violence is gendered, but mediation is gender-neutral, mediators, acting on behalf of the state, force victims of domestic violence (largely women) to be silent in order for them to be seen as "cooperative." Foucault's concept of "serious talk," applied to custody mediation, highlights the state's engagement of systematic suppression of voice and the white-washing of domestic violence as a factor in custody allocation.

CUSTODY MEDIATION AS NORMALIZING JUDGMENT

Foucault (1978) posed the question of sexuality in historical terms; sexuality is a historical construct and not an underlying biological referent. He argued that power is not a commodity, a position, a prize, or a plot; rather, it is the operation of political technologies throughout the social body and suggested that their effects are asymmetrical relations. He argued that domination is fixed throughout its history in rituals and in meticulous procedures that impose rights and obligations. From a Foucauldian perspective, the subject positions "mother" and "father" are outcomes of disciplinary mechanisms such as custody mediation.

The process of mediation produces gender-neutral, co-custodial families headed by biological parents and undervalues gendered and non-biological "parenting." Unfortunately, the subject position "mother" still performs the majority of child-raising duties both within relationships and outside of them, makes less money than those occupying the subject position "father," and does more household labor. Moreover, non-biologically related adults often find themselves in the subject position "mother" without any legal protections. The rights of stepparents and grandparents who take an active parenting role in children's lives have been virtually ignored by the process of custody mediation. Grandparents, who have not been granted legal parent status, but who have raised their grandchildren for significant periods of time, are left out of custody mediation sessions. Stepparents are considered legal strangers and also left out of the mediation process; this is troubling considering stepparents are the fastest-growing class of residential parents, for as many as one in three American children now can expect to spend some of their childhood years living with a stepparent (Seltzer 1994, 235).

Ignoring gender inequality and the role of non-biological parents, mediators (re)produce gendered biological families. Informal sperm donors (biological parents) who have never participated in the life of their child are allowed to mediate for shared custody. In the case of lesbian partners who rely on an informal donor, they can be shocked to find that their donor can be awarded custodial rights. The mediation session, in which two-year olds are treated the same as ten-year olds, also ignores the desires of young children who may have social and psychological attachments to adults who have behaved as parents for considerable lengths of time. The emphasis on biological parenting and the exclusion of children's wishes from mediation discussions highlights the state's interest in continuing to link biology with parenting.

The high percentage of joint physical custody agreements achieved through the mediation process is not likely to be sustained because they rarely fit the behavior of families (Mason 1999). According to Mason, few families can maintain a 50/50 physical and legal sharing arrangement in which the child actually resides with each biological parent one half of the time because the needs and desires of parents and children often change over time. Parents move, remarry, give-in to child preferences for one parent or the other, and inevitably children drift toward a primary parent model. Women often find that over time a "mother drift" occurs which mimics earlier patterns of primary child care, thus she finds herself with *de facto* primary custody but *de jure* co-custody child support (Maccoby and Mnookin 1992). If she is content with primary care giver responsibilities post-relationship due to the "mother drift" but fears a renewed custody battle she will likely keep the child support award configured for shared parenting but behave as a *de facto* primary parent. Thus, the mediation session reproduces unequal, gendered biological parenting.

CONCLUSION

The conclusions reached in this paper suggest the newly emergent phenomenon of gender-neutral child custody mediation post-relationship produces as an outcome asymmetrical co-parenting because there is nothing substantial in the practice that alleviates inequality. Although custody mediation is considered a success by some researchers because it empowers parents to manage conflict creatively, protects father's rights, and reduces the volume of adversarial proceedings, in this chapter I have argued that custody mediation is in fact a disciplinary practice with asymmetrical effects. The normalizing judgment and productive power mediators wield over parents negotiating child custody during mediation sessions reconfigures the relationships between parent and child, individual and state in ways that harm women and children. Mediators reproduce gendered-unequal biological families. The emphasis on biological parenting does not take into consideration the complexity of family structures or the desires of young children.

Foucault's work reveals custody mediation to be a site where the subject "parent" is contested, and, at the same time, a site where the outcomes of "mothering" and "fathering" continue to reflect long entrenched patterns of gender inequality. Gender-neutral custody decisions leave women coming out of divorce and separation settlements with the responsibility of children but with insufficient money to support them. Being responsible for the rearing of children renders women less competitive and less successful in the labor market. The trading of children for money which results in the impoverishment of women prompts a reevaluation of mediation as a system of generating gender inequality as an outcome.

Unlike the adversarial process in open family court where resistance to power is public, mediators, in private mediation sessions, quash resistance and talk that does not count as 'serious'. The adversarial but public trial process provides the weaker parent more protection than mediation which occurs in private. As Martha Fineman (1988, 769) notes:

The public nature of the legal process means that the basis for decisions will be explained, debated, and publicly considered. This process may not be foolproof, but it is better than one in which substantive rules and standards evolve and are implemented behind closed office doors without any possibility of checks from the political system.

Even granting the patriarchal nature of the legal process, the expense of private attorneys, and the discretion of judges, the public adversarial process and the presence of lawyers better serves the weaker party in a child custody case.

The imposition of "gender neutral" custody mediation on gendered parents ignores the consequences associated with continuing a co-parenting relationship with an abusive partner; silences the "weaker parent" (usually women) throughout the process of mediation and family court hearings; and, protects noncompliance by placing the burden on the weaker parent. Foucault's ideas of power as a productive force, 'serious talk,' and normalizing judgment applied to the newly emergent phenomenon of child custody mediation reveal that this decision-making strategy does not constitute a substantive departure from the history of sexism in child custody policy. "Gender-neutral" mediation and the normalizing judgment of mediators is the disciplinary mechanism that reproduces gender inequality in families post-relationship.

Custody mediation is not supposed to privilege the subject position "mother" or "father" but the unintended consequences of closed-door mediation sessions are the impoverishment of women and children and the silencing of domestic violence victims. Mediation sessions operate as a funnel where communication is systematically suppressed and fears and trepidations can not be expressed. Complex ideas get funneled into a very narrow set of legitimated parameters which exclude much and amount to an injustice to one or both parties. In sum, this analysis reveals that custody mediation is a social force that reproduces gender inequality and an important site for feminist study.

NOTES

1. California Family Code 3161: The purposes of a mediation proceeding are as follows: (a) To reduce acrimony that may exist between the parties. (b) To develop an agreement assuring the child close and continuing contact with both parents that is in the best interest of the child, consistent with Sections 3011 and 3020. (c) To effect a settlement of the issue of visitation rights of all parties that is in the best interest of the child. California Family Code 3181. (a) In a proceeding in which mediation is required pursuant to this chapter, where there has been a history of domestic violence between the parties or where a protective order as defined in Section 6218 is in effect, at the request of the party alleging domestic violence in a written declaration under penalty of perjury or protected by the order, the media-

tor appointed pursuant to this chapter shall meet with the parties separately and at separate times. (b) Any intake form that an agency charged with providing family court services requires the parties to complete before the commencement of mediation shall state that, if a party alleging domestic violence in a written declaration under penalty of perjury or a party protected by a protective order so requests, the mediator will meet with the parties separately and at separate times.
2. California Family Code 3177: Mediation proceedings pursuant to this chapter shall be held in private and shall be confidential. All communications, verbal or written, from the parties to the mediator made in the proceeding are official information within the meaning of Section 1040 of the Evidence Code.
3. California Family Code 3182: (a) The mediator has authority to exclude counsel from participation in the mediation proceedings pursuant to this chapter if, in the mediator's discretion, exclusion of counsel is appropriate or necessary. (b) The mediator has authority to exclude a domestic violence support person from a mediation proceeding as provided in Section 6303.
4. California Family Code 3183: (a) The mediator may, consistent with local court rules, submit a recommendation to the court as to the custody of or visitation with the child. (b) Where the parties have not reached agreement as a result of the mediation proceedings, the mediator may recommend to the court that an investigation be conducted pursuant to Chapter 6 (commencing with Section 3110) or that other services be offered to assist the parties to effect a resolution of the controversy before a hearing on the issues. (c) In appropriate cases, the mediator may recommend that restraining orders be issued, pending determination of the controversy, to protect the well-being of the child involved in the controversy.
5. California Family Code 3900: Subject to this division, the father and mother of a minor child have an equal responsibility to support their child in the manner suitable to the child's circumstances.

REFERENCES

Ackerman, Marc, and Melissa Ackerman. 1997. Child custody evaluation practices: A 1996 survey of psychologists. *Family Law Quarterly* 30: 565.

Ahrons, Constance, and Jennifer Tanner. 2003. Adult children and their fathers: Relationship changes 20 years after parental divorce. *Family Relations* 52: 340–351.

Booth, Alan, and Paul Amato. 1994. Parental marital quality, parental divorce, and relations with parents. *Journal of Marriage & Family* 56: 21–34.

Boyd, Susan. 2003. *Child custody, law and women's work.* Don Mills, ON, Canada: Oxford University Press.

Chesler, Phyllis. 1991. Mothers on trial: The custodial vulnerability of women. *Feminism & Psychology* 1: 409–425.

Chodorow, Nancy. 1978. *The reproduction of mothering-psychoanalysis and the sociology of gender.* Berkeley: University of California Press.

Cohen, Aharon Luxenburg, Naomi Dattner, and David Matz. 1999. Suitability of divorcing couples for mediation: A suggested typology. *American Journal of Family Therapy* 27 (4): 329–344.

Demo, David. 1992. Parent-child relations: Assessing recent changes. *Journal of Marriage & Family* 54: 104–117.

———. 2000. Children's experience of family diversity. *National Forum* (80) 3: 16–20.

Dillon, Peter and Robert Emery. 1996. Divorce mediation and resolution of child custody disputes: Long-term effects. *American Journal of Orthopsychiatry* 66: 131–140.

Donzelot, Jacques. 1979. *The policing of families*. Baltimore: Johns Hopkins Press.

Edleson, Jeffrey. 1999. The overlap between child maltreatment and woman battering. *Violence Against Women* 5 (2): 134–154.

Emery, Robert and Melissa Wyer. 1987. Divorce mediation. *American Psychologist* 42: 472–480.

Emery, Robert. 1994. *Renegotiating family relationships: Divorce, child custody and mediation*. New York: Guilford.

Featherstone, Brid. 1999. Taking mothering seriously: The implications for child protection. *Child and Family Social Work* 4: 43–53.

Fields, Jason. 2003. Children's Living Arrangements and Characteristics: March 2002. *Current Population Reports. U.S. Census Bureau*, Washington, DC. P20-547.

Fineman, Martha. 1988. Dominant discourse, professional language, and legal change in child custody decision making. *Harvard Law Review* 101 (4): 727–774.

Foucault, Michel. 1972. *The archaeology of knowledge & the discourse on language*. New York: Pantheon.

———. 1978. *The history of sexuality: An introduction*. Vol. 1. New York: Vintage.

———. 1979. *Discipline and punish: The birth of the prison*. New York: Vintage.

Grillo, Trina. 1991. The mediation alternative: Process dangers for women. *Yale Law Journal* 100: 1545.

Hughes, Robert and Jacqueline Kirby. 2000. Strengthening evaluation strategies for divorcing family support services: Perspective of parent educators, mediators, attorneys, and judges. *Family Relations* 49: 53–62.

Irwin, Howard and Michael Benjamin. 1992. An evaluation of process and outcome in a private family mediation service. *Mediation Quarterly* 10: 35–55.

Johnson, Nancy, Dennis Saccuzzo, and Wendy Koen. 2005. Child custody mediation in cases of domestic violence. *Violence Against Women* 11: 1022–1053.

Johnson, Michael, and Kathleen Ferraro. 2000. Research on domestic violence in the 1990s: Making distinctions. *Journal of Marriage and the Family* 62: 948–963.

Kelly, Joan. 1983. Mediation and psychotherapy: Distinguishing the differences. In *Dimensions and practice of divorce* mediation, ed. J. Lemmon, 33–44. San Francisco: Jossey-Bass.

———. 1991. Parent interaction after divorce: Comparison of mediated and adversarial divorce processes. *Behavioral Science and Law* 9: 387–398.

———. 1993. Developing and implementing post divorce parenting plans: Does the forum make a difference? In *Non-custodial parenting: New vistas in family living*, ed. C. Depner and J. Bray, 136–155. Newbury Park, CA: Sage.

———. 1996. A decade of divorce mediation research: Some answers and questions. *Family and Conciliation Courts Review* 34: 373–385.

Kelly, Joan, Lynn Gigy, and Sheryl Hausman. 1988. Mediated and adversarial divorce: Initial finding from a longitudinal study. In *Divorce mediation: Theory and practice*, ed. J. Folberg and A. Milne, 453–473. New York, New York: Guilford.

Kovrola, Catherine and Astrid Heger, A. 2003. Responding to children exposed to domestic violence. *Journal of Interpersonal Violence* 4: 331–337.

Kreider, Rose. 2007. Living arrangements of children: 2004. *Current Population Reports.* U.S. Census Bureau, Washington, DC.: 70–114.
Kressell, Kenneth. 1985. *The process of divorce: How professionals and couples negotiate settlement.* New York: Basic Books.
Kurz, Demie. 1995. *For richer, for poorer: Mothers confront divorce.* New York: Routledge.
Laue, James. 1987. The emergence and institutionalization of third party roles in conflict. In *Conflict management and problem solving,* ed. D. Sandole and I. Sandole-Staroste, 17–29. New York: New York University Press.
Maccoby, Eleanor and Robert Mnookin. 1992. *Dividing the child: Social and legal dilemmas of custody.* Cambridge, MA: Harvard University Press.
MacKinnon, Catherine. 2001. *Sex equality: family law.* New York, New York: Foundation Press.
Mason, Mary Ann. 1999. *The custody wars.* New York: Basic Books.
Maxwell, David. 1992. Gender differences in mediation style and their impact on mediator effectiveness. *Mediation Quarterly* 9: 353–364.
Millet, Kate. 1970. *Sexual politics.* New York: Doubleday.
National Center for Health Statistics. 2005. Births/Natality. Final Data for 2005, Tables C, 1, 10, 32. *Centers for Disease Control and Prevention,* U.S. Department of Health and Human Services, Hyattsville, MD.
Okin, Susan Moller. 1989. *Justice,* gender and the family. New York: Basic Books.
Rowe, Barbara and Gong-Soog Hong. 1996. The importance of non-residential parent contact for children of divorce. *Consumer Interests Annual* 42: 335–340.
Ruddick, Sara. 1980. Maternal thinking. *Feminist Studies* 6: 342–367.
———. 1989. *Maternal thinking.* Boston, MA: Beacon Press.
Saunders, Benjamin. 2003. Understanding children exposed to Violence: Toward an integration of overlapping fields. *Journal of Interpersonal Violence* 4: 356–376.
Seltzer, Judith. 1994. Consequences of marital dissolution for children. *Annual Review of Sociology* 20: 235–266.
Shanley, Mary Lyndon. 1989. *Feminism, marriage, and the law in Victorian England.* New Jersey: Princeton University Press.
Shiono, Patricia and Linda Sandham Quinn. 1994. Epidemiology of divorce. *Future of Children* 4:15–28.
Stark, Evan and Anne Flitcraft. 1991. Spouse abuse. In *Violence in America: A public health approach,* ed. Mark Rosenberg and Mary Ann Fenley, 123–157. New York: Oxford University Press.
Straus, Murray and Richard Gelles. 1990. How violent are American families? Estimates from the National Family violence Resurvey and other studies. In *Physical violence in American families: Risk factors and adaptations to violence in 8,145 families,* ed. M. Straus and R. Gelles, 95–112. New Brunswick, NJ: Transaction Publishers.
Stull, Donald and Nancy Kaplan. 1987. The positive impact of divorce mediation on children's behavior. *Mediation Quarterly* 18: 53–59.
Thompson, Ross. 1986. Fathers and the child's "best interests": Judicial decision making in custody disputes. In *The father's role: applied perspectives,* ed. M. Lamb, 61–101. New York: Wiley.
U. S. Bureau of the Census. 2001. *People and families in poverty by selected characteristics: 1999 and 2000.* (www.census.gov/hhes/poverty)
U.S. House of Representatives. Committee on Ways and Means. 2000. *2000 Green Book.* Washington, D.C.: U.S. Government Printing Office.
Zelizer, Viviana. 1985. *Pricing the priceless child: The changing social value of children.* New York: Basic Books.

6 Weaving and Unweaving the Rights of Public Woman

The Case of Telephone Operators at the Turn of the Twentieth Century

Jane S. Sutton

> The question of souls is old—we demand our bodies, now.
>
> Voltairine de Cleyre (1914, 350)

Despite recent attempts to frame women as leaders and decision makers, prejudices against women who gain access to positions of authority have not gone away (Eicher-Catt and Sutton 2009; Goldenberg 2007; Han and Heldman 2007; Valian 2000; van Zoonen 2006). On its Web site, The White House Project (2001, 2002, 2005) indicates these prejudices seem stubbornly resistant to change. This chapter concentrates historically on a part of the problem that has not gone away in the United States. Even as women increase their visibility and gain access to positions of authority in the public realm, they are subject to sexual innuendo. According to Kenneth Cmiel, "Residues of ancient taboos persist [in the twenty-first century] far beyond any 'official' end to barriers [in the nineteenth century] against women speaking in public" (1990, 71).

I can't offer a clearer snapshot of this residue than Hillary Clinton seeking the Democratic nomination for the U.S. presidency in 2008. Clinton was depicted in demeaning sexual images on Youtube Youchoose, and some mainstream media also participated in her sexual vilification. In Bill Moyers's interview with Kathleen Hall Jamieson about this sexual vilification of Clinton (*Bill Moyers Journal* 2007), Jamieson makes the case that women acting in the public sphere will have their status as public speakers scrutinized severely, accusing the female speaker/leader of promiscuity (see also Jamieson 1988, 1995). So as scholars from a variety of disciplines in the humanities and social sciences (earlier) note the various modes of exclusion that aim to silence and subordinate women who speak/act as a leader in the public sphere, Cmiel and Jamieson draw our attention to a "social imaginary" (Taylor 2004, 23–30) where women's actions in public are perceived through a lens marking them as harlots—"public women," so to speak.

This chapter frames the social imaginary, particularly honing its opposing ideas, images, and judgments housed in people's actions and language at the turn of the twentieth century about women's status as public speakers, to decipher how working-class women, who, having gained newborn access to the public sphere as telephone operators, are caught within a version of this imaginary that rotates a public woman as "public woman" in an oppositional manner.

Here is how I frame the social imaginary, expose the opposition, and decipher how it works. First, I tell a story of Amelia's arrest. I use this working-class woman and the circumstances in her story as a way to move allegorically to a genre-like figure "Telephone Woman" set in the twin context of the social imaginary and the telephone company. The main character in the allegorical story is not one woman but many working-class women whose story is about judgment, although it does not lead to an arrest. Their stories unfold not in the streets but nevertheless in a *textum*—a weaving connection—where I show their status as public woman and "public woman" shifting between the play—threads—of a dominant opposition (Jakobson 1971). I make sense of the shift with a trope, specifically *paronomasia*. It refers to a kind of playing on the sound and meaning of words that is enactive and thus actualizes "behavioral attitudes" from the structure of the trope itself (Fay 1994, 9). To apply the trope, I set a telephone pole up like a loom with behavior attitudes about women in public hanging like threads from it and I used them to decipher the connections in the social imaginary. The warp and the woof threads illuminate how, during times of sociopolitical change, women's status is altered slightly by entwining emphatically ancient taboos against their public speaking to seal within the social imaginary a view of women in forms of subordination.

THE STORY

The event takes place in December 1895 (see Writ for Amelia Schauer 1895; Must go to the workhouse 1895; The Girl Schauer is set free 1895; The night of horror 1895). Amelia "Lizzie" Schauer, a blue-eyed, comely, working-class "girl" of seventeen, steps out of her aunt's house at 432 Eighteenth Street and walks to Mrs. Dittmyer's house at Sixteen First Street in New York. Maggie Osterburg tells her niece during supper that she is too poor to keep Amelia any longer; but another one of her aunts, Mrs. Dittmyer, has some money and is willing to pay for her housekeeping services.

Amelia stops at a third aunt's house, Mrs. Raff at 620 Fifth Avenue, and borrows ten cents to ride the bridge. This aunt tells Amelia that George H. Mackall, a family friend known within its circle as "Douglass," has agreed to meet Amelia at the bridge and escort her through the city to the Dittmyer residence. Although both Amelia and Douglass arrive at the bridge, presumably at the appointed time, their paths, for whatever reason, never cross.

Around 10:45 that evening, policeman Oppenheimer says he saw Amelia walking up First Street. Forty-five minutes later, another officer, policeman

Reagan, says he saw her talking to two men. Amelia says she is lost. According to her own account, she wonders if Mrs. Dittmyer moved or if she has the wrong address. She stops to ask directions of a man because she says she didn't see the police officer.

In the courthouse policeman Reagan says he saw Amelia talking to "two Italians" in front of a "saloon." He arrests her because "she seemed," Reagan claims, "to be acting improperly" although in cross-examination, Reagan admits he could not hear "what she asked the men." But the fact that an unaccompanied woman is out at night is in the mind of Reagan presumptive evidence that Amelia is soliciting prostitution. Reagan is not alone in his thinking. In the eyes of the law, Amelia is a "public woman," and Magistrate John O. Mott sentences her to the workhouse on the charge of "disorderly conduct" (Must go to the workhouse 1895).

Fortunately, her three aunts employ a lawyer to get Magistrate Mott to reopen the case. Mott agrees but only after the family produces a certificate of examination from a medical doctor. Amelia goes to Dr. J. T. Deyo of 364 Ninth Street to be examined. Amelia proves to be a "strictly good girl." The doctor's examination of Amelia impresses Mott, but it fails to change his judgment of the case (Must go to the workhouse 1895). Some newspapers, such as the *New York World*, make a fuss over Amelia and praise her as a "good girl" (The night of horror 1895). Eventually, Assistant District Attorney Hennessy says the girl's only appeal is to the Court of General Session (Writ for Amelia Schauer 1895). In the end, Justice Andrews, who presided over the Court of General Session, says: "There is no evidence she is a girl of bad character." And he adds: "There is nothing for the Court to do but to discharge the prisoner from custody forthwith." When Peter Conlin, chief of police, read the decision of Justice Andrews, the paper reported Conlin to say, "It always seemed clear to me that the police have no right to arrest women in the street on the bare suspicion . . . that the women are disorderly" (Must go to the workhouse, 1895).

ROTATING THE TROPES/TROOPS

The streets are a way to concretize the oppositional discourse between public woman and "public woman" in the social imaginary. They give Amelia a way to connect with people—her aunts and her job—and make a living as a single, working-class woman. But by going out on the streets at night, Amelia gets into a lot of trouble. This trouble points to the streets as something more than concrete. They are a metaphor for making connections within the context of the social imaginary. The policeman as a viewer/perceiver/auditor connects Amelia to an idea, image, myth, and beliefs to arrive at a judgment: Amelia is a "public woman." But as Amelia gets into trouble being on the streets, she also causes trouble. That "the police have no right to arrest women in the streets" indicates there is unease about seeing women in public surroundings as "public women." The double trouble and contradiction—the trouble Amelia gets into and the troubled social imaginary—suggests that a major dialogue is opening up in the streets over a use of public space (Spence 2007), a dialogue about the bodily and moral excellence of women who gain access to it as speakers. As women enter the workforce as telephone operators, will they be "good girls"? Assuming they are good girls, how might they be viewed working the night shift? Will they be seen as Amelia was seen—as a "public woman?" These are questions to keep in mind as I move to a larger story—that of working-class women—telephone operators—set in the confines of the Bell Telephone Company; and also abstractly in the entwinement of logical extremes—between a public woman and a "public woman."

I use tropes to decipher the oppositional discourse. Remember "public woman" is uttered in *sotto voce*. Because the opposition—between public woman and "public woman"—looks and sounds close enough but yet not exactly (due to the volume), it functions tropically as *paronomasia* (Dupriez 1991, 328–30; Preminger 1974, 602; Sloane 2001, 553–54). Generally speaking, a trope is a turn. Drawing from Friedrich Nietzsche's writing on rhetoric, a trope rallies an army (of images, ideas, words) and mobilizes them like troops to rotate meaning (1989, 250). According to Michelle Ballif and Michael Moran, "one mobilizes the tropes in order to rotate the troops" (2005, 4; see also Mailloux 1993, 299). In the case of Amelia, she is one of many women rising in public and moving out of her (private) sphere, and as she does, the rotation of the trope/troops makes it possible to see her *as* a "public woman." Why are the troops rotated in a manner that vilifies her? As I mentioned earlier, the impropriety associated with public woman constitutes a stubborn theme in history (Jamieson 1988, 76.) A viewer or participant (like the policeman) actively creates the possible premise—Amelia is a "public woman"—through bias and interests circulating in the social imaginary. To the viewer-participant-policeman's credit, his rotation of the subject is neither ridiculous nor is it "false." As he decodes the meaning of the subject—Amelia—being out at night in the streets, he shows his comprehension of the social imaginary.

Now specifically, the trope of *paronomasia* rotates the troops by playing on a pseudo-etymological relationship that easily lets a viewer-participant turn/rotate a public woman into a "public woman." Remember the playful rotations are not one-way streets; they turn in two directions, meaning that *paronomasia* is also a trope of possibility. After all, there is a rotation by which Amelia gains access to the public sphere as a telephone operator. Now we have *paronomasia* as an analytic category for figuring out how the opposition functions to subordinate women as well as the possibility it holds for upsetting this low status. I want to show the action of *paronomasia* solidifying a version of a public woman/telephone woman through the process of weaving. The threads—the warp and the woof threads—stand for the turns from the literal to the imagined or from the proper to

122   *Jane S. Sutton*

the improper. The finished product—the photograph of the mural "Weavers of Speech" (Bond c. 1915) indicates the process is arrested and that a version of a telephone woman/public woman is a sign the social imaginary possesses about how women properly become public women.

Turning from Amelia's story to that of working-class women looking for work, I consider their employment as telephone operators. Female telephone operators were an important part of the Bell Telephone's Company (AT&T) marketing strategy from the 1890s to the later part of twentieth century. Early on, it realized single, white, working-class females between the ages of seventeen and twenty-four could help market the new technology and help spread its growth (Green 1990). How the telephone company realized that females were better than male operators and why they retained female operators as a kind of techno-labor system when automatic switching devices were available are some of the major critical questions that have attracted the attention of those interested in the history of the telephone and of women's labor in the United States (e.g., Green 1990; Lipartito 1995).

THE STORY OF "TELEPHONE WOMAN"

Using the New York Telephone Company's "media"—e.g., a pamphlet and a certain black-and-white picture entitled "Weavers of Speech" (*An Ideal Occupation for Women* [191?]), and diary published in the *Saturday Evening Post* ("The Diary of a Telephone Girl: The Work of a Human Spider in a Web of Talking Wires" 1907), I tell how the telephone company apprehended public woman/"public woman." By December 31, 1895, the Bell Telephone Company had 14,699 employees, and virtually all operators were women (Danielian 1939). As Katherine Schmidt recalls it, by the late 1890s, male operators had moved into higher positions in the Bell organization. Their move up gave women the opportunity to work the night shift (1930). According to the census records, there were approximately 52,000 single female operators in the United States by 1910 (Hill 1929). Now the telephone company, for a variety of reasons, wanted "girls," not "boys," as telephone operators. The reasons why Bell wanted to employ girls, especially native-born white young, single girls, has been thoroughly articulated (Lipartito 1995) and there is no need to pursue them. What is important for purposes of this chapter is that hiring single girls set up the possibility to typecast Telephone Woman as figures of bodily and moral excellences.

"Weavers of Speech" is a black-and-white photograph of a mural. It appears in the New York Telephone Company in a pamphlet, circa 1911 (*An Ideal Occupation for Women* [191?]). It depicts a woman of heroic proportions standing next to a vertical, upright structure set up to hang telephone wires. Holding these wires like threads, "Weavers of Speech" is, therefore, the main character I dub Telephone Woman. To trace out her genre-like character within the social imaginary, I go to the mythic weaver—Penelope, the faithful wife of Odysseus who wards off the suitors' advances by unweaving at night what she has woven by day. Telephone Woman is a weaver at a gigantic loom, the numerous wires "crossing and recrossing as if in the execution of some wondrous fabric . . . a wondrous fabric of speech . . . woven into the record of each day" (Kern 1983, 69). As a laborer, the telephone operator weaves city and factory and farm in a fabric of speech day and night and night and day to produce faithfully the rhetorical space of and for the public, while simultaneously producing the sign of a woman in public.

HER LOOM

The loom is a telephone pole. "Weavers of Speech" places a figure, a goddess or heroine, next to a telephone pole as if the pole were a woman's loom and the telephone lines were her yarn. Upright (*histos*), the telephone pole is at once a sail and a loom, whose beams in ancient Greece stood upright, instead of lying horizontal as in our looms (McEwen 1993). To move from a telephone pole to a loom (*histon*) or to turn a telephone pole into a loom integrates the telephone pole with the whole generic representation of *histon* (loom) that includes not only items associated with weaving but also with what weaving has been associated, namely Penelope.

One of the definitive insights into the rhetorical activity peculiar to women is that they do not speak; they weave (Anonymous 2001; Freud 1953–1974). In Homer's *Odyssey*, silence is signified by Penelope. When she spoke to the bard about the suitors, her son Telemachus ordered Penelope to go to her room "and look to your own province, distaff and loom . . .; public speech shall be men's concern" (Homer 1980, 9). With Penelope in her room, weaving signified a form of silent "speaking" suitable for women and grounds the idea that a woman's performance in the public sphere is not equal to a man's performance but is subordinate to his authority. Weaving is treated as the sign of the silent speaker and unwavering faithfulness since within this mythic context, Penelope unweaves at night what she has woven by day. However, Penelope's faithfulness is also linked to trickiness since she uses her speech/weaving to conceal from the suitors that she is waiting for Odysseus' return. So the female weaver is capable of deceiving men.

This weaver/deceiver is manifest in the myth of Philomela, who was raped and brutalized by her sister's husband Tereus. Tereus cut out Philomela's tongue to keep her from speaking up after raping her. According to Apollodorus, Philomela wove pictures of the rape and sent them to her sister Porcne (1921, 3.14.8). What Philomela does in response to being raped and brutalized provides insight into the semiotic activity of weaving of a "public woman." With speech/weaving, she tricks and thus exposes Tereus. So a woman can use her job as a weaver of speech to overpower man, and this notion grounds the idea that women's weaving/speaking may be improper and needs discipline.

With Penelope and Philomela we have the embodiment of the pseudo-etymological structure of the trope *paronomasia* waiting to be actualized. So with this in mind, I turn to the character Telephone Woman to decipher how she enacts the opposition between public woman and "public woman." Telephone Woman is set up to enter in the public realm, characterized by the icons of industry, agriculture, and city. Based on the company's hiring practices, she is a virginal daughter loyal and obedient to her father, the New York Telephone Company. She is also a sexually ambiguous woman who performs tricks. Like Penelope, Telephone Woman is cast iconically at the telephone pole, which makes her Penelope-like sitting "in her room with distaff and loom" (Homer 1980, 9). In effect, Telephone Woman works apart from the public space that she makes possible through her connections. Nevertheless and at the same time, Telephone Woman's work is devised as a "trick," according to the language of telephony. As Sylvester Baxter explains "trick," it is a "curious technical term in telephony" and is the name applied to "working time" (1906, 237). Telephone operators are classified as "a trick," "b trick," "c trick," and "d trick," according to whether their service is "for morning-afternoon, afternoon-evening, morning-evening, or all night" (237). The "trickiness" of Telephone Woman is that she makes connections and disconnections, plugs and unplugs, wires and unwires, weaves and unweaves. What follows is a full description of how the trope constitutes the process of rotating the tricks of Telephone Woman between public woman and "public woman."

The Woof Threads

As cloth is woven from the top down of the loom, so Telephone Woman is set up to move forward with her work of constructing a social imaginary/fabric through speech. On the top of the beams—loom and telephone—hang the woof threads. The woof threads are fragments of working women positioned in space as "public women" or prostitutes. Whereas popular theology represents women speaking in public in terms of social "pollution" (a sermon of the public function of woman by Theodore Parker preached at Music Hall of Boston, March 27, 1853), the press and editorials represents women in speech as Aspasia-like, leaning on a would-be leader, and exercising undue influence by "sitting in the laps of the highest and lowest" of men (Female depravity 1836). To be a woman and speak publicly is to be labeled a whore by the press; women who came to hear women are also called "whores and harlots" (Morris 1984, 63, 293). That Jezebel and the question of moral speech shadow the body of a woman speaking in public highlights Lucy Stone's description of the difficulties women faced while speaking in public. Speaking on the condition of public women in the United States around the 1890s, Stone says, "Think what it would be like to live perpetually in the midst of scorn and reproach; to [hear], 'This Jezebel has come among us . . . '" (n.d.).

At this point, I should mention that mostly white, middle-class, and unmarried women who worked and spoke up (in settlement houses, as charity workers) outside the home (in public spaces)—such as Jane Addams, Florence Kelley, and Julia Lathrop [appointed first head of the federal government's Children's Bureau in 1912]—could fill out a portrait of the public woman doing good works and speaking well. However, a telephone woman was considered either low or working class (Marvin 1988) and, therefore, easily confused with the political category of a prostitute. The image of a "public woman," therefore, implicates class. That a working-class woman in New York City can be easily conflated and confused with the appearances of prostitution is illustrated by the story of Amelia Schauer.

Telephone women are hired through references, especially the clergy. Those hired to speak on the telephone are inspected and guaranteed as "good girls." For example, "Companies sent 'medical matrons' to visit applicants to determine that the home surroundings [are] healthful and proper" (Lipartito 1995, 1089). Using the Schauer case as a point of reference of public "woman's" impropriety, I find other woof threads. Senator J. M. Sanford, speaking before the California State Senate around 1911, describes what happens to any woman who enters the public sphere. They "lose the esteem" and "respect of men" (Sanford [1911?]). Sir Almroth Wright's *The Unexpurgated Case Against Woman Suffrage* (1913) presents another woof thread. Wright claims that a woman who enters public space has violated a rule of "nature." Violations of nature's rules incur a sanction which acts as proof that such a rule exists. One penalty for defying the rule of natural law that positions woman in the space of the home is the stigma of prostitution. Women who break the law, so to speak, are spoken of as "offensive and evil" (1913, 13).

From arguments against inserting the word *sex* in the Fifteenth Amendment fall additional woof threads. A good example is John F. Crosby's Constitution Essay awarded the Mallory Medal in 1910. Crosby earned praise when he argued that the 200,000 prostitutes in New York City could be "easily induced to vote, and that they would become a very powerful and pliant force" of political rings. Just as "public" women "sell their own souls" so they would "readily sell their votes" (13). Going along with Crosby's line of argument is Mrs. Andrew A. George's statement before the Committee on Woman Suffrage in the United States Senate, April 19, 1913. Public women constitute a real danger to the polity. As Mrs. George put it:

> In Dr. Helen L. Sumner in her book *Equal Suffrage—The Results of an Investigation in Colorado Made for the Collegiate Equal Suffrage League New York State*, on page 84 of which we read: 'Prostitutes generally vote, and their vote is cast solidly for the party in control . . .

And again on page 93, this trained investigator reports: 'The red-light district is freely used by the party in power, and its women [would be] compelled . . . to vote.' (1913, n.p.)

Her "trick" or designated working time (as "a," "b," or "c"), as well as other woof threads hanging from the monumental vertical beam that shade and overlap this trickiness, turns her into a "public woman" as she gains access the working world.

The Warp Threads

The woof extending vertically in one direction is bound together by warp threads traveling orthogonally. Working women had to work. That is an emphatic piece of yarn on which to draw. No one denies that under certain circumstances—the death of a husband—a woman has to perform, has to enter, has to work in public space. Those circumstances create a gap through which to draw the yarn and bear upon the warp of the social cloth. Another gap exploited in transforming a "public woman" into a public woman involves the question of how to judge the sight of a woman in public. In "The Diary of a Telephone Girl: The Work of a Human Spider in a Web of Talking Wires" (1907), the unknown author (probably the telephone company) suggests that women ought to be judged by their background, namely, who their mother and father are, not by their appearances and not by their being on the streets. A related problem is whether long-standing rules of propriety that made it unthinkable for women to be educated (like their male counterparts) entitles a woman to enter public space as a (telephone) speaker. As Fairfax Harrison, president of the Southern Railroad Company, tells his audience before the Alabama Girls' Technical Institute in 1914, "we must recognize the *necessity* for the industrial education of women . . . and acquire this viewpoint" (n.p.). By spinning the yarn of "necessity," the woof threads of "public woman" are designed to contrast with the warp threads engendered by words like those of Fairfax Harrison.

To step back and view the newly emergent public woman, the warp threads projects the "trick" or the work that a woman does in public as a "trick" or work performed in a private space. The proof or the slipknot that closes the gap of choices and assesses her speech as akin to Penelope comes through a spirit of ancient Greece, where women were not involved in public speechmaking (Sutton 1992). Writing against woman's right to vote, Wright summons the spirit of Pericles to protect the telephone women who were working and speaking in public: Quoting Pericles, he proclaims that no evil can be said "of woman in public so long as she confines herself to the domestic sphere" (Wright 1913, 13). That Telephone Woman works in a private space is evident by her Periclean trappings, loom and hearth. Because loom and hearth comprise a formal whole, a unified dominant image, Telephone Woman's work is cast as a form of public speaking in the space of the private or the home. Telephone Woman is a help-mate to the public, but has "no personal contact with the public." She is, therefore, respected and "held in the highest esteem of the land" (*An Ideal Occupation for Women* [191?], 9).

In the logic of domesticity, public woman inhabits public space privately and thus has no real contact with public deliberations. In teaching, for example, we encounter a parallel situation in which women speak in public, but it is fulfilled and influenced by the space of the hearth. Although women were speaking in public as teachers, which had been controversial in light of Paul's dictum in 1 Timothy 2.11–12 that a woman was neither to teach nor to usurp authority over the man (e.g., The doctrine of St. Paul concerning women 1870; St. Paul once more 1870; Paul concerning women 1871), female teachers were regarded as working in a private space. Bronson's analysis of teachers' salaries in 1910 depicts public women/teachers speaking at home. They are in front of children and so remain subordinate to men. "The majority of male teachers are principals, supervisors, superintendents and college presidents or college professors, while the country school teachers, the kindergartners and under teachers are women" (1913, n.p.). Like their teaching counterparts, telephone operators are seen fulfilling their roles as mothers.

Another thread forms public woman with respect to servitude and support associated with the image of the wife. In his remarks "Should Women Vote?," Joseph Gilpin Pyle observes that servitude is the "law" of a good woman ([1913?]). Presumably, "woman" who does not perform the role is sanctioned as "bad." Amuel Gilmore Anderson's sermon *Women's Sphere of Influence* describes the good woman as an out-of-sight support material. "It is the woman just out of sight over the hill who cheers the man . . ." (1898, n.p.). In effect, Telephone Woman completes man's well-being. She is the *hyle*, the stuff, the matter of man's actualization. She is his conduit, his conductor, his cable, his flow area through which public speech passes. Although she could not vote in the 1900 presidential election, Telephone Woman, working for the New York Telephone Company, could read bulletins, handled inquiries, and provided election services to "thirty-two Manhattan clubs and hotels and thirty-five country clubs, hotels, and associations in Westchester County" (Marvin 1988, 219).

In resisting the figure of a "public woman" (in *sotto voce*) that haunted the female speaker in the beginning of the nineteenth century, public women are seen as "devoted servants of male overseers" (Marvin 1988, 26). On the eve of women's suffrage (1920), the image of public woman is becoming dominated by a view that separates her from and resists the image of a prostitute while distinguishing her public speaking as private, providing support for or facilitating life in the public sphere without authority. Telephone Woman stands outside industry, factory, and agriculture while her loom and hearth engenders that space possible. She weaves; she operates lines of communication from a distance and without resisting or interfering with public affairs.

At the beginning of this chapter, I noted a problem of women being sexually vilified today as they seek positions of authority. I also noted that the problem seems stubbornly resistant to change. Let's turn around and look (from the past) toward the future. There is a moment in 1975 when once again the main character is a telephone operator on the streets.

BACKING INTO THE FUTURE

"As I was reading your essay," Michael Huspek wrote me, "I was reminded of my three-year stint as a cab driver in St. Paul and then later Chicago.

> In St. Paul, "Radio Cab Co." had a contract with the Bell Company such that every evening beginning at 10 P.M. and every half hour thereafter a line-up of cabs would be ordered to pick up Bell employees, almost all of whom were women. So at 10 o'clock the call would be for the first 8 cabs in line to proceed to the Bell Company; at 10:30 the call might be for 6 cabs; at 11 o'clock for 14; etc. The employees had strict orders that prohibited them from initiating conversation of any sort with the driver. Similarly, all drivers were under strict instruction to refrain from any and all conversation with the Bell employees. Well, on a hot and humid 4th of July eve, I "forgot myself" and asked one of the employees to roll up her window. "Why?" she asked. "Because kids have been throwing fireworks at passing cabs all evening and I don't want one coming through the window." She audibly shuddered at my response. The next day I received a letter of reprimand from my superiors and was ordered off the Bell-Co. lines for a month. No conversation permitted whatsoever! This was back in the early 1970's. (personal e-mail 2–3–2005)

Huspek's account, at the very least, illustrates that ideas about Amelia/telephone woman/public woman are still at play. While there are other contingencies in the 1970s bearing upon how women are suppose to act as well as be seen in public, the encounter between a cab driver and a Bell employee—like the one between Amelia and policeman—indicates that the space in which women are seen in public is set *paronomasically* in the social imaginary and, as such, "always already" demands discipline and punishment. Although women work, act, and speak in public, the public space itself continues rotating its social imaginary troops, turning opposing discourses to shade, overlap, and bear upon the other in a manner that puts into play an opposition between public women/"public women." As soon as speaking women enter the public, the opposing view of them kicks in, microphysically speaking, and they (and others such as cab drivers) become defined by the opposition, the transmitter of it, and the subject of and to its power. Put another way, the trope called *paronomasia*—embodied as public woman—is still with us and it is actualizing behavioral attitudes from within its enactive microphysics of power.

Now that we know there is a practice of an oppositional discourse, we must attend to it. We must first find or invent a new trope from within the tropical array of the opening and then draw that trope through the warp that I have opened up in oppositional discourse and rotate the troops to make a surprising maneuver. At any rate, if we can do new things with old tropes, public woman may be able to get her body back and with that body emerge as a leader, decision maker, person in charge, deliberator, a woman in public. Looking beyond the scope of this chapter, I want to say the larger goal of looking backwards is not to gain insight into how the opposition is played in particular times and circumstances but rather to use the insight for what Bernard Knox calls "backing into the future" (1994). Backing into the future is a way to see the present more fully. With the thematic entwinement of "public woman" and public woman as a deep historical horizon, we can effect conceptual changes (next time) in the present social imaginary about women's status as leader.

BIBLIOGRAPHY

Anderson, Amuel Gilmore. 1898. *Woman's sphere and influence*. Toledo, OH: Franklin Printing and Engraving Company.
Anonymous. 2001. *Dissoi Logoi*. In *The rhetorical tradition*, ed. Patricia Bizzell and Bruce Herzberg, 48–55. Boston, MA: Bedford/St. Martin's Press.
Apollodorus. 1921. *The library*. Translated by S. J. G. Frazer. 2 vols. Vol. 2, *Loeb classical library*. Cambridge, MA: Harvard University Press.
Ballif, Michelle, and Michael G. Moran. 2005. Introduction. In *Critical rhetorics and rhetoricians*, ed. Michelle Ballif and Michael G. Moran, 1–13. Westport, CT: Praeger.
Baxter, Sylvester. 1906. The telephone girl. *The Outlook*, May 26, 231–39.
Bill Moyers Journal. 2007. PBS 2007 [cited 7 December 2007].
Bond, Edmunds, E. C. 1915. Weavers of Speech, Boston Public Library. (Owner of the photograph).
Bronson, Minnie. 1913. *The wage-earning woman and the state*. Boston: Massachusetts Association Opposed to the Further Extension of Suffrage to Women.
Cleyre, Voltairine de. 1914. Sex slavery. In *Selected works of Voltairine de Cleyre*, ed. A. Berkman, 342–58. New York: Mother Earth Publishing Associations.
Cmiel, Kenneth. 1990. *Democratic eloquence: The fight over popular speech in nineteenth-century America*. New York: William Morrow and Company.
Crosby, John F. 1910. The advisability of inserting the word *sex* before the word *race* in the Fifteenth Amendment to the Constitution of the United States. Washington, DC: Georgetown University.
Danielian, N. R. 1939. *AT&T: The story of industrial conquest*. New York: Vanguard Press.

Diary of a telephone girl, The: The work of a human spider in a web of talking wires. 1907. *The Saturday Evening Post*, October 19, 6–8ff.
Doctrine of St. Paul concerning women, The. 1870. *The Woman's Journal*, 22 January
Dupriez, Bernard. 1991. *A dictionary of literary devices, A–Z*. Trans. A. W. Halsall. Toronto: University of Toronto Press.
Eicher-Catt, Deborah, and Jane Sutton. 2009. A communicology of the Oval Office as figural rhetoric: Women, the presidency, and a politics of the body. In *Communicology: The new science of embodied discourse*, ed. Isaac. E. Catt and D. Eicher-Catt. Madison, NJ: Fairleigh Dickinson University Press.
Fay, Elizabeth A. 1994. *Eminent rhetoric*. Westport, CT: Bergin & Garvey.
Female depravity. 1836. *The Liberator*, August 13.
Freud, Sigmund. 1953–1974. Femininity. In *The standard edition of the complete psychological works of Sigmund Freud*, ed. J. Strachey. Vol. 22, 112–35. London: Hogarth Press.
George, Andrew A. 1913. *Woman suffrage: Argument of Mrs. Andrew A. George before the committee on woman suffrage United States Senate*. Washington, DC: Government Printing Office.
Girl Schauer is set free, The. 1895. *New York Times*, December 10.
Goldenberg, Suzanne. 2007. *Madam President: Is America ready to send Hillary Clinton to the White House?* London: Guardian Books.
Green, Venus. 1990. The impact of technology upon women's work in the telephone industry. Ph.D. dissertation, Columbia University.
Han, Lori Cox, and Caroline Heldman, ed. 2007. *Rethinking Madam President: Are we ready for a woman in the White House?* Boulder, CO: Lynne Rienner Publishers.
Harrison, Fairfax. 1914. *An address before the Alabama Girls' Technical Institute, Montevallo, Alabama, Oct. 17, 1914*, n.p.
Hill, Joseph A. 1929. Women in gainful occupations 1870 to 1920. Washington, DC: U.S. Government Printing Office.
Homer. 1980. *The odyssey*. Translated by W. Shewring. Oxford: Oxford University Press.
Ideal occupation for women, The. [191?]. [New York?]: New York Telephone Company.
Jakobson, Roman. 1971. The dominant. In *Readings in Russian poetics*, ed. K. P. Ladislav Matejka, 82–87. Cambridge, MA: MIT Press.
Jamieson, Kathleen Hall. 1988. *Eloquence in an electronic age: The transformation of political speechmaking*. New York, Oxford: Oxford University Press.
———. 1995. *Beyond the double bind: Women and leadership*. Oxford: Oxford University Press.
Kern, Stephen. 1983. *The culture of time and space 1889–1918*. Cambridge: Harvard University Press.
Knox, Bernard. 1994. *Backing into the future: The classical tradition and its renewal*. New York: W.W. Norton & Company.
Lipartito, Kenneth. 1995. When women were switches: Technology, work and gender in the telephone industry, 1890–1920. *American Historical Review* 99:1075–11.
Mailloux, Steven. 1993. Afterward: A pretext for rhetoric: Dancing 'round the revolution.' In *Pre/text: The first decade*, ed. Victor J. Vitanza, 299–314. Pittsburgh: University of Pittsburgh Press.
Marvin, Carolyn. 1988. *When old technologies were new*. Oxford: Oxford University Press.
McEwen, Indra Kagis. 1993. *Socrates' ancestor*. Cambridge, MA: MIT Press.

Morris, Celia. 1984. *Fanny Wright: Rebel in America*. Cambridge, MA: Harvard University Press.
Must go to the workhouse. 1895. *New York Times*, December 7.
Nietzsche, Friedrich. 1989. On truth and lies in a nonmoral sense. In *Friedrich Nietzsche on Rhetoric and Language*, ed. S. L. Gilman, Carole Blair, and David J. Parent, 246–57. New York: Oxford University Press.
Night of horror, The. 1895. *The New York World*, December 6.
Paul concerning women. 1871. *The Woman's Journal*, March 11.
Preminger, Alex, ed. 1974. *Princeton encyclopedia of poetry and poetics*. Enlarged ed. Princeton, NJ: Princeton University Press.
Pyle, Joseph Gilpin. [1913?]. *Should women vote? Remarks by Joseph Gilpin Pyle at a meeting of the informal club, St. Paul, March 25, 1913*. [St. Paul?].
Sanford, J. B. [1911?]. *Extracts from a speech against woman's suffrage in the California State Senate*: n.p.
Schmitt, Katherine M. 1930. I was your 'Hello Girl.' *The Saturday Evening Post*, July 12, 18ff.
Sermon of the public function of woman, A, by Theodore Parker. Preached at Music Hall of Boston, March 27, 1853. *The Liberator*, April 15
Sloane, Thomas O., ed. 2001. *Encyclopedia of rhetoric*. Oxford: Oxford University Press.
Spence, Sarah. 2007. *Figuratively speaking: Rhetoric and culture from Quintilian to the twin towers*. London: Duckworth.
St. Paul once more. 1870. *The Woman's Journal*, March 26.
Stone, Lucy. n.d. Workers for the cause. In *Blackwell Family Collection, Library of Congress*. Washington, DC.
Sutton, Jane S. 1992. The taming of the *polos/polis*: Rhetoric as an achievement without woman. *Southern Communication Journal* 57:97–119.
Taylor, Charles. 2004. *Modern social imaginaries*. Durham and London: Duke University Press.
Valian, Virginia. 2000. *Why so slow? The advancement of women*. Cambridge, MA: MIT Press.
van Zoonen, Liesbet. 2006. The personal, the political, and the popular: A woman's guide to celebrity politics. *European Journal of Cultural Studies* 9:287–301.
Who's talking? An analysis of Sunday morning talk shows 2006. The White House Project 2001 [cited 10 July 2006]. Available from www.thewhitehouseproject.org.
Who's still talking 2006. The White House Project 2002 [cited July 10 2006]. Available from www.whitehouseproject.org.
Who's talking now: A followup analysis of guest appearances by women on the Sunday morning talk shows 2006. The White House Project 2005 [cited July 10 2006]. Available from www.whitehouseproject.org.
Wright, Almroth E. 1913. *The unexpurgated case against woman suffrage*. New York: Paul B. Hoeber.
Writ for Amelia Schauer. 1895. *New York Times*, December 8.

PART III

Sustained Forces of Democratization and the Effectiveness of Oppositional Discourses

7 Vigilance and Solidarity in the Rhetoric of the Black Press

The *Tulsa Star*

Olga Idriss Davis

The role of the black press in America has engendered scholarly discussion for many years (Jordan 2001; La Brie 1974; Simmons 1998; Wolseley 1990). Its presence creates interesting ways of exploring black life through the discourse of community. When placed at the center of analysis, the black press reveals a world in which journalism becomes a critical act of vigilance and black solidarity that has had a significant effect upon public policy. It locates the tensions between dominance and resistance, the personal and the political, and informs the ways in which stories craft cultural identity and public memory. As with most human constructs of African-American culture, the black press emerges as a response to inferiority, indignity, and inhumanity. Some historians have explored the black press in a number of ways based on its relationship to history and as a vehicle for expression and change, revealing efforts of black newspapers to fight racism, bolster self-esteem, promote militant consciousness, and advocate protest (Jordan 2001, 3). Yet, other historians have examined the press's impact on black opinion, exploring ways in which it crystallized black thought and action against oppression and sometimes diffused black anger and despair with fiery rhetoric (Oak 1948, 133). And yet others have viewed the historical significance of the black press in terms of the way black newspapers fostered black unity or affected African Americans in other ways. Implicit in all of these studies of the black press are the ways in which discourse is a means by which social action creates public memory, defines community, and informs solidarity.

This chapter articulates the ways in which the *Tulsa Star* crafted a space for resistance and solidarity in the struggle for freedom and human rights in the black community of Tulsa, Oklahoma, at the turn of the twentieth century. Situated within a tradition of the black press, this study supports the notion that the press maintains an empowering role in the African-American community by providing its readership the critical lens necessary to deconstruct dominant institutions, and thus potentially serve as an impetus for social change (Huspek 2004, 234). While black newspapers have, historically, countered attacks by the white press against African-American communities, the black press has also occupied a space to engage in the public sphere of critical consciousness. It serves as a voice to protest actions of racist, oppressive behavior when accounts of racism go unreported in the white press (Dates and Barlow 1990, 344; Huspek 2004, 234). Viewing the African American community on its own terms and within the context of power relations, the black press emerges as a critical response to the negotiation and navigation of white control, on the one hand, and resistance to domination on the other. It speaks to the issues of the community, when free expression of alternative views is ignored or disallowed by the white press. While not fully a part of mainstream public opinion and debate, the black press traditionally serves as an arena for African Americans to debate among themselves the alternatives of the dominant culture's ideologies, views, identities, and interests (Jordan 2001, 4).

During World War I, the black press served as a canvas upon which the negotiation of race and the threat of force became the polarities by which white and black relations coexisted as the status of blacks remained at its lowest with lynching of blacks occurring at a high rate (Ellsworth 1982, 19). Resistant groups that had organized such as the Oklahoma Socialist Party, the Industrial Workers of the World (IWW), and other radical groups in the state offered rhetorical support of black rights but faced a resurgence of aggressive white supremacy accompanied by a racist literature well into the 1920's (Ellsworth 1982, 20). The role of the black press in protest to the war, in the crafting of black militancy, and in the rise of black anger, taken together, reveal the making of a discourse in opposition to a mainstream press controlled for the convenience and needs of whites and often at the exclusion of African Americans (Huspek 2004, 232).

Study of the black press also illuminates the internal relations of communities (e.g., Hodge 1979, 157). A critical reading of the *Tulsa Star* reveals how the white and black presses craft social relations by constituting communities—those who produce the paper and those who read it, the community which the paper creates, the world it records, the images and events it presents, and the community which it produces by way of its telling of the story. Each of these communities, interrelated, plays a role in the oppositional relationship between black and white media while the black press serves as a collective force that exposes a broader range of meaning making and opinion (Huspek 2004, 235).

The current study advances the tradition of the black press in its approach to discourse and cultural space. It articulates the concept of a *critical* discourse—a perspective on discourse that reclaims the analytical centrality of power (Hariman 1986, 46)—and explores dimensions of human emancipation (McKerrow 1989, 125). In this light, the aim of the current study is to reveal how discourse is mobilized to empower the oppressed by way of rhetorical strategies. Specifically, a discourse of empowerment suggests transforming unjust social institutions by addressing debates concerning the power dynamics that underlie what counts as knowledge. And in this respect I contend that a rhetoric of vigilance and solidarity serves as an emancipatory wedge between power and hegemony that reveals the power/knowledge dialectic (Collins 2000, 273–74) and seeks to promote social change.

The value of an emancipatory discourse is that it seeks to unmask and demystify power (McKerrow 1989, 125). A critical discourse points to black people's everyday communicative experiences as inherently social, political, and thus inextricably linked to power (Collins 2000, 258; hooks 1990, 47; Jaggar 1998, 65; Smith 1982, 112). In this regard, the *Tulsa Star* created a cultural space to affirm the community's knowledge of its own experience, while at the same time it critiqued prevailing knowledge and enabled the community to define its own realities on its own terms (Collins 2000, 274). Further, the role of the *Tulsa Star* as a discursive and emancipatory presence for social change and community identity prior to the Tulsa race riot of 1921 advances new ways of celebrating the tradition of the black press by charging its progeny of journalists and newspapers to maintain its critical roots in the twenty-first century. A critical approach supports the goal of identifying sources of oppression and finding ways to make systemic changes. It means that critical scholars of the black press place historical conditions in the context of social relations. The *Tulsa Star,* for example, emerges from an exigency that disallowed coverage of a collective voice of African Americans in Tulsa as the historical conditions of Jim Crow laws, segregation, and white supremacy influenced social relations as expressed in the antagonistic relationship between the white and black press.

Similarly, the notion of cultural space links space to the situatedness of self-definition, self-determination, and oppositional knowledge in the search for justice. According to Fine et al. (2000), *spaces* are:

> ... not just a set of geographical/spatial arrangements, they are theoretical, analytic, and spatial displacements—a crack, a fissure in an organization or a community. Individual dreams, collective work, and critical thoughts are smuggled in and then reimagined ... These are spaces where ... social stereotypes are fiercely contested. (122)

The creation of the *Tulsa Star* provides a position of empowerment—a space "to come to voice"—by breaking the silence about oppression, developing self-reflexive speech, and confronting or "talking back" to elite discourses (hooks 1990). Creating a cultural space by way of the black press provided Tulsa's African-American community recuperation, resistance, and vision to reclaim its humanity. bell hooks (1990) reminds that:

> Cultural criticism has historically functioned in [B]lack life as a force promoting critical resistance, one that enabled [B]lack folks to cultivate in everyday life a practice of critique and analysis that would disrupt and even deconstruct those cultural productions that were designed to promote and reinforce domination. (3)

Approaching this study through a critical lens reveals the *Tulsa Star* and its editor, A. J. Smitherman, as beacon lights resisting domination by transforming a rhetoric of vigilance and solidarity into public action. An analysis of a culture of struggle, the crafting of sociopolitical space, and the collective identity of the Greenwood community tell the story of survival and resistance and parallels the relationship between culture and the black press.

THE CULTURE OF NORTH TULSA: GREENWOOD, THE BLACK WALL STREET

The Tulsa race riot of 1921 remains a deep, critical wound that has shaped the contours of contemporary American history. Although regarded as one of the most heinous atrocities this country has ever witnessed, the Tulsa race riot of 1921 is relatively obscure in historical documentation and American public memory. When unearthed, however, its story reveals undercurrents of racial disharmony throughout America in the twentieth century and serves as a provocative study into the system of social relations of blacks and whites and the dynamic social order in which they lived.

The end of southern slavery made way for northern reconstruction, a time when blacks moved from the South into the Midwest and northern states looking for a new beginning and a defining purpose to explore what freedom and hope meant in their lives. African Americans in Oklahoma found themselves released in spirit but shackled by the laws and customs made for slaves. Their battle was a dichotomy of desire to live as free men but surrounded by turbulence and violence resulting from white supremacy and racial hatred. African Americans in Tulsa and other parts of Oklahoma attempted to navigate between appeals to the law and acting affirmatively to confront the terror and lawlessness that threatened black lives and supported the region's racial social order.

A. J. Smitherman, social activist and editor of the *Tulsa Star*, urged African Americans to provide armed protection of potential lynch victims and to take a life if necessary to "uphold the majesty of the law" (Brophy 2002, 8). Black vigilance and intervention was demonstrated in preventing lynching in several cases during 1920 and 1921 (Ellsworth 1982, 23).

But, in 1921, according to reports, the Tulsa race riot started as a result of a young black youth, Dick Rowland, accused by a young white woman, Sarah Page, of attacking her in an elevator of a downtown Tulsa department store. Rowland was arrested and taken into custody. That evening, white men went to the courthouse and demanded that Rowland be turned over with the intent of lynching him. Approximately forty armed black men from the Greenwood section of Tulsa went to the courthouse to protect Rowland from his accusers. Many of the African Americans were veterans of WWI and wore their uniforms in protest against the possible lynching.

Congregating in front of the *Star* newspaper office, black community members of Greenwood heard that the mob of white men had not dispersed from the courthouse. They took up arms and went to the courthouse to offer their services for the protection of the prisoner but they were told to "go home and behave themselves" (*Black Dispatch*, 3 June 1921). A white man is then said to have approached a black man with the attempt of disarming him. A struggle ensued and a gun went off. The race riot had begun. According to Brophy (2002):

> The police commissioned hundreds of white men to put down what they called a "negro uprising," and they marched on Greenwood, followed by a heavily armed mob. Units of the National Guard joined them, disarming and arresting blacks. In Greenwood, armed blacks readied themselves to ward off the assault. But they were ill prepared to match this massive show of force. Black accounts describe the indiscriminate killing, looting, and burning, and the use of airplanes as part of the "invasion" of their community. Commenting on the airplanes, one Greenwood resident noted, "they were invading our district the same as the Germans invaded France and Belgium." While some claimed that the planes dropped nitroglycerin, setting buildings on fire, the evidence on this is inconclusive. At a minimum, though, the planes were used to coordinate the attack on Greenwood and monitor black movement within and outside of the city. (46)

While many historians have speculated on the number of lost lives, there is no consensus. Official estimates claim twenty-four African Americans and ten whites dead; contemporary estimates range from seventy-five to 150 fatalities. One thousand African Americans were left homeless; property damage ranged from $1.5 to $2 million; five thousand African Americans were interred, with release initially pegged to work permits. Blacks successfully fought the effort of city business leaders to develop an industrial district on the land where Greenwood stood and they defeated new city building regulations that would have made it too expensive for blacks to rebuild. Many residents stayed and rebuilt their homes and businesses. But the vibrant community that once existed had dispersed, and the boundaries of Jim Crow had been brutally reinforced. A. J. Smitherman, who had fled to Boston with his family, wrote about "the sting of national indifference" to the terror that rained down on Greenwood and asked, "Will America awake?" (Brophy 2002, 62).

The impact of the riot on race relations, economic empowerment, and community building are still seen today. The Tulsa Reparations Coalition was established by church members in 2001 while The Oklahoma Commission to Study the Tulsa Race Riot of 1921 was established in 1997. The latter became an advisory board which examined issues of the riot including testimony of race riot survivors, and upon their concluding report, presented to the Oklahoma state legislature their findings in the politically charged debate over reparations (Gates 2003, 178–81).

The riot serves as a major turning point in the meaning-making efforts of defining race and class in America. More importantly, the event causes a return to an examination of how black people engaged their world and transformed it in the face of segregation, disrespect, and inhumanity. After a seventy-five-year period of silence, the race riot emerges out of a historical exigency that viewed blacks as inferior to whites. However, what occurred in the community of North Tulsa redefined the myths and stereotypes of Africans in America and reinvigorated enslaved Africans on their renewed quest for citizenship and economic empowerment.

Tulsa's early history began as a Creek nation settlement known as "Tulsey Town" during the latter part of the nineteenth century (Ellsworth 1982, 8). The Cherokees and Creeks were the first settlers of the area that was to become Tulsa. However, by the late 1800s and early 1900s it was seen as a place of opportunity for black pioneers. As the state grew with a boom in population associated with immigration, the oil industry, and of statehood in 1907, African Americans flocked to Tulsa as a place of "new beginnings." After emancipation, African Americans sought meaning for their lives and their new existence of freedom. In their attempts to define what freedom meant in the face of white Southern anger for losing the Civil War, many black pioneers took up roots and journeyed to the North in 1877, the year which saw the end of Reconstruction and the secession of federal troops in the South. Blacks embarked on Tulsa as "The Promised Land."

Theirs was a community burgeoning with black businesswomen and men embracing shared dreams, land ownership, and hope in the future of their offspring. By 1906, blacks comprised about 5 percent of the total population of the city and had established two churches, a black newspaper, the Tulsa *Guide*, one barber, and three grocers among its businesspeople (Ellsworth 1982, 14). Black sojourners included professional and educated African Americans comprised of physicians, Ph.D.s, attorneys, funeral directors, educators, clergy, and bankers. By 1911, another black newspaper was in existence, the Tulsa *Weekly Planet*, keeping abreast of the latest news in the community, such as the first black police officer appointed in Tulsa, and the Dreamland Theater—the first black woman–owned theater in Tulsa—which showed silent movies and live entertainment, along with several other black businesses proliferating on Greenwood Avenue. Juke joints opened to the sounds of jazz, while houses of ill repute indicated Greenwood's underside. By the year of the 1921 race riot, the black population of Tulsa had grown to approximately eleven thousand with two black schools, one black hospital, and two black newspapers, the *Tulsa Star* and the Oklahoma *Sun*, thirteen churches, two black theaters, and a black public library (Ellsworth 1982, 14). North Tulsa, known as "Little Africa" by the white population, was a space carved *into*, rather than *out of*, the American Dream. This space—physical, ideological, and symbolic—was situated in a hotbed of disapproval and a hostile milieu. Nevertheless, the challenge proved ripe for African Americans determined to build a new cultural identity while shaping the course for a new economic class rich in human resources and economic solvency—the black *middle* class.

Situated in the north section of Tulsa, African Americans developed a community willing to abide by the rule of law of American citizenry, though relegated to this part of Tulsa as a result of Jim Crow segregation laws. Largely disenfranchised, Greenwood became the site created to resist Jim Crow laws. The growth of the black business community was in large part due to white Tulsans refusing African Americans to patronize their businesses south of the tracks and in other sections of the city (Whitlow 1973, 5). As a response to this treatment they began building their own community whose members brought money from the South with a vision to build economic sufficiency and independence. Consequently, Greenwood had become the nation's first black community where black citizens were the organizers of a financially, culturally, and economically solvent community.

Standing squarely in the face of Jim Crow laws, blacks in North Tulsa sought entry into the American Dream, particularly after their return from fighting and protecting their country during World War I, with the belief that the constitutional law of equal justice would be accorded to them. Black soldiers returning from the war were imbued with hope, full of optimism and a renewed sense of the possibility of freedom. However, their fight for democracy would pale in the face of white predisposition to a law of control through terror and subordination of black citizens. As Alfred Brophy (2002) points out,

> . . . blacks' search for justice and opposition to violence and discrimination clashed with the attitudes of white Tulsans to spark the riot; how the police and white mobs, in conjunction with the local units of the National Guard, 'ran the Negro out of Tulsa'; and finally, how the city responded to the riot by attempting to prevent rebuilding. Relying on previously unknown court records and unstudied Black newspapers, we can have a richer understanding of the riot itself and of race in Progressive-era Oklahoma. (p. xx) (emphasis mine)

The challenge which faced black Tulsa was whether or not it could prove itself a prototype of black economic and intellectual success, and to seek justice without causing a threat to the dominant structures of power, both socially and economically. Further, the chance for Greenwood's potential success to proliferate into other self-sufficient black towns across the Midwestern region and beyond was a fearful proposition for whites. The success of North Tulsa with its progressive visionary scheme symbolized a shift in the power dynamics of race, domination, and control. But the vision of justice for African Americans was countered by many of Tulsa's prominent, rich, and powerful whites who also were members of the Ku Klux Klan with its ideology of white supremacy.

The fear of the black body and of black economic control fanned the flames which later became the social context for the race riot in 1921. For it was members of Tulsa's white community which began the riot and destroyed the Greenwood business community. Socially held fears and stereotypes of black male hypersexuality and black female promiscuity created a ritualized performance of hate. As Smith McKoy (2001) points out:

> In essence, whiteness simply cannot exist without the existence of the contaminating black social space, and white riots have been the primary mechanism through which this racial balance is maintained. White riots are part of a ritual process of engendering violence into the cultural consciousness. This ritual revolves around the ordering of society around race and the construction of the black body in particular ways . . . (24)

The impetus for the black community was survival. They lived on the precipice of thought and fear that one day whites could come and destroy their efforts. Yet Tulsa, Oklahoma, provided them hope for the future—creating a space to craft a community of resilience, of solidarity in purpose, and of determination in will.

TULSA AND THE BLACK PRESS: THE *TULSA STAR*

Many historians have looked at the role of the black press as an institution which has acted as both a "mirror" of black life in America and as an institution which defines the collective identity for the black community (Jordan 2001). The *Tulsa Star* emerges as a vehicle for creating a black discourse within a public sphere of cultural views, values, identities, and interests which brought black political concerns to the public attention. Ellsworth (n.d.) notes:

The *Tulsa Star*, in particular, not only provided extensive coverage of national, state, and local political campaigns and election results, but also devoted significant column space for recording the activities of the local all-black Democratic and Republican clubs. Moreover, the *Star* also paid attention to a number of quasi-political movements as well, including Marcus Garvey's Universal Negro Improvement Association, different back-to-Africa movements, and various nationalist organizations. One such group, the African Blood Brotherhood, later claimed to have had a chapter in Greenwood prior to the riot. (http://www.ipoaa.com/tulsa_race_riot_story1.html)

Critical ideas in literature and the arts were brought to Greenwood in many ways. During this period, the Harlem Renaissance gave rise to optimism and the promise of equality that had been interrupted by World War I. Black soldiers were returning from war to a nation plagued by riots and lynching as well as a racial climate that denied them the liberty and justice for which they had fought abroad. In literature and the arts, African Americans pushed the margins of discrimination and inequality to create constructs of intellectual, social, and political commentary. For example, the *Tulsa Star* included news columns on the Negro Women's Club work in Oklahoma, black women and voter registration, traveling minstrel shows which came to town, and resident theatre companies, such as the "Smarter Set," were often reported highlights (The *Tulsa Star*, February 28, 1920, 2). Its residents read such vehicles of black political thought as the *Crisis*, published by the NAACP; the *Chicago Defender*, and the *Indianapolis Freeman*. Blacks across the newly recognized state were poised at the margins of a national identity, trying to locate place and situate self in the public discourse of state and nation. Brophy (2002) points out that:

> Together these periodicals alerted Greenwood residents to the legal rights and informed them of recent victories—and setbacks—in the courts and legislatures, as well as in literature and art . . . Veterans also brought ideas to Greenwood. They had seen and lived in a world where Blacks were asked to fight to defend freedom and where they were given more of it than white Oklahomans would generally allow. (3)

Moreover, Brophy goes on to say:

> The Black press made the law a living entity, the province of no single group, the vehicle for advancing claims to justice and equal citizenship. Newspapers like the *Tulsa Star* provided a forum for legal and political activists to test their ideas, develop arguments and propose strategies, and offered a platform for instructing Blacks of their rights and urging them to act. In the 1920 election, the first year women voted in a presidential election, Oklahoma City's *Black Dispatch* ran a front-page call to Black voters. It advised readers to "tell [your registrar] that this is a federal election and you appear before him as a citizen of the United States, which by the way, is just a little bigger than a citizen of Oklahoma." (83)

Though little attention has been given to the impact and significance of A. J. Smitherman's work in the black press and for civil rights, research provides a character view of his tenacity and determination to fight by way of the proverbial rhetorical pen rather than the mighty sword. According to Wolseley (1990, 70),

> [Smitherman] was a versatile lawyer-publisher in the Southwest and East. His specialty in law was criminal trials. His first papers were

published in Tulsa, Oklahoma, a daily as well as a weekly. Both, as well as his home, were lost in race riots in 1921.

The *Star* kept its pulse on the community by reporting the social and political movements vital to the health and welfare of its constituents. Reasons for its stature include the leadership of its editor, its stance against discriminatory actions of state and local government, and its promotion of armed resistance to violence perpetrated on the black community by white mobs. Huspek (2004) notes how the white press serves as an agent of violence when the rhetoric of black leadership is oppositional rather than accommodational toward dominant institutions:

> . . . the black press is a key transmitter of oppositional meanings that may not otherwise see the light of day in a world represented by the white press. The black press appeals to readers who feel anger toward institutions that either inflict class-based damage or deny that damage has been done. It makes visible groups or classes that are invisible or underrepresented in the white press. (219)

Huspek's point is evident when the *Star*'s white counterparts, the *Tulsa World* and *Tulsa Tribune*, both white presses, labeled Smitherman a black activist, criminal and uncivil, and thus failed to publish Smitherman's editorials opposing the manner of reporting on lynching and other pertinent issues of the North Tulsa community. Ellsworth (n.d.) observes:

> Although A.J. Smitherman's editorials regarding lynching were both direct and plainspoken, white Tulsans did not read the *Tulsa Star*, and Smitherman's opinions were not reported in the white press. (http://www.ipoaa.com/tulsa_race_riot_story1.html)

Nevertheless, the black press in Tulsa, under the editorship of A. J. Smitherman, was destined for outspoken and oppositional behavior. From early beginnings, A. J. Smitherman was groomed for leadership. Smitherman was born on December 27, 1883, in Childersburg, Alabama. By 1908 he had moved to Oklahoma, where he worked for W. H. Twine at the *Muskogee Cimiter*, an African American newspaper in Muskogee, Oklahoma. Smitherman was employed as the traveling agent and advertising manager while Twine, an African American attorney, was editor. Here, Smitherman reported the news, raising race issues and educating the readership of politics benefiting the black community (O'Dell 2002, 303). In 1911, Smitherman began publishing his own paper in Muskogee, the *Muskogee Star*. By 1913, he moved his newspaper operation to Tulsa, renaming it the *Tulsa Star*. According to O'Dell (2002), Smitherman and his paper have been underestimated in their contributions to the resistance movement of African Americans in Tulsa up to and during the race riot of 1921 (303).

Trained in criminal law, Smitherman's democratic position of leadership provided an avenue for African Americans to express their political views in a milieu that engendered dialogue within their community. He successfully created an all-black precinct election board composed entirely of black men in his efforts to encourage representation of the black community on issues such as redistricting. As a result, Tulsa had the distinction of being the first and only city in the country to have an election board exclusively of black men (Parrish 1998, 99). This was an audacious act of resistance in the face of Jim Crow laws. The board represented a mechanism for black leadership and governing experience by way of discourse. The potential for political power that could be garnered and developed with such an entity represented symbolically, if not literally, a force to be reckoned with. Smitherman was outspoken in his criticism of the city's administration that, under Mayor T. D. Evans's first official act as mayor, deleted appropriations to a *colored* library. The *Tulsa Star* campaigned against the city's actions toward the black community. According to the *Star*:

> Numerous occasions might be mentioned where hot-headed softskulled white officers have unceremoniously entered business places in the Colored section and without any [kind] of legal excuse or explanation search the person or the patrons of such places, very often when Colored officers are in or near the place, and without invitation or permission from the proprietors ... Sooner or later this practice will provoke a killing of these legal hijacks and when that happens it will require eternal vigilances [*sic*] to prevent a serious race conflict—something no good [man] desires to see. (*Tulsa Star*, January 21, 1921)

Moreover, in the same issue, the *Star* reported the firing of a black officer, Stalie Webb, after he objected to white officers working in the black section of the city as supervisors of the black officers employed and confined to that part of the city by the administration (O'Dell 2002, 305). Smitherman addressed these issues of black sentiment and distrust of the city government in the *Star*. The conflict between the newspaper and city administration would become increasingly tense in the months to come in 1921.

Smitherman and his paper also became a rhetorical voice for blacks to arm themselves and to protect the black community from lynching. The *Star* published reports of any lynching in the United States and every January published the NAACP report on lynching for the previous year. Smitherman had a reputation for showing up at a lynching, reporting on it, and castigating the system that allowed such a heinous crime by whites against blacks. In his narrative account of the Tulsa race riot, Madigan (2001) speaks of Smitherman taking notes in Greenwood's First Baptist Church while listening to a speaker, Dr. Andrew Jackson, on racial issues:

... Andrew J. Smitherman removed a piece of paper and a pencil from his breast pocket and leaned forward in his own pew near the front, poised to capture Jackson's every word. Smitherman, a bulldog-like man, was the irascible editor of the *Tulsa Star,* Greenwood's leading publication and its most authoritative public voice. In the eight years between that night in the church and the great burning to come, Smitherman doggedly chronicled all the local news, from street brawls to potluck dinners. But he also never missed a chance to rail in print against injustices perpetrated against his people, and had intervened personally in attempted lynchings in neighboring towns. An early banner headline summed up his belligerent disposition where race matters were concerned: YOU PUSH ME, the headline promised, AND I'LL PUSH YOU. (8)

Huspek (2004) underscores the oppositional stance and the process of domination to maintain control:

When oppositional meanings become impossible to ignore—the shouts are too loud, or the marches too conspicuous—other techniques may be called for. One is to reinforce existing race and class divisions by driving a symbolic wedge between majority and minority reading audiences, depicting the former as civil and law abiding, and the latter as uncivil and prone to criminal behavior. This exaggerates differences and denies similarities between groups and classes; it also invokes an irrational fear and revulsion toward the so-called uncivil and criminal that can potentially erupt in violence. (229)

In the January 17, 1914 edition of the *Tulsa Star,* an oppositional stance is evident when one front-page headline reads, "Social Equality Conference Hears an Outbreak From a Negro Preacher." Smitherman reports on a Washington, DC, meeting in which a black preacher advised armed resistance in black communities:

Washington, Jan. 8—Negroes were tonight urged to stop buying musical instruments and sending their children to dancing schools, and advised to spend their money for guns and military education by the Rev. T.N. Ross, pastor of a Washington negro church, speaking to a large crowd assembled ... The preacher pleaded with the audience to prepare for war for their social, political and industrial rights. "Prepare for war in times of peace is the policy of this nation," he shouted. "It should be your policy, if you wish to break from oppression from the fetters of this era of new slavery." Cries of "we are with you: that's right," greeted the speaker and the audience rose waving handkerchiefs and urging Ross to "go on." (1)

Smitherman's rhetorical sensibility guided his choice of newsworthy events and activities, specifically as they related to the consciousness-raising efforts upon the community of Greenwood. Contemporary mass media theory suggests that objective journalism supports the notion that reporters do not tell the readers what to *think* but, rather, what to think *about*. It is evident that Smitherman crafted the *Star* as a voice to prepare for the ominous, upcoming race war that was prophesied by black leaders throughout the country. In so doing, he shaped its discourse to engender critical thinking and conversation among black Tulsans of issues pertinent to their political safety and overall social well-being. By reporting on events around the country that concerned black communities beyond Tulsa, the *Star* promoted interstate and intrastate coalition-building efforts, informing the Greenwood community that other black communities, distant in proximity as they might be, experienced similar atrocities and injustices as a part of the black lived experience, and reported on the political and rhetorical means they employed to resist the systems of domination. With newsworthy stories on the black clergy, community leaders, and the importance of the black press, Smitherman maintained at the forefront of his readers' minds the rhetoric of solidarity and vigilance.

In the January 17, 1914 edition of the *Tulsa Star,* Smitherman provided the "platform of principle" of the National Negro Press Association. Here, Smitherman presents the role of the black press in guiding African Americans toward the principles of American justice and democracy. The headline reads, "National Negro Press Ass'n Called." Smitherman writes:

> Nashville, Tenn., Jan. 12— Declaring their loyalty to the flag and the constitution of the U.S. and setting forth plans for the moral uplift of their people, the National Press Association has taken definite action in outlining work for the betterment of the Negroes throughout the United States . . . Through this movement, they have been able to inaugurate many reforms and to help thousands of their race. It is their plan to get at the true condition of the Negroes of the United States, and to report and expose all crime. To assist in this, they have asked all city, county and state officials to co-operate with them by recognizing their official card and their metal membership badge when shown to officials. Long steps toward the alleviation of many embarrassing conditions are already made. In making this call for a mid-winter session they have issued an address to the country. The address, brief but explicit, was authorized by the national body, which convened in Philadelphia last August. It says, "In this fiftieth year since Lincoln's famous emancipation proclamation, the National Negro Press Association enunciates the following platform of principles for the guidance of the Negro people and the good of the American nation. 1. We believe with the founders of this government that there are UNALIENABLE RIGHTS which are the natural dower of every human being born into the world—that the permanent welfare of the nation and of civilization is best advanced by these rights remaining the property of

the legitimate owners. 2. Civilization makes every man his brother's *keeper*—(protector), but no man his brother's *owner*. Whenever the accident of race, nationality, position, power, color or other physical condition enables one individual race or nation to ignore or usurp the inalienable rights of another individual, race or nation, the equilibrium of civilization is disturbed and the progress of humanity interrupted. JUSTICE can only come to man when man is JUST. LIBERTY IS FOR ALL OR FOR NONE. 3. The fate of America and the Negro are inextricably bound together. The Negro has nowhere else to go. We call upon our people to use all their powers to meet the ideals of civilization and the obligations to remain 'bright with freedom's holy light.' We believe not only in the separation of church and state, but that a man's inalienable right to earn his bread should not be confused with the privilege of his neighbor's table. Men may be patriotic fellow-citizens without personal fellowship. Finally, we ask for our people only a square deal: a man's CHANCE to meet civilization's demands of MANHOOD. We think the American people should be willing to grant as a minimum of justice what Abraham Lincoln asked for the Negro: 'All I ask for the Negro is that if you do not like him, let him alone. If God gave him but little, that little let him enjoy.' (1)

This platform demonstrates the reputation of the black press as an effective organization with the intent of demonstrating a unified front to the country's audience comprised of the United States government and other hegemonic systems of domination. With political assertions spanning from slavery to the social construction of black manhood, the National Press Association also intended to unite editors, publishers, and legal minds with the unique purpose of solidifying its voice against military subjugation of black people in America. The black press was often referred to as a "fighting press" and a "crusading press," uniting a mass circulation of readers and outlining an agenda for situating blacks in the national conversation of economic and political empowerment. Moreover, its organizational, rhetorical, and political prowess at once presents a well-defined and well-intentioned infrastructure for the articulation of a national identity among African Americans. Similar to the intentions of the Negro Press Association, the *Tulsa Star* embraced the motto "A Fearless Exponent of Right and Justice. An Uncompromising Defender of the Colored Race. We Fear Only to Do Wrong." The moniker was printed on the front page of each issue. Embedded in this motto was Smitherman's relentless zeal in helping black Tulsans develop a sense of pride and a need for solidarity to resist the racial inequalities of their times.

While the newspaper symbolized for black Tulsans a "beacon light" for raising the consciousness of their community, white Tulsans accused Smitherman of inciting black Tulsans with his outspoken ideas on mob violence and lynching (O'Dell 2002, 308). Ironically, it is unlikely that white

Tulsans were even aware of what black Tulsans were thinking; for although Smitherman's editorials were direct and to the point, it is said that white Tulsans did not read the *Tulsa Star* and that Smitherman's opinions were not reported in the white press, such as the Tulsa *World* and the Tulsa *Tribune* (Ellsworth n.d.).

Some scholars of the black press have compared and contrasted Smitherman to Roscoe Dungee, editor of the *Black Dispatch* in Oklahoma City (Simmons 1998; O'Dell 2002). Both men were concerned about the success of the black race, but their approaches to reporting on discrimination were vastly different. Smitherman was militant in purpose, Dungee an accommodationist who appealed to white readers and, more importantly, was concerned about white business dollars for advertisement in his newspaper. As a result, he was more moderate in his approach to the news, particularly how he treated reports of lynching. In an editorial, Smitherman chastises Oklahoma City blacks and their newspaper, after an editorial by Roscoe Dungee criticized the *Star*'s treatment of a lynching in August, 1920. Smitherman retorts:

> ... No man or set of men have any right to conspire and arm themselves to desecrate the law, but any man or set of men may rightfully and legally take up arms to defend and uphold the law. It is the custom of localities ... for officers, and white men who are not officers, when there is apprehension of trouble between the races, to disarm Colored men while the whites are given absolute freedom going about unmolested whenever and wherever they will. No man should arm himself except for the purpose of self-protection or to uphold the majesty of the law and when he is thus armed no officer has any right to divest him of his arms and he is a coward who would surrender his arms under such circumstances, regardless of the number against him. The Tulsa Star is unalterably opposed to mob violence, regardless of the color of the men composing the mob ... We have had some actual experience with the cowards who compose mobs, which has convinced us that two or three determined men armed for the occasion can thwart the purpose of any mob if they act in earnest and in time. (*Tulsa Star*, September 18, 1920)

Smitherman endorsed and encouraged armed protection of African Americans, which has been suggested was reason enough for whites to target Smitherman and the *Star* with the belief that he had incited the black community with a discourse of violence. As the year 1921 began to unfold, there is no doubt that with increasing tensions and brewing hatred the two separate and unequal communities, black Tulsa and white Tulsa, were destined to meet for the duel of the century.

Madigan (2001) notes the role of *place* as a strategic site for the community of elders, much like an ancestral tribal meeting prior to war:

> ... outside the *Tulsa Star*, where Greenwood's elders had gathered in the crisis, the largest crowd was gathered outside the office of the *Tulsa Star*, the two-story red-brick building almost directly across from his [Gurley's] hotel. (89)

On the night of May 31, 1921, the office of the *Tulsa Star* was the congregating place to discuss and organize a plan for thwarting the possible lynching of Dick Rowland. However, on that fateful night, symbolic language turned into fierce action when a three-day race riot devastated the Greenwood business district. White mobs poured into Greenwood, burned houses and businesses, pillaged, shot black Tulsans on the streets, and devastated the city beyond recognition. Parrish, from the W.P.A. Federal Writers Project of the Oklahoma Historical Society, has noted something of an oddity in the destruction:

> As daylight approached, they (the Whites) were given a signal by a whistle, and the outrage took place ... More than a dozen aeroplanes went up and began to drop turpentine balls upon the Negro residences, while the 5,000 Whites, with machine guns and other deadly weapons, began firing in all directions. (Teall 1971, 205)

After three days of rioting, Greenwood was decimated and reduced to a blackened landscape of charred rubble and smoldering lumber, dashed hopes, and broken dreams. The African American business community of Greenwood was now nothing more than ghostly, crumbling brick storefronts and melted metal of burned-out automobiles. Ellsworth (n.d.) reflects on the devastation:

> ... Gone was the Dreamland and the Dixie, gone was the *Tulsa Star* and the black public library, gone was the Liberty Cafe and Elliott & Hooker's clothing store, H.L. Byars' cleaners and Mabel Little's beauty salon. Gone were literal lifetimes of sweat and hard work, and hard-won rungs on the ladder of the American Dream. (http://www.ipoaa.com/tulsa_race_riot_story1.htm)

A. J. Smitherman and his family escaped the riot of 1921, but lost were their possessions, home, and newspaper office. Wolseley (1990) chronicles the latter years of Smitherman's life after the riot:

> He moved his family to Springfield, Massachusetts, and there began another paper. Then, in 1925 he moved to Buffalo, New York, at first working for other Black papers, but the satisfaction of ownership was missed, so he borrowed one hundred dollars and in 1932 founded the Buffalo *Star*, later called the *Empire Star*, and remained its editor and publisher for twenty-nine years. At his death in 1961 the white press in

Buffalo credited him with having founded the nation's first Black daily, but several such papers of that frequency had been published before Smitherman was born in 1885. The *Star* ceased soon after his death. (70)

A. J. Smitherman, though not a famous name in the annals of journalism and political thought, carved a space within black critical political discourse, making a significant contribution to the role of the black press in the twentieth century. His courage, outspoken views, and dogmatism for justice of African Americans created a rhetorical space for resistance, unification, and cultural identity—the tenets of survival of black America.

FUTURE DIRECTIONS FOR THE STUDY OF THE BLACK PRESS

This chapter has argued that the *Tulsa Star* was a vehicle for creating a black discourse of resistance within a public sphere of social and political crises. It crafted a rhetorical space of vigilance and solidarity in the quest for racial equality at the turn of the twentieth century. While the chapter has explored the journalistic efforts of A. J. Smitherman and the *Tulsa Star* as a prominent voice in the black community of Tulsa, Oklahoma, it also points to future directions upon which further investigation can unearth.

First, we need to learn more of the relationship between black culture and the black press. From this study, it is evident that the black press helped to create and maintain a cultural identity that served as the basis for the ideals of nationhood, citizenship, and economic empowerment. While the nature of this relationship is a historical one, implications of its nuances in the twentieth century suggest interesting ways for examining contemporary relationships today in black communities across the United States.

Second, future studies might explore the black press and its stance on political and legal issues. From a historical perspective, the relationship between the advancement of the progressive/socialist movement and the black press may illuminate rhetorical ways in which the press played a role in the political movements in African American culture. Further study may reveal the ways in which the socialist and black nationalist movements, for example, engaged in a symbiotic relationship with the black press. Subsequent studies may also inform how these movements shaped the African American community and its rhetorical choices in determining the political posture of the black press.

Third, we might benefit from further study of the process of *naming* and how it assisted the community in its journey toward cultural identity. *Naming* is an important tenet in African American feminist and womanist studies, and supports the notion that oppressed people transcend and transform sociopolitical chasms by finding *voice* and by naming their own experience. This points to narrative—the telling of the story of community and of its survival—as a central context for remembering the creation of community. Further, a theory of diaspora (Gilroy 1995) provides a nuanced view of the Greenwood community as a process of "being" and "becoming." According to Gilroy, "Diaspora accentuates *becoming* rather than *being* and identity conceived diasporically, along these lines, resists reification" (24). Gilroy associates "being" with the transhistorical subject and "becoming" with historical situatedness and contingency (Johnson 2003, 42). This suggests further study of how the black press in general and the *Tulsa Star* specifically resisted reification by crafting a conception of sameness (transhistorical) and an idea of solidarity (situatedness and contingency) that did not repress the differences within the community but rather maximized the differences between itself and others (Gilroy 1995, 24). Similarly, as Newkirk (2000, 38) argues, the black press is a significant "counterpoint and counterpart" to the white press; and as Huspek (2004, 218) notes, "Given this logic, the white and black presses do not simply reflect different biases, but operate in opposition, reflecting their respective readers' historical and ongoing struggle over material and symbolic resources" (218). In this study, a rhetoric of solidarity navigated within a performance of community is "situated within history and tradition rounding out the social and political contexts of the times" (Davis 2003, 4). Further study from a diasporic perspective of North Tulsa bears in mind how the *Tulsa Star* created a space for "becoming" a community intent on crafting nationhood and citizenry as well as providing a vehicle for resistance in order to speak out and redefine itself on its own terms.

Finally, what now is the role of the black press in twenty-first-century America? The ongoing questions of how we define *race* and *who* constitutes *community* will create interesting ways for talking about how the black press addresses the needs of the black community in the twenty-first century. Historically, the black press engendered critical thought through public conversation about what it meant to be black. Today, of course, our communities are increasingly more diverse and complex, and this gives rise to such issues as interracial relationships, same-sex marriages, black sexuality, homophobia, the reconstruction and redefinition of *family*, borderland considerations, and the diasporic dilemma accompanied by the contentious debate over "who is defined as *Black*?" These rhetorical questions are shaped in and through the public sphere where we talk about race, community, and blackness in American society. The discourse that emerges must be of a critical nature, whereby the means to engage, illuminate, and elucidate serve to transform silence into sociopolitical action. Tulsa and its black press provided a cornerstone of public memory that illuminates the past and challenges researchers to explore how resistance is currently constituted in black communities throughout America.

BIBLIOGRAPHY

Brophy, Alfred L. 2002. *Reconstructing the dreamland.* New York: Oxford University Press.
Collins, Patricia Hill. 2000. *Black feminist thought: Knowledge, consciousness, and the politics of empowerment.* New York: Routledge.
Dates, Jannette, and William Barlow. 1990. *Split Image: African Americans in the mass media* Washington, DC: Howard University Press.
Davis, Olga Idriss. 2003. Snoop, dig, and resurrect: What can scholars of African American communication learn from the Tulsa race riot of 1921? *Electronic Journal of Communication* 13:2–3, 1–15.
Dungee, Roscoe. 1921. [Editorial]. *The Black Dispatch,* June 3. Oklahoma City, Oklahoma.
Ellsworth, Scott. 1982. *Death in a promised land.* Baton Rouge: Louisiana State UP.
———. (n.d.) The Tulsa race riot. Retrieved March 3, 2005, from http://www.ipoaa.com/tulsa_race_riot_story1.htm.
Fine, Margaret., L. Weis, S. Weseen, and L. Wong. 2000. "For whom?": Qualitative research, representations, and social responsibilities. In *Handbook of qualitative research,* ed. Norman K. Denzin and Yvonne S. Lincoln, 107–31. New York: Sage.
Gates, Eddie Faye. 1997. *They came searching.* Austin, TX: Eakin Press.
———. 2003. *Riot on Greenwood: The total destruction of black Wall Street.* Austin, TX: Sunbelt Eakin Press.
Gilroy, Paul. 1995. "To be real": The dissident forms of Black expressive culture. In *Let's get it on: The politics of Black performance,* ed. Catherine Ugwu, 12–33. Seattle: Bay Press.
Hariman, Robert. 1986. Status, marginality and rhetorical theory. *Quarterly Journal of Speech* 72:38–54.
Hodge, Bob. 1979. Newspapers and communities. In *Language and control,* ed. Roger Fowler, Bob Hodge, Gunther Kress, and Tony Trew, 154–74. London: Routledge.
hooks, bell. 1990. *Yearning: Race, gender, and cultural politics.* Boston: South End Press.
Huspek, Michael. 2004. Black press, white press, and their opposition: The case of the police killing of Tyisha Miller. *Social Justice* 31:1–2, 217–41.
Jaggar, Alison M. 1998. *Feminist politics and human nature.* Totowa, NJ.: Rowman & Littlefield Publishers.
Johnson, E. Patrick. 2003. *Appropriating blackness: Performance and the politics of authenticity.* Durham, NC: Duke University Press.
Jordan, William G. 2001. *Black newspapers and America's war for democracy, 1914–1920.* Chapel Hill: North Carolina University Press.
La Brie, Henry G. 1974. *Perspectives of the black press: 1974.* Kennebunkport, ME: Mercer House.
Madigan, Tim. 2001. *The burning.* New York: St. Martin's Press.
McKerrow, Raymie E. 1989. "Critical rhetoric": Theory and praxis. In *Readings in rhetorical criticism,* ed. C. R. Burgchardt, 124–46. State College, PA: Strata Publishing.
Newkirk, Pamela. 2000. *Within the veil: Black journalists, white media.* New York: New York University Press.
Oak, Vishnu V. 1948. *The Negro newspaper.* Yellow Springs, OH: Antioch.
O'Dell, Larry. 2002. Protecting his race: A.J. Smitherman and the Tulsa Star. *The Chronicles of Oklahoma,* 80(3):302–13.

Parrish, Mary E. Jones. 1998. *Race riot 1921: Events of the Tulsa disaster.* Tulsa: Out on a Limb Press.

Simmons, Charles A. 1998. *The African American press.* Jefferson, NC: McFarland.

Smith, Barbara. 1982. "Toward a Black feminist criticism." In *All the women are white, all the Blacks are men, but some of us are brave,* ed. Gloria T. Hull, Patricia B. Scott, and Barbara Smith, 157–75. Old Westbury, NY: Feminist Press.

Smith McCoy, Sheila. 2001. *When whites riot: Writing race and violence in American and South African cultures.* Madison: Wisconsin University Press.

Smitherman, A. J. 1914, January 17. [Editorial] National Negro press ass'n called. The *Tulsa Star,* p. 1.

———. 1914, January 17. Social equality conference hears an outbreak from a Negro preacher. The *Tulsa Star,* p. 1.

———. 1920, September 18. [Editorial]. The *Tulsa Star.*

———. 1921, January 21. [Editorial]. The *Tulsa Star.*

Teall, Kaye Moulton. 1971. *Black history in Oklahoma: A resource book.* Oklahoma City: Oklahoma City Public Schools.

Whitlow, Henry. 1973. The history of the Greenwood era in Tulsa. *Paper presented to the Tulsa County Historical Society,* 5.

Wolseley, Roland Edgar. 1990. *The Black press, U.S.A.* Ames: Iowa University Press.

8 "From the Standpoint of the White Man's World"
The Black Press and Contemporary White Media Scholarship

Michael Huspek

Despite the distinguished history of the black press and its much-needed presence across the breadth of America's cultural landscape, many contemporary media analysts in the United States have tended either to ignore its significant contributions to public discourse or to outright dismiss them. This widespread neglect, puzzling to say the least, is made all the more so by a relative lack of stated rationale from so many whose work reveals the conspicuous omission. Writings of the prominent media analyst W. Lance Bennett are something of an exception—not because he attends to the black press, for he doesn't, but rather because he offers some rationale for the exclusion. In the second edition of his widely read *News: The Politics of Illusion*, for example, Bennett states an unwillingness to seriously consider the alternative press on the purported rationale that "it is not credible in the eyes of most Americans" (Bennett 1993, 2). And in the third edition of the same book he dismisses writers and readers of the alternative press on grounds that "when people turn to more pointed or radical sources, they become more isolated from the issues and perspectives that shape public opinion and the political agenda of the mainstream media" (Bennett 1996, 9). By the fourth edition of the same text (Bennett 2001), there is not a single reference to the black press or other alternative media, and hence apparently no demonstrable need for the author to continue to rationalize its exclusion.

Bennett's claims reflect a majoritarian bias that is shared by much contemporary mass-media scholarship. The bias includes, first, an uncritical acceptance of majority voice and a concomitant underestimation of ideologies that rationalize majority-based exclusionary practices and, second, a devaluation of minority voice and a concomitant failure to grasp its significance as the basis for ideology critique. An overvaluation of majority voice and accompanying underestimation of majority-based ideology is reflected in Bennett's undefended claim that alternative media are "not credible in the eyes of most Americans." Have most Americans read alternative media such as the black press? It is not clear that they have, but if so, what standards of assessment might inform their view of a presumed deficiency of coverage? To subscribe to this view, would we not need to know the extent to which it may or may not be tied to a host of uncritically examined attitudes or beliefs? Insofar as Bennett's work seems to uncritically advance this empirically unsubstantiated and undefended view, it verges upon being an endorsement.

Similarly, his contention that those who turn to the alternative media effectively isolate themselves "from the issues and perspectives that shape public opinion and the political agenda *of the mainstream media*" (my emphasis) indicates a devaluation of minority voice and an accompanying failure to grasp its significance as the basis for ideology critique. If, as Bennett maintains, a turn to "more pointed or radical sources" does indeed foster isolation from issues and perspectives emphasized by mainstream media, it does not follow that the turn fosters isolation in a broader and more important political sense, viz., that which occurs outside the narrow parameters of mainstream reportage. His position fails to recognize that a turn to alternative media might in fact signal informed discontent as prelude to engaged political action directed against exclusionary practices and the ideologies that offer them supportive rationales. Bennett's majoritarianism thus not only effectively excludes important expressions of minority voice, but also deprives the influential media analyst of a valuable source of critique of media practices and the majority-based ideologies that rationalize them.

In what follows, I develop the twofold claim that any attempt to critically examine mainstream media practices within a democratic order must work to overcome its majoritarian bias, and that this is best accomplished by recognizing and incorporating into one's study alternative media such as the black press. In developing this claim, I first attend to Bennett's work as an exemplar of majoritarian thinking, with special reference to his call for critical analysis combined with his fatally contradictory rejection of the concept of ideology. I then present a brief sketch of a recently completed comparative study of the black press and the mainstream press as a means of demonstrating empirically the analytical utility of minority-based ideology critique and the high cost that comes with its rejection. And I conclude the chapter with a discussion of the need for an alternative to majoritarianism in the form of a discourse-based view of democracy that treats seriously both majority-voiced ideology and minority-voiced ideology critique and that by so doing informs a more fully integrated study of the workings of the black press as supplement and critical counterpart to the mainstream press.

MAJORITARIAN BIAS AND THE IDEOLOGICAL REPRODUCTION OF 'THE WHITE MAN'S STANDPOINT'

Majoritarian bias expresses itself in the contradictory tendency to underscore the importance of majority will as represented in elections and public opinion polls but that fails to adequately appreciate how historically democratic majorities have through such democratic processes effectively excluded groups on account of their nonvoluntary markings such as gender, ethnicity, race, citizenship, status, education, or property ownership (Deveaux 2000; Jagger 2000; Young 1990). On the one hand, majoritarian bias shows interest in how majority configurations reflect the changing dynamics of shifting group alliances and then goes on to assess institutions in terms of how they reflect or respond to majority voice. On the other hand, the bias shows a relative inattentiveness to minority voice that, because of group-based logic, beliefs, or styles of expression, has been deemed nonlegitimate by the socially unmarked majority, thus rationalizing blockage of minority groups' efforts to have their needs successfully integrated into majority-based projects (Calhoun 1992; Eley 1992; Fraser 1990; Huspek 2005).

How institutions can reflect a democratic majority will and be exclusionary at the same time is indicated by the Kerner Commission Report (1966), which noted the numerical underrepresentation of minority citizens across a wide range of institutional contexts that count for success and then emphasized that minority groups' prospects of gaining recognition from majority groups was severely stanched on account of systematic suppression and distortion of minority voice within the mainstream media. Although democracy in the United States was at the time of the report a full century removed from slavery, the commission stressed nevertheless how the mainstream news media continued to report and write "from the standpoint of the white man's world . . . [in which] the ills of the ghetto, the difficulties of life there, the Negro's burning sense of grievance are seldom conveyed" (Kerner Commission 1966, 366). Even today, of course, some four decades after the Kerner Commission Report, many have continued to make a strong case that black issues are still reported and written about by the mainstream media "from the standpoint of the white man's world" (Huspek 2004, 2005; Martindale 1989; Newkirk 2000; Ramaprasad 1996; Wilson II 1991), thereby perpetuating an enduring sense of betrayal felt by citizens who are inoculated with democratic ideals but yet who in significant respects remain hived off from the majority population socially and politically.

Majoritarian bias is present throughout W. Lance Bennett's work. Liberal sprinklings of the mantra *democracy* are accompanied by emphases on the importance of information, voice and an actively involved citizenry but with little substantive discussion of what type of democracy Bennett endorses, what specific information forms he finds most necessary to a working democracy, whose voice and which active citizenry the analyst has in mind. Despite the lack of clarity, however, we can infer from his dismissal of the black press and their readers a majoritarian view of democracy in which minority voice and the kinds of information that flow from it are considered unimportant. This is a serious exclusion that cuts against a fuller discourse-based view of democracy that values equally minority as well as majority voice (Huspek 2005). It also significantly undercuts the effectiveness of those who seek, as does Bennett, to offer a critical assessment of media practices; for a dismissal of devalued other—here in the form of minority groups and their principle vehicles of self-expression—amounts to a rejection of a valuable source of critical discontent with mainstream media practices by those who may be best positioned, both as outsiders and targeted others, to articulate media shortcomings that otherwise go undetected by those responsible for them.

Majoritarian bias is reflected no less in Bennett's weak and somewhat confused articulation of ideology—a concept for which he claims to have found no evidence in mainstream press practices: "In order to find ideological bias in the news, we would have to assume that the procedures in news organizations designed to edit bias out of news stories are either ineffective or, worse, they are part of a clever *liberal* media conspiracy to let bias through" (Bennett 2001, 3) (emphasis added). He then counters those who would seek to hold onto the concept: "To the contrary, the avoidance of political partisanship by journalists is reinforced, among other means, by the professional ethics codes of journalists, by the editors who monitor their work, and *by the business values* of the companies they work for" (Bennett 2001, 33) (emphasis added).

We will here forgo raising the question as to whether Bennett searched for evidence of a clever *conservative* ideological bias or considered whether writers' and editors' practices can indeed be effectively disentangled from "the business values of the companies they work for." Instead, we focus on the apparent contentedness to deploy the concept of ideology on a narrow liberal-conservative spectrum as it is so frequently done in mainstream media pop commentary. So doing, of course, strips the concept of much of its explanatory power. Consider, for example, Stuart Hall's work on ideology which identifies two types of racism in media practices, overt and inferential, the latter being both "more widespread—and in many ways, more insidious, because it is largely invisible even to those who formulate the world in its terms" (Hall 1990, 13). As ideology, inferential racism discourages agents from recognizing the full nature and consequences of prevailing practices or beliefs while at the same time doing so in a way that escapes their conscious awareness; and it is this "invisibility" that explains how disturbing contradictions within society go largely unrecognized by majority populations over long stretches of time. Note again the Kerner Commission Report that pointed to a historically entrenched ideology that rationalized writing and editing "from the standpoint of the white man's world." This was expressed not only in unsatisfactory coverage of black issues and a failure to adequately amplify black community voice, but also with an apparent unawareness on the part of writers and editors that "an appreciable part of their audience [was] black" (Kerner Commission 1966, 383). This state of ideological blindness was not the sole province of either liberals or conservatives; nor were the ideologically informed practices explained by reference strictly to either liberal or conservative bias. Rather, the commission indicted the entire mainstream mass-media industry and suggested that its ideologically cast practices escaped easy detection and correction by journalists and editors because they practiced their craft within an institutional environment in which assumptions regarding audience, voice, issue significance, institutional legitimacy and, of course, race, went unchallenged.

Bennett goes on to claim that the analytical utility of the concept of ideology is lacking, and once again appeals to his majoritarian bias in defense of the claim: "people who see a consistent ideological press bias . . . are seeing it with the help of their own ideology. This generalization is supported by opinion research showing that people in the middle see the media as generally neutral, whereas those on the left complain that the news is too conservative, and those on the right think the news has a left-leaning bias" (Bennett 2001, 34). Here Bennett does not attempt to clarify the concept in such a way that it might transcend the vagaries of public opinion: Are all claims of ideological bias equally valid? So doing might have entailed considering views of ideology outside the domain of majority public opinion—e.g., those that have been conceptualized by social and political theorists. But instead, Bennett appears content to simply acknowledge a certain ideological egalitarianism within the general public, and then uses such as rationale for jettisoning altogether ideology as a working concept.

If Bennett's rejection of ideology and the need for ideology critique is problematic, his proposed alternative is even more so, and both merit a fuller treatment than I have thus far provided. To that end, I here briefly sketch out the conclusions of a recently completed case study that contrastively analyzed mainstream and black press reportage. This turn is meant as substantive contribution to an understanding of how the black press positions itself oppositionally to its mainstream counterpart and how, in so doing, it reveals otherwise undetected ideological tendencies in mainstream press news coverage. It will then serve as empirical basis for continued discussion of Bennett's ill-fated dismissal of the black press, the significance of the failing for contemporary mass media research, and the need to develop alternatives to it.

OUTLINE OF A CONTRASTIVE ANALYSIS OF WHITE MAINSTREAM AND BLACK NEWS COVERAGE

A recently completed case study (Huspek 2004) contrastively analyzed two Southern California newspapers—the *Riverside Press-Enterprise*, a white-owned and -operated mainstream daily that boasts a circulation of 170,000 (Scarborough Report 2000), and its counterpart, the *Black Voice News*, a weekly publication with a paid circulation of fewer than 10,000 though with an estimated readership of 40 to 60 thousand in the Riverside metropolitan area. The analysis focused specifically upon coverage of the 1998 police killing of Tyisha Miller, a nineteen-year-old African American woman who died in a hail of twenty-four bullets fired by four white

Riverside police officers. The case proved controversial in many respects, beginning with concerns about whether police were justified in shooting the victim who sat in her car with a nonworking pistol on her lap but who appeared to be unconscious when police fired upon her. The question of race contributed to the controversy and was fueled when witness accounts surfaced that the police officers had directed racial slurs at Ms. Miller both before and after the shooting as well as engaging in questionable celebratory displays immediately after the shooting—none of which was noted in lengthy investigative reports filed both by Riverside's Police Department and the district attorney's office. Race concerns surfaced again when over two hundred of Riverside's 343-member police force responded to the job terminations of the four shooters and their supervisor by shaving their heads in a public ceremony.

Both the white-owned and -operated *Press-Enterprise* and *Black Voice News* diverged in their approaches to and interpretation of significant aspects of the story, including: use of sources; definition of the story; linguistic packaging; and representations of fact.

Use of Sources

Differences between the two newspapers were readily apparent in their use of sources. In a total of twenty-eight news stories of eight hundred words or more that appeared in the *Press-Enterprise* during the six months subsequent to the shooting, the white newspaper cited police officials and representatives from the district attorney's office 413 times (66+ %) as opposed to 209 (33%) citations of nonpolice witnesses and local black community leaders. In contrast, of fifteen 800+-word stories written over the same time period by the *Black Voice News*, local black community leaders, Ms. Miller's family, relatives and friends, and eyewitnesses to the shooting were cited 194 times (77%) as compared to fifty-six citations (22+%) of official law enforcement sources. (See Table 8.1.)

Definition of Story

The newspapers' different use of sources quite likely contributed to the way each framed the story. The *Press-Enterprise* focused primarily upon Ms. Miller's personal history as well as her actions and state of mind at the time she was fatally shot, and this is in contradistinction to an almost total exclusion

Table 8.1 Official v. Community Sources

	# of stories	police	D.A.	Police/D.A.	non-police	total
Press-Enterprise	28	307	106	413(66+%)	209(33%)	622
Black Voice News	15	41	15	56(22+%)	194(77%)	250

of interest in the four officers and their supervisor—all Caucasian—who were not identified by name until some two weeks after the killing. Interest in Ms. Miller included lengthy stories about her level of intoxication (.13 alcohol level)—e.g., one *Press-Enterprise* headline read: "Tyisha Miller Was Drunk Test Shows"—her behavior during the hours preceding her death, several police-based stories about her past (albeit minor) brushes with the law, unsubstantiated claims she had gang affiliations, and a district attorney's assurances that she "was a tough girl" and a "bad student" who earned low grades in school. The *Black Voice News*, in contrast, directed attention to those who participated in the killing, and raised questions regarding discrepancies in police accounts of the event, pointed to the fact that the police issued multiple statements about Ms. Miller's personal history well before divulging the names of her killers, and noted that there appeared to be no investigation of rumors from eyewitnesses that the four shooters and their field supervisor had directed racial slurs at the victim both before and after the shooting.

Linguistic Packaging

Over the weeks and months following the shooting, stark differences between the two newspapers' coverage persisted. A poignant example is how the newspapers responded when the majority of Riverside's police force shaved their heads in protest of Ms. Millers' killers being dismissed from their jobs. The *Black Voice News* immediately reported that the protesting cops looked like "skinheads" and printed follow-up stories that spotlighted Congresswoman Maxine Waters's statements that the officers who shaved their heads had marked themselves as "Neo-Nazis" whose skinheads were "symbols of racism," "modern day equivalents of sheets." In contrast, the *Press-Enterprise* did not print the term *skinhead* but instead used terms like *buzz cuts* and *hair cuts*. Only in the specific context of Maxine Waters's speech was the term *skinhead* used, and this only as embedded in her statements, while all subsequent articles resorted to linguistic gymnastics in avoiding use of the term: "officers with close-shaved scalps"; "wearing shortened haircuts"; "with their hair cut close to the scalp."

Representations of Fact

Yet another dimension of contrast between the newspapers was reflected in coverage of Miller's killers. This was especially the case regarding accounts by Officer Rene Rodriguez, who arrived at the scene only seconds after the killing. Rodriguez reported to his supervisors that he witnessed the four officers and their field supervisor laughing, whooping it up, and slapping each other on the back in what appeared to be a celebration. Shortly after, as family members of Ms. Miller began to arrive at the scene, according to Rodriguez, the field supervisor warned his subordinates to keep their "high fives" to a minimum and then said: "We need to get you guys out of here.

These animals are arriving in busloads." Although Rodriguez verbally conveyed to his superiors the inappropriate behavior he had witnessed, his allegations were not entered into the 1,500+-page official police report or the subsequent 2,000+-page district attorney's report. Nor was Rodriguez ever asked by his superiors to repeat, clarify, or further elaborate on his claims, though the gist of his allegations circulated widely through the Riverside Police Department's rumor mill.

It was not until some seven months after the shooting that the *Press-Enterprise* reported upon Rodriguez, who, in a complaint filed with the State Department of Fair Employment and Housing, "charged that some of the officers exchanged high fives after the Miller shooting, used obscenities to describe their victim, called her grieving family members 'animals,' and joked that perhaps her relatives would feel better if they knew that she had been shot with black bullets" (*Press-Enterprise* 1 September 1999). The 2,400-word story also mentions that Rodriguez made "damaging allegations" about the racial climate within the Riverside Police Department, including that "white officers engage in rampant racial profiling by pulling over black and Hispanic motorists and then manufacturing reasons to search their vehicles; and that white officers routinely make racist jokes and ridicule minority officers." Rodriguez himself was reported to have had a stink bomb placed in his patrol car and that frequently he was not given the kind of backup support that all officers routinely expect when they pull over motorists or make an arrest. Finally, the story reports that Rodriguez had been rendered unable to work on account of fear for his own safety and that he returned to his job only after the supervising officer at the Tyisha Miller shooting appeared unannounced late in the evening at his home with a "return-to-work" order form in one hand and a police baton in the other.

The *Press-Enterprise* report was foundation for additional stories that circulated both regionally and nationally, including a 1,900-word story in the *Los Angeles Times* and a 500-word account by the Associated Press. The contents of the story were extremely troubling, of course, and shed negative light upon the Riverside police. Although the *Press-Enterprise* stopped short of validating Rodriguez's charges—"Everyone must be careful about putting too much on one man's say-so"—the newspaper printed a cautiously worded editorial that criticized the department: "It's not how Riverside looks; it's what Riverside is. And, slowly, but inescapably, a lot of people have moved toward the reluctant conclusion that Riverside is not anywhere near what it should be—or where they thought the city was—in terms of racial attitudes by the police" (*Press-Enterprise* 5 September 1999).

Standing alone, the liberal mainstream newspaper's editorial appeared not to have pulled any punches. But an examination of the *Black Voice News* shows otherwise. In contrast to the *Press-Enterprise*, the black newspaper provided its readers with more detailed coverage. Whereas the *Press-Enterprise* reported that Rodriguez arrived at the scene only seconds after the shooting, *Black Voice News* coverage revealed what its white counterpart did not, viz., that Rodriguez subsequent to the shooting escorted one of the shooters to police headquarters and then remained with all four and their supervisor over the next six hours (*Black Voice News* 2 September 1999). That omission was key: it was at police headquarters that one of the shooters allegedly went home to pick up an underground videotape of police-involved shootings that all the officers then watched while cheering as if at a football game; and it was on the way to police headquarters that Rodriguez alleges to have heard his escort state: "After the shooting stopped I capped her twice in the head" (*Black Voice News* 2 September 1999). Similarly, although the *Press-Enterprise* noted some examples of Rodriguez suffering recriminations from his colleagues in the Riverside Police Department, *Black Voice News* coverage reveals that the mainstream newspaper failed to mention the death threats against the officer or a most telling case in which Rodriguez, putting an arrest upon a violent suspect who was directing verbal abuse at the officer, was visited by a fellow officer who, upon hearing the arrestee's racist remarks, hung a heavily tattooed arm outside his patrol car window, clenched his fist, yelled "White Power!" and drove off without providing assistance to Rodriguez. Finally, *Black Voice News* coverage reveals that the *Press-Enterprise* failed to report that police internal affairs never investigated Rodriguez's voiced concerns to his superiors regarding the behavior of his peers. The black newspaper, unlike its white counterpart, also revealed that although high-ranking officers in the Riverside Police Department knew of Rodriguez's allegations, his statements were absent from both the official police and the district attorney reports.

These omissions in the *Press-Enterprise* coverage are significant: Had the *Press-Enterprise* more comprehensively reported upon the behaviors by the four officers and their field supervisor in the wake of the shooting, the newspaper's weak suggestion that the Riverside Police Department perhaps contained racist elements might have had to give way to a concern that racism was pervasive throughout the institution. Had the white newspaper revealed the officer's admission of having "capped [the victim] twice in the head," logic might well have dictated the question: Should Ms. Miller's death have been treated as a criminal homicide? And had the same newspaper duly acknowledged the failure of Rodriguez's superiors to act upon his disturbing allegations, consideration of the possibility of a police cover-up of a serious crime might have been difficult to suppress.

CRITICAL ASSESSMENT OF MAJORITARIAN-INFLUENCED MEDIA STUDY

That the preceding questions and so many like them were not raised, combined with a consistent alignment of reportorial decisions and practices, suggests that the mainstream newspaper's coverage reflected an identifiable ideological bent that steered its readers away from serious consideration that racism was prevalent in a wide array of institutional practices throughout Riverside's law enforcement community. The newspaper consistently pulled up short when, as *Black Voice News* coverage suggested, thoroughgoing critique of official law enforcement structures and practices was called for. And, at least as important, the newspaper failed to seriously consider the possibility that its own coverage was itself in need of critical evaluation.

It is, therefore, only with much skepticism that we entertain Bennett's assurances that citizens need not "get worked up over the ideological biases of journalists," for even "if reporters lose their perspective, there are editors to correct them" (Bennett 2001, 3). So, too, skepticism is called for in the face of Bennett's proposal, against those who engage in ideology critique, for a "more sensible approach," which is to "look for those universal problems that hinder the efforts to citizens, whatever their ideology, to take part in political life" (Bennett 2001, 34). But so as not to reject the proposal prematurely, we here look at what Bennett claims to be four ("universal") characteristics of news that stand out as reasons why public information in the United States does not advance the cause of democracy: personalization, dramatization, fragmentation, and authority-disorder bias.

Personalization Bias?

"If there is a single most important flaw in the American news style, it is the overwhelming tendency to downplay the big social, economic, or political picture in favor of the human trials, tragedies, and triumphs that sit at the surface of events" (Bennett 2001, 35). Bennett calls this tendency "personalized news" and defines it "as the journalistic bias that gives preference to individual actors and human interest angles in events over larger institutional, social and political contexts" (Bennett 2001, 47). Against this tendency he posits the need for institutional analysis (Bennett 2001, 41). Yet it is important to note that his critique and correction are offered without reference to alternative media—an omission that is significant in light of what black press otherness often contributes in the way of understanding white, mainstream practices. Reference to the foregoing detailed study of black press coverage of the police killing of Tyisha Miller suggests that personalized news itself is not so much of a problem as is the ideology that generates its specific uses within the mainstream press. In its coverage of the police killing and subsequent events, the mainstream *Press-Enterprise* did indeed personalize the case when it reported on Ms. Miller's personal history as well as her actions and state of mind at the time she was fatally shot. This included an initial story on Ms. Miller that relied upon police sources who hastily dredged up the victim's past brushes with the law—two misdemeanor charges of battery (both dismissed) and one misdemeanor count of disturbing the peace. Focus upon the victim also raised questions as to why Ms. Miller appeared to be unconscious and foaming at the mouth prior to being shot and killed. But if the mainstream press's personalization of Ms. Miller was noteworthy, so too was its failure to provide a similarly personalized coverage of the police officers responsible for her death. The otherwise not so conspicuous absence of personalization of the police is rendered transparent by *Black Voice News* coverage which, in contrast to the *Press-Enterprise*, asked: Who were the officers? Had they used their weapons before? Why were toxicology reports of Ms. Miller's alcohol-content level and her background released within days of the shooting while the names of the officers responsible for her death were not released until several weeks later? What were the results of toxicology reports for the police officers? And, finally, why did there appear to be no investigation of (eventually validated) rumors from eyewitnesses that the four shooters and their supervisor had directed racial slurs at the victim both before and after the shooting?

The preceding suggests that the personalization bias to which Bennett refers is not problematic in itself but, more pointedly, only in the specific ways it is used or not used in the service of ideology. This is no less true for Bennett's recommended antidote to personalization, viz., institutional analysis. For here, too, comparison of white and black press coverage indicates that over and above institutional analysis per se we need to be concerned with who is offering the analysis as well as their assumptions and beliefs. In fact, the *Press-Enterprise* did offer institutional analysis when, several weeks after the shooting of Tyisha Miller and continued community protest, it raised questions regarding the level of training demanded of Riverside police and whether the department was more prone to use force than other comparatively sized departments. Yet the limitations of the *Press-Enterprise*'s institutional analysis were brought to light by the *Black Voice News*' alternative line of questioning regarding the possibility that racism pervaded the culture of the Riverside Police Department. Would the officers have carried out an identical plan had Ms. Miller been white? Would the same plan have been implemented had some of the officers been black? Of course such questions—well founded in light of eyewitness allegations of grossly inappropriate conduct on the part of the officers—point to the need for a quite different focus of institutional analysis, viz., not level of training but rather that of racial attitudes within an institutional culture.

Dramatization Bias?

A second problematic news bias, according to Bennett, is that of dramatization. "News dramas emphasize crisis over continuity and the present over the past or future" (Bennett 2001, 36). "The most obvious effect of dramatization," he laments, "is to trivialize news content" (Bennett 2001, 55). Yet, as is true with personalization, it is perhaps not dramatization that is itself problematic so much as how the drama is used. Once again contributions of the black press offer instructive value. Consider, for example, the head-shaving protest launched by a majority of Riverside's police officers in response to the police officers involved in the killing of Ms. Miller being removed from their jobs. This kind of protest was no doubt intended to be dramatic, a point not lost upon the *Black Voice News*, which reported immediately that the protesting cops looked like "skinheads," and were indistinguishable from "real skinheads" who were present at the local high school where the head-shaving ceremony was held. In contrast, the white mainstream press here downplayed the racist symbolism of the event and instead dutifully printed the skinhead officers' assurances that their gestures were meant solely as "signs of mourning" and "a show of solidarity."

If Bennett's critique of dramatization is problematic, so too is his recommendation that in place of drama the media engage in more analysis. Although such a prescription on its face appears valid, its force is weakened in the absence of consideration of the ideologies of journalists who are commissioned to engage in analytical writing. Who, for example, is conducting the analysis? And what are their aims and assumptions? *Press-Enterprise* coverage of the invited appearance of the "outsider" Jesse Jackson is relevant here. The day before Reverend Jackson's arrival in Riverside, the white mainstream newspaper printed a 1,600-word analytical piece—"Jesse Jackson: Drawn to Trouble" (*Press-Enterprise* 15 February 1999)—that focused on whether Jackson's involvement in issues of social conflict "heals or harms" the community. The story, as framed, appeared well researched and balanced, though it ironically drew upon a black conservative Los Angeles radio host (another "outsider") to state the case against Jackson's effectiveness. But the story's pretense was itself questionable: Was an analysis of this sort really needed? Or was it not perhaps likely to stir the emotions of some readers in a situation in which emotions were already at a high pitch? Did the analysis aim to inform? Or was it written so as to feed strong racist sentiment that already existed among segments of predominantly white Riverside? In short, it is not at all obvious that analysis of the sort Bennett recommends, in and of itself, is sufficient correction to dramatized coverage; for analysis can be deployed in ways that produce effects no less unsatisfactory than those of dramatization.

Fragmented News Bias?

A third problematic, according to Bennett, is that news tends to be fragmented, a central tendency of which is to "emphasize individual actors over the political contexts in which they operate" (Bennett 2001, 38). Against this purported shortcoming he offers two recommendations: more historical analysis and more stories "with active citizens in mind." Although at a surface level such critique and corrective seem valid, when advanced in conjunction with a dismissal of the importance of the alternative press, they appear naïve and inconsistent. The naïveté is evident in Bennett's call for more historical analysis without apparent consideration that history can be written in different ways from different standpoints, depending on who is writing and who the writing is about. This is borne out by the white mainstream *Press-Enterprise*'s use of history in its coverage of the police killing of Ms. Miller. Less than a month after the shooting, the *Press-Enterprise* printed a 2,000+-word feature story on two African-American community activists—both cousins of Ms. Miller—who were acting as primary spokespersons for the Tyisha Miller Steering Committee. The thrust of the story was historical in that it raised questions about both community activists' past brushes with the law. The story noted how one cousin had been jailed (but then released) on suspicion of assault and attempted murder, how the other cousin had been arrested (but later released) in connection with a slaying, and how he also had once been tried for assaulting a police officer (charges dropped after jury deadlock). Written from another point of view, a writer might have opted to use the arrests as illustration of the history of law enforcement's disproportionate targeting of young black males. But the *Press-Enterprise* instead opted to hold up "the [historical] prism of crime and violence associated with many members of the Butler's extended family."

In turning to Bennett's antidote to fragmentation, it appears somewhat inconsistent to dismiss the importance of the alternative press and its readers, on the one hand, and to then offer on the other hand the prescription that "more coverage of grass-roots citizen participation would provide models for others to follow" (Bennett 2001, 66). But beyond the apparent inconsistency there again looms the recurrent inattention to ideology—here specifically as it applies to how different forms of coverage of grassroots participants can be presented, and to what end. The *Press-Enterprise*, in keeping with Bennett's prescription, gave extensive coverage to the grass-roots citizen participation of community protesters and their leadership. But a brief examination of the coverage suggests that it did not constitute much of an advance over fragmented news. Rather, the thrust of the mainstream newspaper's coverage was to effectively equate protestation with crime or incivility. This was evidenced in the newspaper's coverage of a street demonstration that spilled over onto a highway that runs through the heart of downtown Riverside. The *Black Voice News* cited firsthand accounts that the marchers—escorted by a cavalcade of police—simply brought the typical midday traffic crawl to a halt. The *Press-Enterprise*, in contrast, led with the front-page headline: "Miller shooting protest snarls traffic on Highway 91; about 40 demonstrators nearly cause a 'disaster', police say" (*Press-Enterprise* 2 November 1999), and then offered the following description: "Protesters of the Tyisha Miller shooting—some with children—marched onto Highway 91 and forced the closure of the Westbound lanes after they nearly caused a 'catastrophic' accident, police said." Further: "A gasoline tanker truck nearly jack-knifed when the driver slammed on the brakes to avoid a pick-up, Riverside Police Sergeant Jay Theuer said." (Theuer, incidentally, primary source for the story, was an outspoken representative of the police officers' union that had gained attention earlier when a majority of its members shaved their heads.)

The *Press-Enterprise* then printed a strongly worded editorial that described the highway demonstration as "a near-catastrophe, purposely arranged . . . It demonstrated first and foremost an astonishing unconcern for public safety" (*Press-Enterprise* 3 November 1999). The unsigned editorial then called for citations and arrests of the marchers for an assortment of violations, including child endangerment. A day later *Press-Enterprise* columnist Dan Bernstein weighed in, calling the demonstration's leader a "knucklehead" and "doofus," and lambasting "his clique of hangers-on" for "grabbing a headline, even as they tarnish the memory of their meal ticket, Tyisha Miller" (*Press-Enterprise* 4 November 1999). Finally, in the days following the highway protest sixteen letters expressing opposition to the protest and its leaders outweighed one letter that likened the protest to Southern civil rights marches in the 1960s. The total of seventeen letters contrasts with the white newspaper's treatment of the police "skinhead" protest, which, marked by a complete absence of letters or editorials on the matter, offered the impression that the community had no strong opinion on two hundred of Riverside's finest shaving their heads. Although this coverage appears consistent with Bennett's exhortation to cover grassroots activity, it is not at all apparent that it constitutes an advance over the news bias of fragmentation that he perhaps rightly finds to be problematic.

Authority-Disorder Bias?

Bennett's fourth problematic characteristic of news points to a continuum of authority and disorder whereby a tendency of "the authoritative voices of officials to take center stage" is sometimes offset by coverage that concentrates on the failings of elected officials. States Bennett: "with the balance tipping more in the direction of negative and disturbing news, the authority-disorder bias can become distorted to the point of seriously misrepresenting society and politics" (Bennett 2001, 64). Against this bias, Bennett suggests that news institutions become less reliant on authoritative voices of officialdom and more "reflectively critical in their orientation" (Bennett 2001, 41). Here again, however, Bennett's call for critical reflection in the absence of consideration of the white mainstream press's ideological bent appears to be problematic. It was, for example, precisely an institution engaging in critical reflection when the *Press-Enterprise* criticized other news agencies for practicing "parachute journalism" in their use of race to "exploit unique or sexy angles," albeit this kind of critical reflection may not have squared with the facts of the case. For in the estimation of the black press, crucial facts all pointed to the likelihood that racism was indeed pervasive throughout the Riverside Police Department; and in the estimates of this writer the mainstream newspaper's coverage—e.g., its criminalization of black community activists, its institutional deafness to the black community's alarm at having armed and uniformed skinheads patrolling their streets, its refusal to consider racial aspects at numerous levels of the case—amounted to institutional complicity with those who killed Ms. Miller as well as those who went skinhead and scared the wits out of Riverside's black community. But as indicated throughout, Bennett's critique is blind to the possibility that a racist ideology might be at the base of much of mainstream media practice, including its inclination to be critically reflexive in some respects but not others.

DISCUSSION

The foregoing analysis shows clearly that Bennett's recommendations, offered conscientiously without sensitivity to ideology or a need to critically assess it, are seriously flawed. The problematic characteristics he finds in mainstream press coverage of the news to some degree may exist, but their significance is reduced in the absence of consideration of their ideological character. As argued earlier, personalized bias, dramatization, fragmentation, and lack of critical reflection within the news may or may not be problematic in and of themselves. But they are clearly so if motivated by and used to support dominant ideology and the practices of exclusion it legitimates. This is no less true of the well-intended antidotes Bennett offers. The call for increased institutional and historical analysis, informed by critical reflection and carried out via careful analytical writing, is all well and good but rings hollow if not advanced with a sensitivity to how such practices can be and have been deployed in ways consistent with and in support of a pernicious ideology.

We should not, therefore, underestimate the role of ideology as it disguises exclusionary institutional practices carried out under the auspices of democracy. Ideology legitimates exclusionary practices while at the same time it seals itself off from critical inquiry. In this sense the ideological forces at work in the mainstream press may not be readily apparent either to those who advance them or to their audiences, including third-party analysts. This points to the pressing need to critically examine mainstream media practices through the lenses of excluded others. And in this case, the lens has been provided by the black press and used to discern an otherwise undetected skein of racist ideology within the mainstream media that misrepresents African Americans—sometimes ignoring them, sometimes inflicting real symbolic violence upon them. As indicated by the brief contrastive analysis of the mainstream *Press-Enterprise* and *Black Voice News*, on multiple dimensions—use of sources, framing of stories, linguistic packaging, selective representations of fact—the former consistently reported and commented upon the police killing of Tyisha Miller in ways that discouraged meaningful discourse on the possibility if not likelihood that racism was present during the killing itself, in its official investigations, and in its defenses. This amounted to a systematic distortion of the case to a point that verged upon media complicity with Riverside's law enforcement institutions.

It may be worth reconsidering at this point Bennett's twin rationale for dismissing the importance of alternatives to mainstream media such as the black press and their readers: lack of credibility and ineffective political action. Regarding the first, we might here grant provisionally Bennett's claim that the majority of U.S. citizens do not find the alternative press to be as credible as the mainstream press, although so doing entails that we ignore the increasingly swelling ranks of readers who are turning to the alternative press as either supplement to or counterpoint of the mainstream. But the claim itself, informed by a majoritarian bias as it is, not only fails to consider that the majority viewpoint on this matter may be mistaken but that the mistakenness itself may be derived from the public's ongoing exposure to mainstream press reportage. It may well be, that is, that some readers of the *Press-Enterprise* hold racist attitudes and beliefs that are consistent with those furthered by the mainstream newspaper; but it is also conceivable that some readers of the *Press-Enterprise* might find those attitudes and beliefs to be abhorrent were they to be made transparent in public dialogue. But as analysis of the *Press-Enterprise*'s coverage suggested, there could be no genuinely open discourse because of the mainstream newspaper's denial that race was a significant factor in the case of Tyisha Miller or its own coverage of it.

The suggestion throughout this chapter is that a hypothetical reader exposed to both the mainstream and black press would likely find good reason to question the credibility of the former, perhaps even more so than the latter. For it was the *Black Voice News* that consistently sought out counters within the community to Riverside law enforcement's official handling of information that raised tough questions without skirting the issue, and that thereby opened public discourse in opposition to its containment as found in its mainstream counterpart. Whether the black press was indeed a more effective contributor to open, democratic discourse of course remains a claim to be considered elsewhere (Huspek 2005). But here it is of signal import to note that such a claim can be given no serious attention if the role of the black press as counterpart and counterpoint to the white mainstream press is dismissed on unexamined majoritarian grounds.

Bennett's second rationale for dismissing the black press, viz., that readers of such alternative sources are certain to alienate themselves from effective involvement in the political order, beyond reflecting the problematicity of a majoritarian bias, is also clearly mistaken. In fact, the contrastive treatment of the *Press-Enterprise* and *Black Voice News* presents conclusions directly antithetical to Bennett's. For it was not the readers of the *Press-Enterprise* who were on the street protesting on a weekly basis, putting pressure upon Riverside's law enforcement and politicians to deal justly with the officers who shot and killed Tyisha Miller and the institutional culture that may have abetted their act. Indeed, at virtually every level the

Press-Enterprise's treatment of the case deferred to officialdom and did so while simultaneously discrediting the protest and its leadership. In contrast, and against what has been called the mainstream press's logic of containment (Huspek 2004), the *Black Voice News* offered its readership a logic of challenge that recognized the value of public displays of active citizen discontent in the face of institutional unresponsiveness on the part of law enforcement and mainstream media.

My reference to one of several recent contrastive analyses of black and white newspapers (Huspek 2004, 2005; Clawson, Strine IV, and Waltenberg 2003; Jacobs 1996; Martindale 1989; Ramaprasad 1996; Strohm 1999) has been meant to reveal the shortcomings of Bennett's call to dismiss the significance of the black press. It also has pointed to the hazards of rejecting the significant role ideology plays in contemporary news coverage. Attention to the black press, minimally, is a necessary supplement to contemporary mass media study that can tell us a great deal about a significant segment of the population, its history, and current responses to contemporary affairs and issues. But beyond this the black press has always provided a vitally needed ideological counterweight to the white mainstream press and, in this capacity, brings to light exclusionary practices and their rationales—that exist contrary to the ideals of democratic openness—that might otherwise go undetected.

Finally, the much-needed turn to the black press and other alternative press venues points to the need to abandon majoritarian thinking in favor of a more discourse-based approach. Against a tendency to ask whether media news coverage adequately reflects majority opinion, examination of the black press should be seen as an opening up of discourse that aims to bring all citizen perspectives into the democratic public sphere. This not only ensures a more comprehensive approach to citizen voice and its vehicles of public expression, but it promises to be a more just approach as well. As any reading of the black press shows, its coverage, analyses, and viewpoints are not merely an addition to mainstream voice but a critical response to it. In this sense the black press must be seen as attempting to engage all citizens in open public dialogue that is otherwise lacking in mainstream news coverage.

CONCLUSION

Since publication of the first issue of "Freedom's Press" in 1827, the black press in the United States has encountered formidable obstacles. Vilified and harassed by opponents, intimidated by government agencies (Nerone 1994), and always in dire need of adequate financial backing (Rhodes 1994), the black press has had to swim upstream against a very strong current (Huspek 2005). Today, not only do many of those obstacles continue to exist, albeit in slightly different guises (Kessler 1984), but also a new set of challenges has arisen in the form of a loss of talent to white mainstream papers (Wilson II 1991), intruding corporate interests, and ever-greater hegemony of mainstream-advanced interests and values, including the uncritical promotion of democracy as majoritarian practice and belief.

In the face of such challenges, and perhaps because of the very nature of its enduring upstream struggle, the black press has presented a strong moral voice that remains uniquely suited to comment upon the majority-based practices and their rationalizations that shape the flow of public discourse, the force and direction of which today often goes unrecognized. This is not to say, of course, that the alternative as expressed by an oppositional black press can claim a higher moral purchase of the rightness of political practice and belief than that which is expressed within the mainstream press. But there is evidence to suggest that the black press, more so than its mainstream counterpart, seeks to open up an egalitarian flow of discourse between minority and majority that negates a condition whereby mainstream is synonymous with downstream (Huspek 2007). As critical hermeneutics has so valuably taught us, out of such discourse potentially emerges an awareness of and reflection upon the limits of one's ideologically shaped understanding of self and other. In this regard, contemporary media study might play an essential part, even more so than it has done in the past.

BIBLIOGRAPHY

Bennett, W. Lance. 1993. *News: The politics of illusion*. 2nd edition. White Plains, New York: Longman.
———. 1996. *News: The politics of illusion*. 3rd edition. White Plains, New York: Longman.
———. 1998. The uncivic culture: Communication, identity and the rise of lifestyle politics. *PS: Political Science and Politics* 31:741–61.
———. 2001 News: *The politics of illusion*. 4th edition. White Plains, New York: Addison, Wesley, & Longman.
Black Voice News. Riverside, California.
Calhoun, Craig. 1992. Introduction: Habermas and the public sphere. In *Habermas and the public sphere*, ed. Craig Calhoun, 1–31, Cambridge, MA: MIT Press.
Clawson, Rosalee., H. C. Strine IV, and E. N. Waltenberg. 2003. Framing Supreme Court decisions: The mainstream versus the black press. *Journal of Black Studies* 33(6):784–800.
Deveaux, Monique. 2000. *Cultural pluralism and dilemmas of justice*. Ithaca, NY, and London: Cornell University Press.
Eley, Geoff. 1992. Nations, publics and political cultures: Placing Habermas in the nineteenth century. In *Habermas and the public sphere*, ed. Craig Calhoun, 289–339. Cambridge, MA: MIT Press.
Fraser, Nancy. 1990. Rethinking the public sphere: A contribution to the critique of actually existing democracy. *Social Text* 25/26:56–80.
Hall, Stuart. 1990. The whites of their eyes: Racist ideologies and the media. In *The media reader*, ed. M. Alvarado and J. O. Thompson, 9–23. London: British Film Institute.

Hurwitz, Jon, and Mark Peffley. 1997. Public perceptions of race and crime: The role of racial stereotypes. *American Journal of Political Science* 41(2):375–401.
Huspek, Michael. 2004. Black press, white press, and their opposition: The case of the police killing of Tyisha Miller. *Social Justice* 31(1–2):217–41.
——. 2005. Introduction: Contributions of the black press to human and civil rights. *Journal of Intergroup Relations* 32(3):2–8.
——. Huspek, Michael. 2007. Habermas and oppositional public spheres: A stereoscopic analysis of black and white press practices. *Political Studies*, 55, 4: 821–843.
Jacobs, Ronald. 1996. Civil society and crisis: Culture, discourse and the Rodney King beating. *American Journal of Sociology* 101(5):1238–72.
Jagger, Alison. 2000. Multicultural democracy. In *Deliberation, democracy and the media*, ed. S. Chambers and A. Costain, 27–46. New York: Rowan & Littlefield.
Kerner Commission. 1966 [1988]. *The Kerner Report: National Advisory Commission on Civil Disorders*. New York: Pantheon.
Kessler, Lauren. 1984. *The dissident press*. Beverly Hills: Sage.
Martindale, Carolyn. 1989. Selected newspaper coverage of causes of black protest. *Journalism Quarterly* 62, Fall:920–24.
Nerone, John. 1994. *Violence against the press: Policing the public sphere in U.S. history*. Oxford: Oxford University Press.
Newkirk, Pamela. 2000. *Within the veil: Black journalists, white media*. New York: New York University Press.
Press-Enterprise. Riverside, California.
Ramaprasad, Jyotika. 1996. How four newspapers covered the 1992 Los Angeles Riot. In *Mediated messages and African-American culture*, ed. V. T. Berry and C. Manning-Miller, 76–95. Thousand Oaks, CA: Sage.
Rhodes, Jane. 1994. Race, money, politics and the antebellum black press. *Journalism History* 203–4):95–106.
Scarborough Report. 2000. Profile report on the Riverside Press-Enterprise. Los Angeles: Scarborough Research.
Strohm, Susan. 1999. The black press and the black community: The Los Angeles Sentinel's coverage of the Watts riot. In *Framing friction: Media and social conflict*, ed. M. Mander, 58–88. Urbana and Chicago: University of Illinois.
Wilson II, Clint. 1991. *Black journalists in paradox*. New York: Greenwood.
Young, Iris Marion. 1990. *Justice and the politics of difference*. Princeton: Princeton University Press.

9 Exposing the Hypocrisies of State Power
The African-American Press and the Holocaust

Felecia G. Jones Ross and Sakile Kai Camara

Black owned and operated newspapers represent and advocate African-Americans' interests and concerns that the mainstream media have marginalized or ignored (Huspek 2004, 217; Hutton 1993, 26; Kessler, 1984, 21; Lacy, Stephens and Soffin 1991, 8; Wilson and Gutierrez 1995, 41; Wolseley 1990, 6). Appealing to principles of democracy and human rights, the black press has challenged the self-righteousness of dominant society and its oppression and mistreatment of African Americans in the United States as well as other groups worldwide. In editorials, articles and political cartoons, black press news coverage during both world wars pointed out the hypocrisy of a nation that symbolized democratic freedom to the world yet mistreated its own citizens at home (Kornweibel 1994, 155; Washburn 1986a, 73). Human rights abuses anywhere, they argued, threatened human dignity and security everywhere (Carson, 1998, 40–50).[1] This was especially true regarding black-owned and -operated newspapers' uses of the Jewish Holocaust of the 1930s and 1940s as an opportunity to expand their human rights advocacy for groups other than African Americans. Although the mainstream press in the United States published vivid reports of the Nazi brutality, it did not focus on the immorality of the practices in the way the African-American press did. Drawing upon two leading newspapers, we will highlight how *The Chicago Defender* and *The Pittsburgh Courier*, in contrast to mainstream coverage, underscored the importance of human rights as they related to issues of the Holocaust.

This study thus seeks to remedy a tendency in a century's worth of academic description and analysis of the black press in the United States to place little or no emphasis on black newspaper coverage of foreign issues. We believe our remedy is needed in order to provide a fuller understanding of the advocacy role of the black press, not only as it relates specifically to the African-American experience, but also for its contributions to the larger political culture as well.

We selected the *Defender* and *Courier* as sites of examination because during the 1930's and 1940's they were well established, nationally circulated newspapers that regularly commented on the Nazis' mistreatment of Jews on the one hand, and that protested whites' mistreatment of African Americans on the other. We emphasize editorials and political cartoons as our bases for analysis not only because they best exemplify both newspapers' advocacy function, but also because there was little information on the atrocities in either of the newspapers' general news sections. With respect to the Holocaust, we specifically analyze themes common to both papers as well as those unique to each paper. We also compare the comments of these alternative newspapers with those of the general, mainstream press.

DEVELOPMENT OF AFRICAN-AMERICAN NEWSPAPERS

By the end of the First World War, black newspapers evolved from a small number of short-lived publications serving limited readerships to a large number of stable publications serving readers in all regions of the country (Bayton and Bell 1951, 8–15; Kessler 1984, 21; Tripp 1998, 3; Wolseley 1990, 69). African Americans relied on these publications to address specific issues and to advocate their interests in the early years of Emancipation and Reconstruction.[2]

Although black newspapers existed prior to Emancipation, most were published in northern cities where non-enslaved African-Americans resided (Bryan 1969, 2; Kessler 1984, 21–23; Tripp 1998, 23–26).[3] Although these pre-Emancipation newspapers provided a foundation for future endeavors, they were noted principally for advocating the abolition of slavery and many stopped publishing after slavery ended (Bryan 1969, 6–8; Kessler 1984, 34–39; Tripp 1998, 17 and Wolseley 1990, 25–42).

As the growth of the black press coincided with the growth in African-American literacy and movement of the black population to different regions of the country, it reflected the challenges of newfound freedom in the face of many obstacles (Domke 1994, 131; Kessler 1984, 15–20; Ross 1995b, 107 and Tripp 1998, 15–16). After the Civil War, amendments to the U.S. Constitution respectively prohibited slavery, granted all African Americans citizenship rights and granted African-American men voting rights. But in the following 50 years, U.S. Supreme Court decisions such as Plessy vs. Ferguson formally eroded these rights while the specter of mob violence always threatened to entirely destroy them. African Americans turned to their newspapers not only as they articulated these impediments to freedom but also as a beacon of hope along the long and painful quest for full citizenship rights. By the beginning of the First World War, black newspapers were so highly influential in the African American community that the government called on editors and publishers to use their influence to encourage African Americans to support the war effort (Kessler 1984, 54–64; Kornweibel 1994, 155–158).

The Chicago Defender (1905) and *The Pittsburgh Courier* (1907)[4] were established during this 50-year period (Buni 1974, 227; Ottley 1955, 7, 80, 81–95; and Walker 1996, 9–24) and their long, continued existence, as of this writing, represented the stability and assertiveness of African-American newspapers.[5] The *Defender* and *Courier* did not hesitate to scrutinize human rights issues relating to African Americans in the US and to provide strategies for successfully redressing these wrongs.

They did not limit their protest to domestic issues, however, but joined other black newspapers in criticizing the United States and its allies' global policies and activities that adversely impacted people of color. For example, both the *Defender* and *Courier* opposed the U.S. Marines' presence in Haiti[6]—the *Defender* contrasting conditions in Haiti with the American South's lawlessness and social proscription (Suggs 1988, 33). And between the world wars, the papers covered and criticized Italy's invasion of Ethiopia—the *Courier* framing the conflict as just one more example of white imperialists exploiting people of color (Walker, 1996, 4–17). It was within this tradition that both newspapers, upon learning of Hitler's persecution of Jews, strongly denounced the practice.

THE AFRICAN AMERICAN PRESS AND OTHER HUMAN RIGHTS ISSUES

A primary goal of the black press was to act as an advocate for the African-American community, and it did so by paying attention to the human rights abuses—often downplayed or dismissed by white society— in order to seek accountability, promote respect and to reform the rigid structures responsible for such abuses. Such issues included women's rights, war, imperialism, political activity and military justice for other cultural groups (Hutton 1993, 36; McBride 1996, 325–348; Weill and Castañeda 2004, 537). The black press recognized, for example, the double oppression of racism and sexism and advocated for women's suffrage and their full participation in all aspects of life (Bryan 1969, 4; Hutton 1993, 26–35). In order not to excuse Germany's war against Jews, the Black press supported America's involvement in the war, but

Exposing the Hypocrisies of State Power 177

continued to hold the nation accountable for its moral failure to provide equal rights at home (Clark 1943, 417; Kornweibel 1994, 155;Washburn 1986a, 73).

The black press has consistently stressed active African-American political participation by advocating the acquisition and exercise of voting rights (Reeves 1997, 25–43). Throughout its history, the black press has promoted specific political agendas and has pushed candidates or parties deemed to be in the best interests of the community (Barger 1973, 645; O'Kelly 1980, 313; Ross 1993, 87–92; 1995a, 53; Stevens and Johnson 1990, 1090). Black newspapers have also revealed flaws in the criminal justice system ranging from police brutality to jury selection (Barger 1973, 645; Huspek 2004, 217; O'Kelly 1980, 313; Ross 1999, 48), and they have exposed how the health care system has exploited (Tuskegee Experiment) blacks (Pickle, Quinn and Brown 2002, 427) and other groups (e.g., Native Americans as related to the issue of smallpox). It is within this tradition that the *Defender* and *Courier* joined mainstream publications in recognizing and denouncing the brutal treatment of Jews (Lipstadt 1986, 13–39; Tifft and Jones 1999, 217–220) and used these atrocities as a forum to reiterate their protest against the mistreatment of people of color worldwide.

In the remainder of this study, we raise and explore the following questions: How did the two black newspapers react to specific events of the Holocaust? What themes are common to both newspapers? What themes are unique to each paper? And how did these themes differ from the comments and information in the mainstream press? In addressing such questions we hope to broaden the scholarship on alternative media's voice and relevancy during historical, human rights milestones and, in this specific case, illustrate how the black press' distinctive view of the Holocaust fulfilled its role as America's moral conscience.

Method and Procedure

Reading all of both black newspapers' issues published from 1933 to 1945,[7] we selected editorials and editorial cartoons that directly or indirectly referred to Nazi Germany's persecution of Jews. Direct references were headlines and texts of editorials and cartoons that either used words such as race/Jewish persecution/terror in Germany or focused on a specific Holocaust activity as listed in The Holocaust Timeline.[8] Indirect references were the headlines and texts of editorials or cartoons that focused on the ideologies and tactics of Hitler and Nazis as they related to African Americans and other people of color. For *The Pittsburgh Courier*, our method produced a total of 44[9] editorials, and 0 editorial cartoons. For *The Chicago Defender*, our method produced 30 editorials and five cartoons.

RESULTS

Comments On Specific Events of the Holocaust

Of the 277 incidents listed on the Holocaust Timeline between January 30, 1933 and April 30, 1945, 11 were the subject of editorials published in either the *Defender* the *Courier* or both.[10] Although all of the listed incidents either directly or indirectly affected the treatment of Jews, the editorials that made a direct reference to this treatment form the gist of our commentary.

Olympics

In 1936 Berlin hosted the quadrennial summer Olympics. By that time, the world had already heard reports of the way Nazis had been mistreating Jews. Hitler and his regime used the Olympics as a means for gaining world favor, showing Olympic spectators hospitality while simultaneously hiding its persecution practices from public view. Editorials concerning the German-hosted event began appearing in the *Courier* a year before and referred to the concerns of white Americans participating in an event in a foreign country that mistreated its own citizens; but the editorials focused also upon such concerns in the context of how white-dominated America treated its own people of color.

For example, in its first editorial titled "Much Ado About Olympics," on August 10, 1935, the *Courier* wrote that it was "laughable" that America was making an uproar about the Nazi persecution of the Jews when Americans had virtually exterminated the Indians and continued to discriminate against African-Americans. And in keeping with the spirit of human rights, the *Courier* reiterated its denunciation of the way the Jews were being treated.

In a subsequent editorial, the *Courier* disagreed with a letter published in another newspaper that called for African American athletes to boycott the Olympics as an open protest against Hitler's ideology of Nordic supremacy. While the *Courier* praised the motive behind the call, it pointed out in an article title "Unwise Counsel," on August 31, 1935, that a greater blow to Hitlerism would be for African-American athletes to beat the Nazi athletes: "it will lift the prestige of the despised darker races and lower the prestige of the proud and arrogant Nordic."

The boycott issue appeared again in later editorials specifically related to a threat by all Olympic teams to withhold their participation and that caused Germany to pull its anti-Jew signs and placards. The issue of American hypocrisy returned. Two editorials following the Olympics titled "The Nazis Bow to Agitation," on November 16, 1935, and "After Berlin—What?" on August 22, 1936, questioned whether or not the United States was going to show its appreciation to the victorious African-American athletes by allowing them to fully benefit from the fruits of American society.

Kristallnacht

Also known as "The Night of the Broken Glass," is an incident that took place in November of 1938 in which German storm troopers, along with SS and Hitler Youth, beat and murdered Jews while vandalizing their synagogues and places of businesses. The broken glass represented the shattered windows of the vandalized stores.

The *Defender*'s editorial titled "It Can Happen Here," on November 26, 1938, warned that the same type of incident could occur in the United States because of the effectiveness of hate propaganda. The editorial pointed out that African-Americans would be in worse shape in this event because they do not have the financial support or places to appeal for assistance, and the editorial urged African-Americans to reach out to other oppressed minorities

Common Themes

Editorials reacting to Nazi atrocities appeared in the *Courier* and *Defender* respectively in March and June of 1933. By the time of the *Courier* editorial, Hitler was already Chancellor of Germany and the notorious SA and SS men had law enforcement powers. By the time of the *Defender*'s comments, concentration camps had already been opened and functioning and the infamous Gestapo had been mobilized. Neither editorial focused on any one particular incident of the Holocaust, but both reflected awareness that atrocities against Jews existed and related them to the experiences of African Americans in the United States.

A unifying theme of the editorials was the connection between mistreatment of German Jews and African Americans, from which Hitlerism and American Hypocrisy emerged as sub-themes.

American Hypocrisy

These editorials and cartoons were analogous to the saying: "People who live in glass houses should not throw stones." Through simple juxtaposition, they called for white and Jewish Americans to denounce the mistreatment of African Americans in the United States in the same way that they denounced such treatment of Jews in Germany. The earliest editorials in both papers focused on the hypocrisy theme. In an editorial offering reasons for the Jewish persecution, an editorial in the *Courier* titled the "Economic Background of Mobbism" on April 8, 1933, criticized Jewish Americans for not reaching out to or showing outrage against the persecution of African Americans:

> They are ready to denounce the discrimination practiced against Jews in Germany, but seldom have anything to say about the discrimination practiced against Negroes in America. Jewish merchants, bankers and hotel proprietors are not noted for any unusual liberality and helpfulness toward ambitious and talented young Negroes emerging from colleges with scholastic honors but no jobs.

Both the "glass house" analogy and lack of sympathy toward African Americans were evident in the *Defender* titled "Sen. Robinson Decries Jewish Persecution" on June 17, 1933, reacting to a U.S. senator's denouncement of the persecution:

> White men cannot march into the palace of justice gushing with high-sounding words and critical analysis of other nations and their cruelty toward their subjects, when they themselves are unable to conceal their own hands stained with the blood of our defenseless people and against which they have uttered no public word of complaint.

This "glass house" analogy was also illustrated in a 1939 Defender cartoon titled "You Made Me What I Am Today" on December 9, 1939, in which an American white man wearing clothes labeled "American hatred (?) for Nazi ideals" is putting out a man looking like Hitler carrying a black doll wearing a tag labeled "Race hatred, disfranchisement, segregation, brutality to minorities."

A number of editorials under the hypocrisy theme such as: "Whither Catholics and Jews?" on October, 22, 1938; "American Hypocrisy," on July 22, 1933; "The A.F. Of L. and the Nazis," on January, 6, 1934; "Blind Bill Green," on November 28, 1936; and "Hitler Learns from America," on August 12, 1933, continued through the Second World War and were seen in topics including Jewish prejudice against African Americans, physicians protesting Hitler, American Federation of Labor boycotts of German products, and the German use of American race legislation as a model for its racist practices.

While denouncing the hypocrisy, as noted in an editorial titled "American Hypocrisy," on July 22, 1933, the Black press did not hesitate to preface it with denunciations of persecutions in general and with statements of sympathy for Jewish victims:

> While we join in the denunciation of the vicious Hitler regime and our sympathies go out to persecuted individuals everywhere regardless of race, creed or politics, we cannot tolerate the nauseating hypocrisy of those who are all against race prejudice and intolerance in Germany, but are unable to see it in the United States.

In an editorial titled "Sen. Robinson Decries Jewish Persecution," on June 17, 1933, we find a similar sentiment:

> We also include in our efforts any people, in any country and of whatever race, who are victims of oppression, hate and prejudice. Our sympathies are accentuated by the belief that freedom, liberty and love of fellow man are the only witnesses to the existence of a just God.

Hitlerism

Editorials like "The Silver Lining of Hitlerism," on November 25, 1933; and "A Startling Comparison," on March 15, 1941, used this term to describe Hitler's oppressive tactics and the racist ideologies behind them. It was not uncommon to see phrases such as "policy of the 'Hitlerites'" and " . . . there is Hitlerism much closer to us . . . ."

Defender cartoons used the term *Hitlerism* to depict the discriminatory treatment against people of color in America and the fact that it was occurring at the same time Americans were fighting in Europe. A cartoon titled "If the Democracies Win,—What?" on May 17, 1941 shows a white foot labeled "British and American Attitude Toward Darker Races" stepping on a dark-skinned couple holding a note to Florida Senator Claude Pepper[11] asking if this was what the democracies were offering in place of Hitlerism. Another cartoon titled "The Enemy Is Still Here," on August 23, 1941 shows an American soldier with Hitlerism written across his shirt stepping over his Negro buddy. Just in front of him is a sign that reads "Democratic America." Over his shoulder is a cloud labeled Hitlerism in Europe.

Cartoons showing Hitler's likeness depicted politicians as supporters of legislation that discriminated against African Americans. A cartoon titled "Bed (Bad?) Fellows," on December 16, 1939, showed U.S. Senator Martin Dies[12] in bed with Adolph Hitler. On the foot of the bed is "Persecution of Minorities and Hypocrisy." Another cartoon titled "Artist's Conception of Gov. Talmadge," on July 26, 1941, showed Georgia Governor Eugene Talmadge[13] being made to look like Hitler with the word Georgia pinned on one lapel and a button with a swastika on it with the words race hatred pinned on the other lapel.

These commentaries reminded readers of American hypocrisy, and were used to unite all oppressed groups. The *Courier* stressed this unity in an editorial titled "Hitler Invades America" on April 7, 1934, which revealed Nazi recruitment efforts in American cities:

> It appeals to American race prejudice, and that is sufficient to win favor in the eyes of large numbers of citizens. It should sweep the South. Negroes had better organize to fight this Nazi movement and seek alliance with the Jews, Catholics and non-Aryans, and do so quickly.

An editorial titled "The Silver Lining of Hitlerism," on November 25, 1933, suggested that Hitlerism had caused Jews who had been previously indifferent to racism against African Americans to more critically question ongoing practices of white supremacy in the United States:

> The Jews are properly aroused. They are beginning to see that their position here is not as secure as they have been led to believe. . . . The "Aryan" racial superstition has been flayed and ridiculed.

Themes Unique To Each Paper

Each paper had one theme that distinguished it from the other. The *Defender* tended to link human rights values to democratic values. The *Courier*'s editorials tended to focus more on Jewish resistance to Nazi oppression.

The Chicago Defender stresses human rights. A *Defender* editorial titled "Germany Will Repent," on July 22, 1933, predicted that the Nazi government's mistreatment of Jews would one day haunt the German nation. Rather than focusing on the oppression of African Americans, this editorial focused on the immorality of persecution and linked moral principles to the principles of democracy.

> ... but the day will come when this ghost now frightening the Jewish people of Germany with poverty and destruction will reappear to haunt the lives—if not of the Germany of today—the Germany of tomorrow. The constitution and liberty of a nation when invested in the power of one man is destined to be destroyed by idiosyncrasies of self-adulation. This alone would be sufficient to retard future Germany, but coupled with this will be the apostate of a world opinion massed on the side of right against the sinister influences of evil.

Human rights values and their connection to democracy were also evident in a *Defender* editorial published just after the start of World War II[14] titled "Truth Cannot Be Crushed," on September 9, 1939 noted:

> Fascism means war. Fascism means the death of democracy. Fascism means an increase of mass unemployment, starvation, mob terror and violence, the material and spiritual degradation of men, women and children, the destruction of the church and of the family.

Resisting Oppression

The *Courier* used editorials like "A Successful Boycott," on March 24, 1933; Jewish Pogroms in Germany," on April 1, 1933; "The Economic Boycott," on April 15, 1933; and "How the Jews Do It," on September 16, 1933, to describe Jewish resistance to the Nazis as a guideline for African Americans to use against their own oppression. Most of the resistance-themed editorials focused on how American Jews effectively used boycotts against German businesses and products to mobilize support and to lessen the persecution of their "brethren in Germany."

While pointing out the effectiveness of Jewish resistance tactics, the editorials chastised African Americans for their failure to support organizations such as the NAACP and hence African Americans' inability to mobilize support to protect or advance their civil rights. The editorial excerpted below from "Jewish Pogroms in Germany," on April 1, 1933, is typical of this sentiment:

We do not adequately support the National Association for the Advancement of Colored People, our one efficient defense organization. Even during times of crisis we contribute only grudgingly to it . . . And they [Jews] are powerful because they are organized. Four million American Jews have more influence on Congress than twelve million Negroes, not just because they have votes and know how to use them, but because they are able to bring financial and commercial pressure to bear on those who oppose them.

Themes Distinctive from Mainstream Press

Although the American news media overall denounced the persecution of Jews, the mainstream press and its black counterpart differed in the way that they denounced it. Although the mainstream press claims to present the truth in an unbiased way, the way it handled the Holocaust reflected particular biases. Specifically, the mainstream newspapers' skepticism of the atrocities reflected that they did not identify with Jewish oppression in the way African-American newspapers did. It was not unusual to see editorials and people quoted in articles suggesting that the reports of oppression were exaggerated, and was part of a Jewish agenda for political power and financial support (Lipstadt 1986, 43; Tifft and Jones 1999, 218). Furthermore, they tended to provide reasons for the anti-Semitism with some editorials suggesting that the mistreatment reflected German unhappiness with losing World War I, while other editorials blamed it on Jewish activism[15] (Lipstadt 1986, 43–45).

As with black newspapers, the mainstream press highlighted the question of whether American athletes should boycott the 1936 Olympics to protest Jewish persecution, allowing for both sides of the debate to be reflected. But black newspapers as a whole tended to oppose the boycott. Some mainstream newspapers reflected the African-American call for American athletes to beat the German athletes; but the overriding reasons for the mainstream's opposition of the boycott was based on a relativist principle that the United States should not get involved in Germany's internal affairs. The mainstream press exhibited blindness toward its own hypocrisy so as to avoid confronting the reality of racial division and mistreatment of minority groups in the United States (Lipstadt 1986, 67).

While black newspapers expressed fear that African Americans could be subjected to a Kristallnacht-type terror, mainstream papers avoided the issue. In their condemnations of this German atrocity, they suggested that it represented not racial or ethnic hatred but merely the frustration of German citizens in response to their poor financial conditions (Lipstadt 1986, 42).

Neither did the mainstream press frame the Holocaust in the context of human rights values. Rather, they tended to treat the reported atrocities as isolated incidents rather than as a Nazi grand plan to exterminate the Jews (Lipstadt 1986, 15, 18; Tifft and Jones 1999, 218).

ANALYSIS

The *Defender* and *Courier*'s treatment of the Jewish Holocaust was consistent with the general historical mission of the black press, i.e., being a tool of advocacy in the interests of African Americans. Since its birth in the early 19th century, black press protest of racial discrimination has been a crucial element of this mission. The Hitler regime's record of persecution against Jewish people gave credence to black newspapers' protestations and complaints; however, this time the oppression was not limited to African Americans. Reporters and editors of black newspapers understood that tactical messages of hate were not limited to people's color, but may have been effectively directed against anyone regardless of their wealth, social status, or religious belief.

The Holocaust was one of many news events that received the attention of the black press between the two world wars. This was a time when mainstream society's traditional beliefs about race were challenged on a number of fronts. Black newspapers devoted space to Joe Louis' heavyweight boxing championship, African-American athletes' triumphs at the 1936 summer Olympics, the Scottsboro Case, the invasion of Ethiopia, as well as vigilantly advocating for legislation to outlaw lynching and other forms of domestic terrorism. The reporting of athletic accomplishments challenged the belief of white supremacy.[16] The Scottsboro Case brought to light southern racial injustice (Carter 1979, 5–10, 11–50; Pfaff 1974, 72; and Ross 1999, 48).[17] The Ethiopia invasion brought to the forefront an African nation led by a person of color, thereby negating unflattering mainstream perceptions about black intelligence and leadership. This coverage served to reaffirm African Americans' rights to full citizenship.

As in World War I, black newspapers were an influential voice leading up to the start of World War II. And its discourse was even more strident than during earlier years as African Americans between the wars were willing to outwardly, and sometimes violently, demand their civil rights.[18] The black press, even in the face of intimidating surveillance and other harshly intrusive governmental practices (Washburn 1986b, 73–86), was an instrumental agent in the struggle for human recognition. Indeed, it was always positioned at the vanguard in the quest for human freedom and dignity.

CONCLUSION

We believe that our study clearly shows that black press news coverage and analysis, filtered through the African-American experience, are relevant to all Americans. Black press coverage of the Holocaust provided specifically an opportunity for African-Americans to learn resistance tactics from Jews, and ultimately to ally themselves with Jews and other victims of discrimination when such alliances became a key element in the civil rights victories of the 1960's and 70's.

Beyond this, newspapers like the *Defender* and *Courier* pointed to German atrocities against the Jewish people, contextualized those atrocities within a larger historical framework, and, later on, revealed America's hypocrisy as it castigated Hitlerian practices, on the one hand, but turned a blind eye to oppressive practices in its own backyard, on the other. In this sense, the black press challenged not only how the news was collected and reported upon by the mainstream press but also shined a critical light upon the values and biases that informed mainstream practices.

To conclude, our critical treatment of the role of the black press in what might be considered by many to be a non-African-American event points up the need to elevate the value of alternative media and to do so in a way that also broadens our understanding of the mainstream media. The mainstream media is clearly not the only voice for democracy, and as our analysis indicates, sometimes it may not even be the best voice for democracy. Greater consideration of contributions of the black press across a wide historical spectrum of human affairs provides, minimally, ways of critically assessing the mainstream press which, in the absence of scholarly treatment of the black press and its African-American experiential point of view, have otherwise gone unacknowledged, not only by mainstream reading audiences but by contemporary media analysts as well.

NOTES

1. This is a modification of Dr. Martin Luther King, Jr.'s statement in his "Letter from Birmingham Jail": "Injustice anywhere is a threat to justice everywhere."
2. The Emancipation to Reconstruction years were during 1863–1877.
3. Five black newspapers were published in the South despite laws prohibiting teaching African Americans how to read.
4. Some sources list the starting date as 1910; the year it began continuous publishing.
5. These include *The Philadelphia Tribune* (1884), *The Baltimore Afro-American* (1892), *Norfolk Journal and Guide* (1900) and *The New York Amsterdam News* (1909).
6. Other newspapers opposing the presence were the *Norfolk Journal and Guide*, *The Baltimore Afro-American*, *The Philadelphia Tribune*, *Boston Guardian* and *The New York Age*.
7. Black owned and operated newspapers did not always provide news coverage of issues commented upon in editorials. Such comments appeared weeks after the events occurred. Thus, it is necessary to read each issue of the newspaper. Furthermore, black newspapers during the 1930s and 1940s were not indexed.
8. This timeline is part of *The History Place*; an Internet-only publication that focuses on the history of humanity.
9. There were no editorial comments about Jewish persecution in Germany during the year 1937 in *The Pittsburgh Courier*.

10. The events were "The Night of the Long Knives," June, 1934; the Nazi occupation of the Rhineland, March, 1936; Berlin Olympics, 1936; "Kristallnacht," November, 1938; Nazi seizure of Czechoslovakia, March, 1939; Nazi invasion of Poland, September, 1939; Nazi invasion of Paris, June, 1940; France's armistice with Hitler, June, 1940; Nazi invasion of the Soviet Union, June, 1941; German surrender at Stalingrad, February, 1943; and Allies land in Sicily, July, 1943.
11. Senator Pepper supported civil rights.
12. The cartoon erroneously stated that Representative Dies was a senator. Dies represented a district in Texas where the Ku Klux Klan was active and where he had spoken at several Klan rallies. Dies co-created the House Un-American Activities Committee which was criticized for failing to investigate the activities of the Ku Klux Klan.
13. Governor Talmadge opposed civil rights legislation to the extent that it caused Georgia's public colleges and universities to lose their accreditation.
14. In the week prior to the publication of this editorial, Germany had invaded Poland and Britain, France, Australia and New Zealand had declared war on Germany.
15. These were the very boycotts the black press wanted to emulate.
16. Joe Louis was not the first African-American heavyweight boxing champion. Jack Johnson held that title in 1910; however, Louis was not as controversial as Johnson and thus presented a more acceptable image to the mainstream society. Furthermore, Louis's defeat of white opponents during an era when the Nazis were claiming Aryan superiority made his accomplishment significant.
17. The Scottsboro case involved nine young African-American men falsely accused of raping two white women in the South. This case drew national attention because of the involvement of Communists in the defense of the men and because of the credibility of the alleged victims and questionable trials.
18. The Harlem and Detroit riots are evidence of this assertiveness. This was also known as the era of "The New Negro," a time in which blacks were willing to take direct action as in boycotts and marches rather than depend on established civil rights organizations for redress of grievances.

REFERENCES

Barger, Harold M. 1973. Images of political authority in four types of Black newspapers. *Journalism Quarterly* 50: 645–51.

Bayton, J.A., and A. Bell. 1951. An explorative study of the negro press. *Journal of Negro Education* 20: 8–15.

Bryan, Carter R. 1969. Negro journalism in America before emancipation. *Journalism Monographs* 12: 10–17.

Buni, Andrew. 1974. *Robert L. Vann of the Pittsburgh Courier*. Pittsburgh: University of Pittsburgh.

Carson, Clayborne.1998. *The autobiography of Martin Luther King, Jr*. New York: Intellectual Properties Management.

Carter, Dan. 1979. *Scottsboro: A tragedy of the American South*. Baton Rouge: Louisiana State University.

Clark, Kenneth B. 1943. Morale of the Negro on the home front: World Wars I & II. *ournal of Negro Education* 12: 417–28.

Domke, David. 1994. The Black press in the 'nadir' of African Americans. *Journalism History* 20: 131–138.

Huspek, Michael. 2004. Black press, white press and their opposition: The case of the police killing of Tyisha Miller. *Social Justice* 31: 217–241.

Hutton, Frankie. 1993. *The early Black press in America, 1827 to 1860*. Westport, Conn: Greenwood Press.

Kessler, Lauren. 1984. *The dissident press: alternative journalism in American history*. Beverly Hills, CA: Sage Publications.

Kornweibel, Theodore Jr. 1994. "The most dangerous of all Negro journals": Federal efforts to suppress the Chicago *Defender* during World War I. *American Journalism* 11: 155–158.

Lacy, Stephen, James M. Stephens, and Stan Soffin. 1991. The future of the African-American press: A survey of African-American newspaper managers. *Newspaper Research Journal* 12: 8–19.

Lipstadt, Deborah E. 1986. *Beyond belief: The American press and the coming of the holocaust 1933–1945*. New York: Free Press.

McBride, Genevieve. G. 1996. The progress of 'race men' and 'colored women' in the Black press in Wisconsin, 1892–1985. In *The Black Press in the Middle West, 1865–1985*, ed. Henry Lewis Suggs, 325–348. Westport, Conn: Greenwood.

O'Kelly, Charlotte.G. 1980. Black newspapers and the Black protest movement, 1946–1972. *Phylon* 41: 313–324.

Ottley, Roi. 1955. *The lonely warrior. The life and times of Robert S. Abott, the founder of the Chicago Defender newspaper*. Chicago: H. Regnery Co.

Pfaff, D.W. 1974. The press and the Scottsboro rape cases, 1931–32. *Journalism History* 1: 72–76.

Pickle, K., S. C. Quinn, and J. D Brown. 2002. HIV/AIDS coverage in black newspapers, 1991–1996: Implications for health communication and health education. *Journal of Health Communication* 7: 427–444.

Reeves, Keith. 1977. *Voting hopes or fears?* New York: Oxford University Press.

Rhodes, Jane. 1998. *Mary Ann Shadd Cary: The Black press and protest in the Nineteenth Century*. Bloomington: Indiana University Press.

Ross, Felecia G. J. 1993. The Cleveland *Call and Post* and the New Deal: A change in African-American thought. *Journalism History* 19: 87–92.

Ross, Felecia G. 1995a. Fragile equality: A Black paper's portrayal of race relations in late 19th Century Cleveland. *Howard Journal of Communication* 6: 53–68.

Ross, Felecia G. J. 1995b. The Brownsville affair and the political values of Cleveland Black newspapers. *American Journalism* 12(2): 107–122.

Ross, Felecia G. J. 1999. Mobilizing the masses: The Cleveland *Call and Post* and the Scottsboro incident. *Journal of Negro History* 84: 48–60.

Stevens, Summer E., and Owen V. Johnson. 1990. From Black politics to Black community: Harry C. Smith and the Cleveland *Gazette*. *Journalism Quarterly* 67: 1090–1102.

Suggs, Henry Lewis 1988. The response of the African-American press to the United States occupation of Haiti, 1915–1934. *Journal of Negro History* 73: 33–45.

Tifft, Susan E., and Alex S. Jones. 1999. *The trust: The private and powerful family behind the New York Times*. Boston: Little, Brown and Company.

Tripp, Bernell. 1998. Extending the boundaries: 19th-Century historical influences on Black press development. Paper presented at the annual meeting of American Journalism Historians Association, October 8–11, in Louisville, Ky.

Walker, Juliet E. K. 1996. The promised land: The *Chicago Defender* and the Black Press in Illinois: 1862–1970. In *The Black press in the Middle West, 1865–1985*, ed. Henry Lewis Suggs, 9–50. Westport, Conn: Greenwood.

Washburn, Patrick.S. 1986a. J. Edgar Hoover and the Black press in World War II. *Journalism History* 13: 26–33.

Washburn, Patrick S. 1986b. *The Pittsburgh Courier*'s Double V Campaign in 1942. *American Journalism*, 3, 73–86.
Weill, S., and Castañeda, L. 2004. "Empathetic rejectionism" and inter-ethnic agenda setting: Coverage of Latinos by the Black press in the American South. *Journalism Studies* 5: 537–550.
Wilson, Clint II, and Felix Gutierrez. 1995. *Race, multiculturalism, and the media: From mass to class communication*. Thousand Oaks: Sage.
Wolseley, Roland. 1990. *The Black press U.S.A*. Ames: Iowa State University Press.

PART IV

Normative Contours of State and Oppositional Discourses

PART IV

Formative Contexts of
State and Oppositional
Discourse

10 The Philosophical Foundations of the Discourse Society

Darryl Gunson

The work of Jürgen Habermas places discourse at the heart of morality. The claim that is embodied in Habermas' Critical Theory is that the contestation of norms in modern societies must be constrained by the demands of reason and its requirement of universalism. This manifests itself as a "Discourse Ethics" which is devoid of any substantive ethical commitments and offers what are the minimal but rationally binding procedural rules for the resolution of contested normative claims. If this implies that we need to talk more, it is a modest conclusion. However, there is more to this framework than the surface banality of its conclusion might suggest, and this is best appreciated by considering the more philosophical justifications that Habermas provides. The philosophical context that makes Habermas' work so interesting and relevant, both theoretically and practically, lies in the way the "communicative solution" is presented as being the only way of engaging with, and overcoming, the philosophical problems that a "discourse of modernity" has revealed.

INTRODUCTION

In the contemporary academic climate it may sound archaic to approach social-theoretic questions from a perspective that places *rationality* and *universality* at its centre. Indeed, the notion that we should still hold onto this legacy of the Enlightenment has come under sustained attack from many sources and may therefore seem extremely naïve. It may be Foucault's (Foucault 1967) theses concerning the historical discourses on reason and "unreason" and how madness is, in some sense, a construction of such discourses that makes this standpoint seem outmoded. His later claims (Foucault 1977) that the technical rationality exemplified in modern science and technology is at the service of regimes of discipline and surveillance also seems at odds with such an approach. Jean-François Lyotard's (Lyotard 1984) distrust of universalising rationalist philosophy, with its rejection of the "grand narratives" of modernity, has also been highly influential in this regard. The work of Foucault and Lyotard, amongst others, represents a cultural shift in thinking about the legacy of the Enlightenment, ushering in a deep-rooted suspicion of enlightenment-type thinking. Despite this cultural shift, Jürgen Habermas remains the leading advocate of a social philosophy that does have a rational, universalistic basis (Habermas 1984, 1987a) and he has, over the years, elaborated a detailed account of the central role these concepts play in linguistic communication and how this can serve to underpin the "project of modernity"; a project that is, he argues, unfinished (Habermas 1996)[1].

The concepts of rationality and universality provide the philosophical grounds for his argument that the progressive ideals of modernity can best be served by a culture where open discourse is the preferred way of settling important normative questions. Indeed, as we shall see, the charge of naivety is attracted not because of Habermas' fondness for discourse, for most social theorists and philosophers see a role for it, but rather for his contention that disagreements that arise out of discourses can be resolved *rationally*. The general problem here according to critics is that rationality has become suspect, especially when it is conceived along *universalist* lines. This is because it is thought to marginalise the voice of "the other" and consequently runs roughshod over the diverse forms of human thought and practice that our (post) modern situation requires us to appreciate.

Opposed to this suspicion, Habermas' work, controversially, aims to tie social theory to a particular version of the philosophy of language. The basic idea here is that the realm of morality in modernity can be understood by paying attention to certain norms embedded in the linguistic process of consensus formation where questions of truth, right or wrong, or sincerity emerge. These rules or norms are the rational scaffolding upon which morality rests. It is, however, important to note that Habermas' theory refers to norms at two distinct, but related, levels. The first level concerns norms that actual communities agree as valid and are immanent to the process of deciding truth, right from wrong or establishing what the best course of action might be. Mere agreement, however, is not sufficient to establish such norms as valid. They must be the upshot of a process leading to a *rational* consensus rather than one that is merely *defacto*, and therefore there is considerable emphasis by Habermas on the inner logic of moral argumentation. Even at this level of abstraction we can note the implied connection between normativity, reason and justice. A rational consensus will be above the influence of subjective power, which tends to distort normativity to fit the interests of the powerful.

The second level refers to norms that operate at the meta-level. These norms are those that form the framework that governs the conduct of discourse. They are the presuppositions of discourse: no-one should be excluded; all have the right to have their views heard, and to criticise those of others; only those norms that can be accepted by all as regulating common or general interests are valid. These are those norms that are thought to embody the Enlightenment ideals of universalism and rationality and

The Philosophical Foundations of the Discourse Society 193

they are thought to yield a framework that is minimal, but rationally binding. It lays no claim to adhere to particular values, but outlines a procedure by which norms may be established. It is by considering the process by which norms are generated that the rationality of decisions concerning social ends may be assessed.

The "project of modernity" that Habermas sees himself defending has the aim of increasing the scope for rational decision making and increasing freedom in our societies. The thought is that rationality can be emancipatory because it is embodied in the basis of our communicative competence and *communication* is essentially freedom enhancing. It is therefore essential that morality and its normativity more generally, are rational. The content of morality is the upshot of the rational processes that Habermas champions, whose foundations have an essential connection with the pragmatics of communication. It is the reconstruction of our basic linguistic competence that is supposed to yield the blueprint of meta-norms to guide discourse.

It is important to note here that the framework to which I referred above is one that can be understood and assessed as a heuristic that *presupposes* the domain of the moral. It is therefore a prescription as to how moral matters should be rationally settled which might be endorsed or rejected for many different reasons by theorists: for being too complicated, too expensive or for taking too much time. Put like this, we have two things[2]: first a thesis about the pragmatics of communication and a recommendation for using certain principles therein as a blueprint for assessing the rationality of decisions for social action, but also, and importantly, there is a thesis regarding the realm of morality itself upon whose foundations the first thesis rests.

It is my contention that when seen aright, the idea that discourse or communication is at the heart of a free society is not just an optional extra, not something that we can choose from a host of alternatives, but something that is inextricably linked to freedom, and something that is, as I said earlier, rationally compelling. However, as already mentioned, this idea has come under attack from some very influential sources and the viability of such a project has been questioned. It is the argument of this paper that despite the fashionable distaste for universalism, there is still enough in Habermas' project that is viable. That is, there is enough to secure the theoretical credentials of the "discourse society" which may itself serve as a blueprint for enlightened societies of the twenty first century.

COMMUNICATION, DISCOURSE AND FREEDOM

Communication

The linguistic turn that Habermas' work took during the 1980s was focussed on the quite abstract business of drawing out the structure of speakers' linguistic competence. The project of *Universal Pragmatics* (Habermas 1979) is significant in its treatment of language not in terms of syntax, nor in terms of its semantics, but in terms of its pragmatic properties. It sought to focus on the things that speakers do when they use language; on speech acts. Insofar as it did this, the overall ambition for the project was that of "reconstructing the validity basis of speech." (Habermas 1979, 4). If the emphasis on speech-acts provided the thesis with its pragmatic orientation, then the universal part of the project had to do with the contention that there are basic competencies that are part of one's linguistic "know-how" that are genuinely universal. *All* competent speakers of *all* languages, it was argued, possess a core of implicit, practical knowledge which is structurally equivalent to the others. This is the foundation for the ability to use language that is routinely displayed in everyday, often mundane situations.

This project therefore has a kind of quasi-transcendental character since the task of making the presuppositions of linguistic competence explicit is similar in some respects to Kant's transcendental arguments regarding what reality must be like if humans are to have any knowledge of it at all. It is, however, only *quasi*-transcendental because it contends that its conclusions are not just based on pure aprioristic deduction, but are constrained by empirical observations of actual speech (Habermas 1979, 21–25; Wood 1984, 154–57).

Drawing on a novel mixture of speech-act theory and Kant-influenced Weberian concepts of cultural *rationalisation* and *differentiation,* Habermas first makes the controversial claim that underlying all potential uses of language is the primary objective of reaching an understanding through consensus. More fully he argues (Habermas 1979, 2) that a number of claims are always implicit whenever we try to communicate with others. A speaker is:

1. *Uttering* something understandable
2. Giving (the hearer) *something* to understand
3. Making himself *understandable*
4. Coming to an understanding *with another* person

The speaker selects and uses an expression that is, in convention with the dictates of that particular language, comprehensible. In so doing he is also at the same time providing the hearer with an object of understanding with the intention of communicating something true, or at least a content that is valid, in order to share knowledge with the hearer. Intentions, it is suggested, should also be uttered sincerely so that the hearer can *believe* the speaker. Finally, the utterance that is chosen must be right, or appropriate, in accordance with the normative background that governs linguistic usage. It is through observations such as these that he gives substance to his view that fundamental to all speech is the type of action aimed at *Verstandigung,* reaching understanding. And that goal—the "inherent *telos* of speech"—is to bring about "an agreement ... that terminates in the intersubjective mutuality of reciprocal understanding, shared knowledge, mutual trust and shared accord with one another." (1979, 2).

These presuppositions of communication are fleshed out even further by the suggestion that communication inevitably involves the raising of certain "validity claims", which correspond to certain "domains of reality". Reciprocal understanding, shared knowledge, and mutual trust are based on the recognition of the various corresponding validity claims that are routinely raised in communicative contexts. These validity claims are: truth, rightness, truthfulness and comprehensibility (1979, 14).

Whenever language is used with the aim of communicating something, validity claims are raised. Offering anything at all as a possible object of understanding entails an obligation on the part of the speaker to explain, if asked, what the utterance means. Thus, failure to respond satisfactorily to the question "what do you mean?" invites the charge of irrationality. Such a response will, quite obviously, appeal to the norms and conventions of the particular language and may, often, be redeemed immanently by making them explicit. Habermas' point here is that it is a presupposition of all communication that speakers can, at the very least, come to a consensus about the meanings of words and therefore the meaning of speech-acts. Whenever there is disagreement as to meaning, the fact that we are routinely able to communicate anyway suggests that there is a rational pragmatic obligation on the part of co-conversationalists to enter into a discourse about the correct meaning of words and expressions, and that our competence suggests that rational consensus on such matters is possible.

Moreover, whenever we aim to communicate something of a factual nature about the world, we do, implicitly at the same time, claim to be able to legitimate our assertion. It is part of the structure of the pragmatics of constative speech-acts that speakers be able to redeem the implicit claims they entail. So, part of our competence is constituted by the requirement to be able to answer, satisfactorily, according to the appropriate norms, the question: "how do you know?" Suitable ways of redeeming validity claims about the objective world might be: "I've seen it with my own eyes" or "I've just read it in a scientific journal" and so on. When the norms appealed to are rejected, or queried, the fact that we are able to communicate and arrive at consensus suggests that speakers are able to enter into a theoretical discourse aimed at resolving differences as to the appropriate norms relating to evidence necessary for redeeming the validity claims of contested constative speech acts.

Similarly, normative or regulative speech-acts, relating to the "social world", always rest on implicit validity claims. For any speech-act that purports to moral or normative correctness, the utterer is required, as a matter of rationality, to provide grounds for their act. To use a simple example, the Professor who asks the student to leave her class, is required, so the theory goes, to be able to give an appropriate response if the student requires further justifications. "Why should I leave?" needs to be met by at least indicating the norms that make it appropriate that the Professor may, in this context, make such a request. However, just as with constatives, mere identification of the relevant norms may not suffice to ensure the success of the speech act. When a norm is disputed the supposition is that parties to the dispute are able and rationally required to undertake a discursive examination of the norms in question with a view to coming to a consensus about them.[3] That is, a "practical discourse" is required when the *identification* of a norm is not sufficient. The supposition is not just that this is rationally required, but also, importantly, that consensus is achievable; that speakers could, if the occasion demanded it, *actually* come to a consensus over disputed norms.

Finally, with speech-acts of the expressive mode referring to "'My' world of internal nature" the implicit claims are not quite those of the previous categories; not so much truth or rightness, not so much an obligation to provide proof, nor one to highlight the normative framework being appealed to, but rather one of providing grounds for belief in the truthfulness of the utterer. That is, grounds for the co-conversationalist to believe that the speaker is sincere. Such grounds may well be assurances from the speaker, or consistency with past and subsequent behaviour, but the point is, again, that the structure of communication has an implicit normative dimension.

Discourse

What has all this to do with discourse, one might reasonably ask? The connection with the pragmatics of linguistic usage and discourse lies in the nature of validity claim redemption presupposed by linguistic competence. The suggestion is that the empirical fact of our general competence with language presupposes that we are also potentially capable of resolving normativity rationally through discourse; at the heart of our linguistic usage is a communicative rationality. It is through an examination of language —a project of "reconstructive science"—that Habermas hoped to forge the blueprint for a social ethics based on discourse.

What is this Discourse Ethics? The short answer is that Discourse Ethics lays claim to revealing the procedural framework that is necessary for resolving disputes, particularly those with normative implications, in a rational manner. One might say that the rational society is the moral society, which is at the service of freedom, and increasing freedom[4] is the emancipatory ideal that Habermas takes to be the legacy of the Enlightenment.

Developing this thought we may say that a society begins to fulfil its emancipatory potential when the preconditions for rational practical discourses are institutionalised. Such preconditions are, it should be noted, universal. They are meant to be applicable across the board to any society and this is one of the core ideas that have, as we shall see in a moment, attracted the ire of some commentators. Thus, not only is the rational society one which employs instrumental reason in deciding how to achieve social ends, but it also employs communicative reason when those ends themselves, or the general norms which constrain such ends, are contested. Communicative reason is that which is employed in coming to an understanding or consensus and is inherent in communicative competence. In practical discourse, it is claimed that speakers aim to, and consider it possible that they can, achieve a rationally motivated consensus regarding the contested norms. Here it is considered important to distinguish between a *de facto* consensus and one that is genuine or rationally motivated. It is only the latter that has the potential to increase freedom and justice, since it is only a rationally motivated consensus, it is claimed, that can strip away distortions in the discourse that arise from particular strategic interests. The consensus must be at the service of the *general interest*. Insofar as the practical discourse is in the service of such an interest, it must meet certain requirements, requirements that are already presupposed in everyday communicative contexts. The presuppositions of such competence, taken together, constitute what Habermas calls the ideal speech situation.

The ideal speech situation is, as the title suggests, not to be found in actual practical discourses, but is rather a counterfactual presupposition that all speakers cannot but anticipate. Its key element is the absence of all constraints on participants in a practical discourse except those demanded by reason. So, participants should be free to employ all communicative speech acts, to raise questions and to provide evidence constrained only by the minimal validity claims associated with communicatives that require speakers prove to be intelligible. In addition, stemming from the analysis of representatives, it is contended that all participants in a discourse be allowed the opportunity of putting forward their attitudes, feelings and intentions regarding the issues at stake, thereby going some way to ensuring that the ensuing discourse is free from constraints which may distort the communicative process. The underlying validity claim is, as already noted, that speakers are sincere in their arguments. The corresponding institutional constraints on the discourse must be such that speakers are able to be sincere without the threat of pressures or sanctions either internal or external to the speech situation.

Similarly, all participants in the discourse should be free to use regulative speech acts. That is, they should be free to raise issues, forbid arguments and question the normative contexts that may militate against the appropriateness of some arguments rather than others. This would go some way to ensuring that norms invoked to block some arguments and allow others to proceed are not one-sided, or invoked without scrutiny from the strategic perspective of some of the participants in the process. So, not only does this validity dimension constrain the discourse by requiring that the appropriateness of arguments be agreed upon, but it also allows (due to the second normative aspect of regulatives) that participants be able to question those very norms invoked as redemptions as to the appropriateness of specific arguments raised in the debate.

We have here a model of communication, with its analysis of speech acts, the types of validity claims that may be raised and their modes of redemption, from which an ethical theory—Discourse Ethics—is derived. Social justice requires rational norms to serve as guides for action, which are procedurally determined under conditions that approximate to the ideal speech situation. Thus the institutionalisation of the conditions for realising the ideal speech situation becomes one of the central objectives of Critical Theory. Put like this, the project of Critical Theory in late modernity becomes one of encouraging, supporting and persuading that more, not less, open conversation, debate—discourse—is the mark of a rational society. But, importantly, one of the key marks of rationality in this sense is adherence to the universal principles of Discourse Ethics.

Freedom

There are many examples of how this basic framework has been used to illuminate both the potential and the limits of communication for increasing freedom. One application in the British context has been the attempt to assess the rationality and the justness of policy decisions arising from government-ordered public inquiries (Kemp 1985). Others have explored the usefulness of Habermas' framework in understanding the dynamics and obstacles to the success of government-led urban renewal "partnerships" in the West of Scotland (Gunson and Collins 1997). Habermas himself (Habermas 1989) is well known for supporting the idea that the "public sphere" that emerged in Europe, initially among the intelligentsia, might yield valuable insights for contemporary societies as to how an area of public life, where intersubjective agreement on values and standards has been reached in order to further socio-political ends, might exist relatively autonomously of the state. Habermas' studies into this phenomenon are instructive precisely because they indicate the ways in which discourse is important to a free and rational society, but also in that they provide useful clues as to the conditions in which the public sphere becomes less effective. For example, the period where this arena for public discussion and debate was most effective was before its structural transformation in the eighteenth and nineteenth centuries. With the onset of industrial capitalism, the public sphere was opened up to more voices, which paradoxically led to a narrowing of the interests effectively expressed. This "privatisation of the public sphere", a liberalisation of market relations that reduced the autonomy of the public sphere from state interference, actually led to an undermining of the very aspect that had proved to be most effective; its tendency to set aside special interests in the pursuit of the common good. Habermas, of course, argues that an increased inclusiveness ought not to go hand in hand with the narrowing of interests subject to rational public discussion.

It is instructive that the contemporary and historical examples that might approximate to anything resembling Habermas' framework do not, on closer inspection, measure up very well to the ideal. Indeed, such a paucity of examples as to how all this could be practised merely adds to the growing suspicion, noted earlier, that this kind of social theorising has had its day. Such scepticism is particularly vivid when we begin to make the link between Habermas' technical, philosophical work and that which is closer to sociology and social policy. Even though there is an intimate link between the often highly abstract and technical work and that which seems directly related to politics and practical decision making, it is not always easy to tell what the core issues are between Habermas and his detractors and so the force of some of the technical arguments may get lost against the background of objections to the work that are more practically orientated.

Habermas has placed a large burden upon the more philosophical aspects of his work, emphasising the more technical justificatory programme. The thought here is that although history and contemporary study may show that the rational communication society may never have existed, there is an important sense in which this is bypassed by the philosophical programme. That programme, it could be argued, aims to secure the blueprint as an *ideal* rather than an actuality. It is designed to show the *coherence* of the philosophical vision and persuade of its validity as a regulatory ideal. This being so, it is important to look a little more closely at the philosophical justification that Habermas provides. For it is by looking at the underlying philosophy that we will be able to understand why anyone would object to such *prima facie* sensible ideas and thereby understand more clearly the idea of a rational society that has discourse at its heart.

DISCOURSE AND THE PROBLEM OF MODERNITY

When we consider the question of the basis upon which social change does, or possibly could, proceed, it is useful to draw a distinction between those who think that the central category here is power and those who think ethical concepts such as justice have conceptual priority. From the perspective of the former camp, considerations of justice may be paid lip service whilst at the same time recognising that this is a necessary, perhaps Machiavellian, charade to maintain power. Or, following Nietzsche, it may be thought that any such ethical concepts are merely a manifestation of a "slave morality" which is that of those too weak to recognise the "will to power" as the basis of all human activity. Habermas quite clearly falls into the second camp, for it is central to his project that even though political activity is about power, power is in some sense a phenomenon that is derived from and legitimated by the communicatively agreed norms that form the ethical basis of social and political activity. Indeed, we may take this point a bit further and suggest that pursuing the "project of modernity" is precisely the project of showing how "just" norms are possible and of trying to foster the institutional arrangements to allow them to become actualised.

When Lyotard[5](Lyotard 1984), xxiv) wrote that the postmodern condition was one of "incredulity towards metanarratives", he was quite explicitly making the point that any blueprint for society based on a universalist social philosophy could no longer bear scrutiny. This positions him in the opposite camp to the Habermasian project. The enlightenment idea of material, social and moral progress, through reason, turns out to be suspect because those ideals themselves, that purport to be the vehicles of justice, lack independent "legitimation" and turn out to be just another manifestation of power. Habermas' Discourse Ethics with its central premise of speech orientated to consensus is precisely another example of a grand narrative offering a set of *universal* principles by which all action is to be judged. In so far as this is what Habermas is doing, it represents no less than an act of "terrorism"; an act of forcing the multi-shaped heterogeneous "language games" that constitute society into the round holes of an ultimately arbitrary system.

Lyotard does not object to Habermas' project on the grounds that it is, as a heuristic device, unhelpful, unproductive from a pragmatic point of view. Rather the objection is to the whole philosophical tradition of which Habermas is part. Habermas' crime is not that he has overlooked some technical detail or other, nor is it that he fails to give due consideration to the metatheoretic presuppositions of his project. No, his crime is that he has dared to engage in large-scale normative philosophy at all. Matters are only made worse in the eyes of Lyotard when the normative content of modernity is cashed out in terms of progress, rationality, justice and universalism. Why? Simply because the normativity inherent in these concepts is itself not something that is subject to scientific ratification; the ideas are inherently philosophical and the philosophies are merely narratives on a grand scale.

Universality is suspect because it requires principles to be applicable to everyone in the same manner and therefore is incompatible with difference and diversity. Rationality is, likewise, suspect in that it is, first, too closely interlinked with the concept of the universal. This has the consequence that whoever gets to define rationality and reason[6] is also in a position to judge those that do not measure up. Here the idea is that there is a direct link between universal rationality as it manifests itself throughout history and the Gulag[7], where dissent and difference are eradicated by sheer force. Second, reason has long since been suspect because of its instrumental nature. Therefore, this line of thought continues, we cannot pin our hopes on reason as recent human history is replete with examples of cultures that seem, at least on the face of it, to be rationally advanced, and yet are capable of, and in some cases recruit the resources of reason to execute, some quite horrendous plans[8]. How can reason be emancipatory when it "allows" or "participates in" something like this? Reason is just what the powerful want it to be.

Let us then take Lyotard as broadly representative of the current anti-enlightenment intellectual climate and ask whether or not Habermas' views on the nature and role of discourse in a modern society are really apt targets for this kind of critique? Let us start with the very idea of modernity itself. Habermas quite clearly situates himself within a tradition that encompasses, for the most part, what we might call traditional German philosophy, which means that he is continuing the "conversation"[9] that begins with Kant, through Hegel, Marx, Weber and the Frankfurt School. Since Habermas regards Hegel as the first philosopher of modernity and it is also Hegel that is cited by Lyotard as an example of the grand narratives of modernity, let us sketch this Hegelian context that Habermas sees himself as operating within.

As Habermas observes, (1987b) Hegel inherited from Kant the idea that reason is differentiated (scientific, moral-political and aesthetic) and the associated view that one of the problems of modernity is that of providing the rational grounds for the norms that govern these domains. For Hegel, however, modernity can no longer rely on criteria from the past to anchor its normative project. It can no longer rely on authority, tradition or, indeed, religion. Modernity is seen as a *new* historical age that is conscious of the necessity for constant vigilance regarding the supposed break with the past, and of the need to develop criteria to ground the norms governing Kant's differentiated spheres of rationality, in ways that are "internal" rather than imposed from outside the culture of modernity. As Habermas himself has put it, "modernity has got to create normativity out of itself" (1987b, 7). Reason, as manifest in the new sciences and philosophy (and perhaps aesthetic discourse), is to be the final arbiter when knowledge claims are assessed.

Indeed, with Hegel, modernity's emphasis on critique is taken to new heights because the very activity of critical philosophy can no longer be taken for granted. Thus, the differentiation of reason must itself be subject to critique. In other words, philosophy has to become reflexive. Coupled with the question of modernity's awareness of time[10], we have the prospect that the Kantian categories are uncritically historically relative to that era in which they were written and, therefore, do not fully capture the force of a new age creating normativity "out of itself". That is, the radical reflexivity of philosophy seems to undermine the main premise of the modern project: that there is available to people, absolute, neutral or non-partial, reason that can yield objective knowledge and thus further the emancipatory idea of increasing freedom. If reason itself is historically relative, reflecting the society of the day, then the prospect of rational progress along Enlightenment lines is dim. This radical reflexivity actually ushers in the prospect that history will (and must be) just the story of change, not progress[11]. Furthermore, it is precisely this kind of critique that lies behind postmodern approaches.

Hegel's attempt to resolve the problem of modernity with history becoming the story of the universal subject—absolute reason or spirit—finally becoming aware of itself is, Habermas agrees (with Lyotard), a failure. Its all-encompassing unity of absolute reason seems to deny any place for the individual and so only represents freedom in a highly contentious and ambiguous way. Absolute reason becomes conscious of itself in the form of a rational state. Freedom is thus the freedom to accept the principles of the rational state, but of course, if the individual is not free in this sense, then they must be forced to be free. In other words, there is the very real danger of modernity becoming totalitarianism. Habermas is obviously keen to distance himself from this[12]. However, whereas those such as Lyotard would want to see the Hegelian failure as evidence that there is no emancipatory potential inherent in reason, Habermas remains convinced that there is a way out of this philosophical dilemma.[13].

Is Habermas' Discourse Ethics merely another metanarrative? Do we try and rescue the core tenets of the Enlightenment—progress through reason—or do we capitulate in the face of power? Do we pursue the problem through the search for universalistic principles or do we accept that a perspectival, relativistic view of the world and its activities is all we can expect? Perhaps, but it is still worth examining how Habermas defends his vision of the "discourse society".

AN AVERSION TO THE UNIVERSAL?

We have already seen how the project of modernity in Habermas' hands has two central, interlinked, philosophical pillars supporting the edifice. One of these is the response to Hegel's and Weber's "entrapment" within the paradigm of instrumental reason by identifying another side of reason, the communicative which emphasises that communication cannot exist without, at root, a basis in mutual understanding and consensus.

The other pillar is the universalism that props up Discourse Ethics. Even though both ideas have a lot of justificatory work to do, the concept of the universal is the most important. It is so because one could, conceivably, imagine a situation where even Habermas' most trenchant critics allow that open communication is important or even necessary for groups in forming robust identities and formulating their needs and interests, but deny that this openness extends into the arena of politics where power, in the form of the state or other powerful groups, is encountered. That is, critics could deny the universalism here whilst endorsing a watered-down version of the "discourse society". Even if one accepts the general thesis that discourse can be emancipatory, there is still the question as to what makes it fair, just, and rational. We know that the answer is based on ideals that have universalistic credentials. So it is important, I think, to look at what can be said in support of this pillar.

The concept of universality is, arguably, one of the central components of what one might call a naïve Enlightenment fundamentalism. The argument is that progress will consist of universal knowledge: truths about the natural world in the form of the laws of nature, normative principles that hold for everyone in the form of truths about justice and morality more generally. The truths of science are not, so the thought goes, relative to time and place, to society or culture; they are either true (absolutely) or false. The same goes for principles by which to organise societies and, indeed, individual lives. Of course, such a naïve view has come under attack from a number of sources. There are those that stress the irreducible differences of social lives and those that live them, such that there can be no universal principles; no "one size fits all". Indeed, in these postcolonial times, the very idea that there are moral codes that are universally valid is considered absurd. The dominant mode of thought is relativism, with all its attendant problems of incommensurability and its foreclosure of the possibility of critique of the "other".

What may be said, philosophically, in defence of universality? One central point to recognise is the way in which Habermas modifies the concept from its original Kantian formulation. Kant's moral philosophy is notable for its formulations of the "categorical imperative"; one version of which says: "Act only on the maxim whereby thou canst at the same time will that it should become a universal law" (Kant 1988, 38). The demand for universalisable maxims is a demand that the principles we propose to adopt are appropriate for all. Habermas accepts this demand for universalisability as the starting point for any attempt to overcome the problem of modernity. However, one major criticism of Kant's view is that it is essentially "monological", characterising moral reasoning as an essentially individual, private matter. The image here is of individual thinkers engaged in their own private thought experiments regarding their actions and the maxims that they might imply. The question is: can they *will* it to be universally applicable?

The *individualistic* formulation notwithstanding, the core idea here is that nothing could be a moral principle if it cannot be a principle for all and, importantly, that this test of fitness for moral duty is developed without reference to any objectivist or subjective conceptions of 'the good' and does not lend weight to any particular set of values, beliefs or desires. In this regard it does seem to encapsulate the boundaries of morality in a way that respects the demand that modernity develop "normativity out of itself". For Kant it is the structure of reason itself that provides the universalist character of the categorical imperative. That the framework is minimal is the source of its strength and its weakness. It is a weakness, some contend, because of its formalistic nature; it is empty of content and therefore offers no guidance on what people ought to do in specific circumstances. The strength of this lies in the fact that it does not propose to tell us what to do, only that we can test those actions and the principles so implied, for moral fitness.

Habermas takes this basic idea—that reason demands universalisability—and makes it "dialogical". That is, it is not sufficient for an individual person to reflect on the issue of whether or not they can accept the norm, rather, *all* interested parties must discursively test norms. This principle of morality makes its appearance as one of the keystones in Habermas' Discourse Ethics, where every valid norm must be such that:

> (U): *All affected can accept the consequences and side effects [which] its general observance can be anticipated to have for the satisfaction of everyone's interests* ...

This in turn supports the principle of Discourse Ethics:

> (D): *Only those norms can claim to be valid that meet (or could meet) with the approval of all affected in their capacity as participants in a practical discourse* ... (1990, 65-6).

Principle D presupposes that we can already justify our choice of norm and U is the rule of argumentation that says what it is to provide such a justification.

Sceptics may well ask what of the principle (U) itself? What of this new twist to the tale of modernity? What could justify the principle of universalisability? Indeed, if justification is not forthcoming, or if it is unconvincing, then even on its own terms modernity may be accused of being self-defeating. Certainly, no purely *deductive* justification seems to be possible for there seems to be no candidate fact from which such a principle would validly follow. However, Habermas does not leave the matter there, for he is acutely aware of the need for justification. The justification that is sketched (1990, 80) relies on the concept of a *performative contradiction*. Such a contradiction occurs when: "a constative speech act k (p) rests on non-contingent presuppositions whose propositional content contradicts the asserted proposition p" (1990, 81). So when Descartes tries to doubt the fact of his existence he cannot because the very act of doubting presupposes the existence of the doubter. It is a kind of logical impossibility. Something similar holds, it is argued, for the principle U when faced with the sceptic. So the burden is to show that:

> ... every argumentation, regardless of the context in which it occurs, rests on pragmatic presuppositions from which the propositional content of the principle of universalism (U) can be derived (1990, 82).

The argument is sketched in some detail by Habermas, which need not detain us here, but the gist is that in trying to mount an *argument* to refute U, the sceptic must make certain presuppositions[14], which themselves are constitutive of the very foundation for U. The sceptic is caught in the logical grip of the performative contradiction. The next step in Habermas' justificatory schema is to point out that it follows from the rules of discourse that a contested norm cannot actually meet with the consent of all interested parties unless U holds:

> Unless all affected can *freely* accept the consequences and the side effects that the *general* observance of a controversial norm can be

expected to have for the satisfaction of the interests of *each individual* (1990, 3).

Once U is secured, as an unavoidable rule of the logic of practical discourses, then the principle D can also be shown to have more justificatory substance then mere preference.

How does this serve to rebut the claims of the Enlightenment sceptic described above? The concept of universality has a central role in the discourse-ethical project that Habermas advances. It features as the basic moral principle: norms must be acceptable to all and applicable to all. This principle is justified to the extent that the sceptic who tries to mount an *argument* is necessarily caught up in the *performative contradiction*. The force of such an argument is meant to be that once the sceptic realises the contradiction, they will concede that even their position presupposes the basic moral principle, and thus the foundation of Habermas' system will be secured. Of course, the transcendental argument only works if the sceptic is willing to articulate his objections in the form of an argument. It has no force in the face of a rejection of rational discourse. The opponent who refuses to enter into debate is not vulnerable to this argument, but it does serve to demonstrate the limits of reasonableness as well as its normative force.

CONCLUDING COMMENTS

Is the project a failure and must we conclude, along with the sceptics discussed in the foregoing pages, that the desire to have a society where discourse and rational debate are central is hopelessly naïve, clinging to some indefensible enlightenment legacy? In short, I think the answer is no.

However, although I have described his thesis that communicative rationality is prior to instrumental-strategic rationality, I have not defended it. I have not attempted to defend Habermas against the sceptic who argues that he has not shown us that *all* language use is dependent on some moment where the primary aim is of coming to a consensus. Such a thought suggests that we do not always anticipate that such a consensus is possible and therefore, if sustainable, may weaken the thesis that normative ideals admit of cognitive validation. It is true the sceptic who consistently refuses to admit that ethical concepts such as justice can be rational, except in an instrumental way that reflects power asymmetries, has not been rebutted.

Nevertheless, let us be mindful of what has been established here. The moral principle U secures all that is necessary to appreciate the fundamental role that discourse must play in modern societies. *That* principle is the test for the validity of norms. It stipulates that *all* must agree. In so far as it does this, it provides a basic formal, but not entirely empty, criterion of the moral. What it does not do, of course, is at the same time demonstrate that somehow a *rational* consensus is possible. The principle assumes that this is the case, it being the burden of the arguments that constitute Habermas' Universal Pragmatics to support this assumption. Without this premise it is always possible for the sceptic to criticise the position by pointing out that any consensus will always be *de facto*, since all such phenomena ultimately rest on power. Indeed, this is precisely the kind of view that Lyotard takes of the matter. However, even without a sustained defence of *that* aspect of Habermas' work here[15], it is my contention that we need not yield the ground to the sceptic. We need not, therefore embrace the relativism and the view of politics as essentially *agonistic* that this would seem to entail.

It is all very well to place an emphasis on cultural differences and the supposed divergence between the values that people may hold and which might therefore guide their action. Indeed, it seems unavoidable that one accepts that certain projects or plans for action can seem perfectly rational in light of the aims that the actors have. What one might disagree about, of course, is whether those aims are rational or consistent. But to say that there can be no rational consensus regarding the aims, or *telos* of action is to *over*emphasise difference. There may well be plenty of historical examples, or obscure anthropological cases, of cultures manifesting "other" rationalities, but it is not clear that now, in the contemporary global climate, that there really are cases of such radical incommensurability.

It may be true that people, groups or indeed nations, want different often incompatible things, but it is not the case that we have no convergence on the norms of rational argument that may be used to justify claims to those things. Thus, an emphasis on *difference* and a suspicion of universality comes up against its *limit* in the discourse on rationality. Therefore, in situations where discourse is the *preferred* means of addressing common issues, it may well be that there is disagreement as to what *is* in the common interest, but at least that is something that could be discussed reasonably. So even if one is not convinced that Habermas is able to demonstrate the whole thesis, it is plausible that there will still be sufficient common ground to act as the basis for processes aimed at coming to shared understandings and rational consensus.

If the preceding point addresses the sceptic who rejects the possibility of rational consensus, it does nothing to assuage the worries of that sceptic who rejects the moral principle U: that only those norms that are accepted by all will be valid. Of course, the argument a few paragraphs above suggested that the force of the performative contradiction that he is caught in silences this kind of sceptic. However, there is another possibility that Habermas raises (1990, 99) where the sceptic is not caught up in the aforementioned contradiction simply because he refuses to be drawn

The Philosophical Foundations of the Discourse Society 207

into the "game" of providing argument and legitimation for his position. Recall, it was the very attempt to deny certain rules of argumentation that led to the sceptic contradicting himself since *this* act of negation presupposes the very thing supposedly negated:

> The *consistent skeptic* will deny the transcendental pragmatist of a basis for his argument. He may, for example, take the attitude of an ethnologist vis-à-vis his own culture, shaking his head over philosophical argumentation as though he were witnessing the unintelligible rites of a strange tribe. Nietzsche perfected this way of looking at matters, and Foucault has now rehabilitated it (1990, 99)

As Habermas points out, at this point there ceases to be dialogue. One is no longer talking *with* the sceptic, but rather *about* him. Thus the process of discourse and rational discussion is circumvented and contradiction avoided by silence. It is therefore acknowledged that a willingness to argue, to engage in discourse, is a *sine qua non* for the plausibility of the view that morality is a cognitive business.

Although it may seem that the refusal to speak, to enter dialogue, will avoid the contradiction, this is a far more difficult stance to maintain than it first appears. Even though the sceptic may well turn her back on the moral principle by refusing to argue, she certainly cannot turn her back on the wider communicative community of which she is part. Given that this is not possible, short of suicide or severe mental illness, the sceptic must operate within a community that does have argumentation as the basis of reaching understandings and planning for action. There can be no form of socio-cultural life that is not geared towards maintaining communicative action through argumentation, even if this is in a very rudimentary and undeveloped form. No matter how good a "drop out" she may become, the sceptic cannot avoid the communicative practices that being a member of a community entails, and these are "at least partly identical with the presuppositions of argumentation as such" (ibid, 100). In this sense we can see how fundamental such presuppositions are.

In the foregoing pages I have been concerned to elaborate Habermas' core idea that a society that encourages discourse is more likely to serve the interests of its citizens than one that does not. Put like this, the idea is hardly likely to seem contentious or even remarkable. And yet the radical critique of this idea implies that such a view is merely one possible way of organising the social and intellectual energy of a society and further, that the alternatives are equally valid. The reason for this is that the philosophical basis for the discourse society is thought to be lacking. What I hope to have shown is that this basis is rather more robust than it might first appear.

APPENDIX

Candidate rules for the conduct of all discourse

At the logico-semantic level

1. No speaker may contradict himself.
2. Every speaker who applies predicate F to a object A must be prepared to apply F to all other objects resembling A in all relevant respects.
3. Different speakers may not use the same expression with different meanings.

These are rules that by themselves are purely logical and have no ethical import whatsoever.

Pragmatic presuppositions in the search for truth

1. Every speaker may assert only what he really believes.
2. A person who disputes a proposition or norm not under discussion must provide a reason for wanting to do so.

The process of communication

1. Every subject with the competence to speak and act is allowed to take part in the discourse.
2. Everyone is allowed to question any assertion whatever.
3. Everyone is allowed to introduce any assertion whatever into the discourse.
4. Everyone is allowed to express his attitudes, desires, and needs.

No speaker may be prevented, by internal or external coercion, from exercising his rights as laid down (foregoing) (Habermas 1990, 9).

NOTES

1. As Mitchell Stephens aptly put it: "A debate has been raging in the world of scholars and intellectuals. On one side are the 'postmodernists'–the thinkers whose ideas inspired the playful, hybrid buildings, outfits and artworks that now grace the American landscape; the thinkers who encouraged a generation of graduate students to 'deconstruct' such long treasured notions as 'reason' and 'justice'. The major figure on the other side of this debate is Jürgen Habermas" (Stephens 1994).

2. It is, I argue, essential to understand that both of these theses are part of the discourse-ethical project, and that one cannot adequately consider the two theses in isolation from each other. Furthermore, we will be able to see more clearly how Habermas intends that Discourse Ethics is not really an optional heuristic, but it is the only rational route available to us.
3. I have referred to the discursive obligations discussed here as having a " 'double normative' context" (Gunson and Collins 1997, 283), but I don't think that is quite right. All the contexts are doubly normative in the sense that rationality requires that one *ought* to redeem validity claims if required by referring to the conventional norms for doing so (or at least the ones that are being appealed to) and also, where this does not suffice, one *is rationally required* to enter into discourse about the status of the normative framework that is being appealed to. What is, perhaps, slightly different with respect to "regulatives" is that they are already normative in the sense of aiming at changing peoples' behaviour, whereas "constatives" and "representatives" are not.
4. Of course 'freedom' itself is a controversial concept, but I cannot go into this matter here except to add that by freedom I do not (just) mean that bulwark of modern liberalism-the negative freedom of Isaiah Berlin-freedom to do just anything without external constraint, but rather I have in mind an account that is, perhaps, more Hegelian. That is, a free society is one that has maximised its own internal self-rule; it provides freedom to pursue the rational course of action, not from an individualistic perspective, but from the perspective of the general good.
5. To be sure, when Lyotard wrote, "Consensus has become an outdated and suspect value. But justice as a value is neither outdated nor suspect. We must thus arrive at an idea and practice of justice that is not linked to that of consensus." (1997, 66), it certainly does not look as though he fits straightforwardly into the dichotomy between justice and power. But, despite this self understanding with its co-option of the concept justice, it is my view that unless we are to slide into a kind of relativism about these matters where justice concerning clashing ideas (language games) really is impotent and therefore reduces to power, we have to see that modernity requires that we fall back on precisely those resources of rationality and discourse that Habermas deals with.
6. The idea that rationality might be subject to definition, competing ones at that, captures, I think, the notion that even this touchstone of the Enlightenment may not be neutral, but is itself an effect of the more basic phenomenon of power. This motif crystallizes the philosophical burden placed upon Habermas, for without addressing the radical point that reason is always a reflection of the societies that champion it, Habermas has done nothing more than offer a system that cannot but exclude and alienate those who somehow do not 'measure up'.
7. This point, originally made by Sarup (1993, 92), is worth quoting in full. Speaking of the "new philosophers", amongst whom we may include Lyotard, Sarup suggests that: " . . . they contend that there is a direct line between Hegel to the Gulag. The stages are these: first there is Hegel's invention of Absolute Spirit with its teleology of history. Then Marx relocates this teleology within history conceived in materialist terms. Finally the annulment of contradiction at the end of the teleological process becomes (with Stalinism) an abolition of differences through sheer force. Absolute Spirit becomes the knock at the door in the name of history, of the secret police."
8. One of the most obvious examples here is that of the Holocaust. In some ways this is an example of a very rationally advanced culture: materially, socially and perhaps even aesthetically, too. And yet the instrumentality of reason is put at the service of killing in industrial quantities.

9. By 'conversation' I allude to the literary device employed in his *The Philosophical Discourse of Modernity* where he imagines all the 'great' thinkers involved in a discourse regarding the problem of modernity.
10. That is, modernity's self-understanding as an historical phenomenon (Habermas 1987, 1–22).
11. This rather abstract point is structurally analogous to the debate within the Philosophy of Science that addressed the implications of Thomas Kuhn's (Kuhn 1970) work. Imre Lakatos' (Lakatos and Musgrave 1986) charge that Kuhn reduced the concept of scientific progress to 'mob-psychology' carries the implication that science does not 'progress rationally' but is subject to major disruptions that have an irrational element akin to faith. Something analogous to this is present in the tension between those who perceive the project of modernity as being about progress based on reason and those who reject this view. One candidate for the latter position is Michel Foucault with his view of history as the process of dominant discourses being replaced by others, a process that is not progressive but one that reflects asymmetries of power.
12. It is, of course, not just Hegel that is the problem. If Hegel's attempt to outwit the 'dialectic of enlightenment' by conceiving reason as totalising and embodied in the state leads to totalitarianism, then so too, it may be argued, does Marx's materialist version of Hegel which sees reason as embodied in that another universal subject, the proletariat.
13. This is the dilemma of totalizing reason on the one hand and tradition on the other.
14. As set down in rules which are suggested as examples for the conduct of all discourse (see Appendix).
15. This part of the project has attracted quite a lot of criticism (Culler 1984; Thompson 1981; Wood 1984), however Habermas has defended it strongly and convincingly (Habermas 1982, 269–74).

BIBLIOGRAPHY

Culler, J. 1984. Communicative Competence and Normative Force. *New German Critique* 35:133–44.

Foucault, M. 1967. *Madness and Civilisation*. London: Tavistock.

———. 1977. *Discipline and Punish*. London: Penguin.

Gunson, D, and C Collins. 1997. From the I to the We: Discourse Ethics, Identity and the Pragmatics of Partnership in the West of Scotland. *Communication Theory* 7 (4):278–300.

Habermas, J. 1979. *Communication and the Evolution of Society*. Boston: Beacon Press.

———. 1982. A Reply to My Critics. In *Habermas: Critical Debates*, edited by J. B. Thompson and D. Held. Cambridge Mass: MIT Press.

———. 1984. *The Theory of Communicative Action, Vol 1, Reason and the Rationalisation of Society*. Translated by T. McCarthy. Boston: Beacon Press.

———. 1987a. *The Theory of Communicative Action, Vol.2, Lifeworld and System: A Critique of Functionalist Reason*. Boston: Beacon Press.

———. 1987b. *The Philosophical Discourse of Modernity*. Cambridge: Polity.

———. 1989. *The Structural Transformation of the Public Sphere: An Inquiry into a Category of Bourgeois Society*. Cambridge: Polity.

———. 1990. Discourse Ethics: Notes on a Program of Philosophical Justification. In *Moral Consciousness and Communicative Action*. Cambridge Mass: MIT Press.

———. 1996. Modernity: An Unfinished Project. In *Habermas and the Unfinished Project of Modernity*, edited by M. P. D'Entreves and S. Benhabib. Cambridge: Polity.

Kant, Immanuel. 1988 (1785). *Fundamental Principles of the Metaphysics of Morals*. Translated by T. K. Abbott. Amherst, NY: Prometheus Books.

Kemp, R. 1985. Planning, Public Hearings and the Politics of Discourse. In *Critical Theory and Public Life*, edited by J. Forester. Cambridge Mass: MIT Press.

Kuhn, Thomas. 1970. *The Structure of Scientific Revolutions*. Chicago: CUP.

Lakatos, I, and A Musgrave, eds. 1986. *Criticism and the Growth of Knowledge*. Cambridge: CUP.

Lyotard, J. F. 1984. *The Postmodern Condition: A Report on Knowledge*. Manchester: MUP.

Sarup, M. 1993. *Post-Structuralism and Postmodernism*. Hemel Hempstead: Harvester Wheatsheaf.

Stephens, M. 1994. Jürgen Habermas: The Theologian of Talk. *Los Angeles Times Magazine*.

Thompson, J. B. 1981. *Critical Hermeneutics*. Cambridge: CUP.

Wood, A. 1984. Habermas's Defence of Rationalism. *New German Critique* 35:145–64.

11 Habermas and Oppositional Public Spheres
A Stereoscopic Analysis of Competing Discourses

Michael Huspek

In his reflections on *Structural Transformation of the Public Sphere* (1989) [1962], Jurgen Habermas considers the question "of whether, and to what extent, a public sphere dominated by mass media provides a realistic chance for the members of civil society, in their competition with the political and economic invaders' media power, to bring about changes in the spectrum of values, topics and reasons channeled by external influences, to open it up in an innovative way, and to screen it critically" (Habermas 1992, 455). He then answers: "It seems to me that the concept of a public sphere operative in the political realm, as I developed it in *Structural Transformation*, still provides the appropriate analytical perspective for the treatment of this problem" (Habermas 1992, 455). He also acknowledges, however, that the analytical perspective is not sufficient by itself but requires "considerable empirical research" (Habermas 1992, 455), thereby posing a challenge to those who may be tempted to study the public sphere while drawing upon his discourse-centered theoretical approach.

At stake here is the emancipatory potential of the public sphere and its capacity to deepen and extend the possibilities of democratic life. Yet despite the theoretical richness of Habermas's work and its empirical-analytical promise, researchers have by no means been quick to take up the challenge (but cf. Gunson and Collins 1997; Forester 1985). Instead, much contemporary research on the public sphere has only directed obligatory nods toward the grand sweep of Habermas's thesis before shunting aside its idealized scaffolding in favor of more concretely rigorous empirical approaches (e.g., Alexander 1995; Barkley Brown 1995; Gregory 1995). Perhaps the most often cited reason for such is his very concept of the bourgeois public sphere which has been the subject of much debate as critics have expressed concern about an underestimation of its historical record of exclusionary practices as well as the counterpractices of excluded groups who have formed "shadow publics" in response (e.g., Calhoun 1992; Fraser 1990; Kluge 1993; Negt and Eley 1992). In acknowledging such concerns, Habermas has stated the need for a "stereoscopic view" that might reveal how a "mechanism of exclusion that locks out and represses at the same time calls forth countereffects that cannot be neutralized" (Habermas

1992, 427). Yet the statement has received no serious follow-up, as Habermas has provided few specifics for fusing together the analytical with the empirical in terms of articulated method, scope, and design (Blaug 1997; Ruane and Todd 1988). This omission becomes all the more significant when considered in light of the normative dimension of his work. For short of a successful integration of descriptive and analytical statements it is not clear that we can know how or where to hold up emancipatory ideals as a means of critically assessing contemporary public-sphere practices.

This chapter addresses these considerations through a series of three claims. First, I argue that although critics of Habermas's thesis are right to point to its underestimation of both the public sphere's record of exclusionary practices and forms of otherness spawned as a result, his responses have been sufficiently corrective, albeit sketchy and in need of additional filling in. Second, I maintain that a satisfactory response that begins with explicit reference to Habermas's discourse-centered theoretical approach needs also to take into account exclusionary practices and forms of oppositional otherness—a need that has heretofore not been sufficiently met. So doing should not in any way diminish the broad arch of Habermas's theoretical edifice but in fact may point to new and theoretically powerful applications to empirical domains. Indeed, my third claim is that it is only by wedding together Habermas's discourse-centered theoretical approach with empirically grounded practices of power and opposition that the full normative potential of his theory can be realized.

In demonstrating the analytical utility of all three claims, I offer a preliminary sketch of a stereoscopic analysis that focuses on public sphere practices and counterpractices—specifically those of the *New York Times* as exemplar participant of bourgeois publicness and the black-owned and -operated *New York Amsterdam News* as its oppositional counterpart— that applies Habermas's discourse-centered theoretical approach to exclusionary discursive practices on the one hand, oppositional responses on the other, with special consideration given to their bearing on questions regarding the normative basis for ideology critique as it pertains to a public sphere dominated by mass media.

HABERMAS'S THEORY OF THE BOURGEOIS PUBLIC SPHERE AND CHALLENGES FROM OTHERNESS

Habermas has proclaimed the emergence of the bourgeois public sphere as a radically new development in the seventeenth and eighteenth centuries when private citizens begin to assemble in free and open spaces, relatively unfettered by inequalities of status or role. He describes the phenomenon as "an intermediary structure between the political system on the one hand, and the private sectors of the lifeworld and functional systems, on the other" (Habermas 1996, 393), which provides a forum where citizens openly and freely interact with the intent to motivate others to act in concert toward collectively held goals. This is made possible by a bracketing out of social inequalities whereby all participants are recognized as communicative equals who share a normative background of mutually recognized validity conditions regarding what counts as uttering true, sincere, and just speech acts, and who are committed to purely symmetrical forms of discourse that allow those shared validity conditions to be freely and openly brought into play. This entails an embrace of normatively based procedures such as mutual recognition, hermeneutic sensitivity, and reciprocal perspective taking, all meant to ensure that validity claims can be produced, questioned, and contested without reservation. Insofar as such procedures themselves carry a prescriptive force, they may be said to exemplify an emancipatory potential.

Critics of Habermas's thesis have expressed dissatisfaction with its apparent underestimation of the bourgeois public sphere's historical record of exclusionary practices. Fraser, for example, has argued that the bourgeois public sphere should be recognized not so much as a domain of freedom and openness but rather as "the arena, the training ground, and eventually the power base of a stratum of bourgeois men, who were coming to see themselves as a 'universal class' . . . and who excoriated alternative public spheres in an effort to block broader participation" (Fraser 1990, 61). A parallel line of critique by Negt and Kluge (1993) has underscored the class-based character of the bourgeois public sphere which delegitimated those who lacked private property or cultural capital. And yet others have linked the bourgeois public sphere in the United States to an ideology of racial supremacy that portrayed the black world "as an irrational, illiterate, owned, nonbourgeois community of chattel," its potentials denied, and public membership being out of the question (Baker 1999, 271). These critics also note Habermas's relative neglect of excluded groups, voiceless in the bourgeois public sphere but not silent in their alternatively constituted lifeworld practices that at different points have crystallized into contestatory public spheres from which social movements have been launched (Calhoun 1992). Indeed, it is likely that the bourgeois order blocked broader participation of these groups because they *were* often combative (as well as highly literate) and posed a significant challenge to the dominant public sphere. As Eley notes, by neglecting excluded oppositional other, Habermas misses the extent to which the public sphere was always constituted by conflict, and not solely conflict with absolutism, for "it necessarily addressed the problem of popular containment as well" (Eley 1992, 306).

Habermas has granted the validity of these concerns but without relinquishing his core theoretical proposition: exclusionary practices and the pressures behind them may indeed work at cross purposes with the ideals of open and free communication, and in so doing they represent a degradation of the public sphere; yet admitting this does not undercut the idea that open and free communication instantiated itself within the public sphere qua prescriptive ideals that by their very presence posed a critical challenge to emergent or residual rationales for exclusionary practices. Habermas's defense is not that the communicative ideals of the bourgeois public sphere have effectively overcome any and all practical obstacles, but that the articulated emergence of such ideals, however contradicted by nondemocratic ideologies and the exclusionary practices they support, nevertheless has radically transformed the landscape of public discourse. Power-based intrusions within the public sphere, on this view, are admittedly troublesome, but Habermas argues that these kinds of exclusionary practices, irrespective of who wields them or their targets, have been difficult to uphold because of public-sphere expectations that they discursively validate themselves out in the open where any and all validity claims may be critically assessed and publicly contested (Habermas 1996, 373–76; Keane, 1988). States Habermas: "independently of their cultural backgrounds all the participants intuitively know quite well that a consensus based on conviction cannot come about as long as symmetry relations do not exist among the participants—relations of mutual recognition, reciprocal perspective-taking, a shared willingness to consider one's own tradition with the eyes of the stranger and *to learn* from one another, and so forth" (Habermas 1998, 169).

Habermas also concedes that he may have underemphasized the import of counterpublics that developed in response to the bourgeois public sphere's exclusionary practices (Habermas 1992, 427). But again he argues that greater consideration of alternative public spheres should not necessarily weaken his thesis; for alternative publics may be presumed to share with the dominant the same normatively backed conditions for producing, questioning, and contesting validity claims, as well as the procedures that ensure that such conditions are realized. Here he distinguishes between two forms of excluded otherness, one having been vividly detailed in Foucault's works where "there is no communication between those within and those without," and where "[t]hose who participate in the [dominant] discourse do not share a common language with the protesting others" (Habermas 1992, 429). A second emerges with bourgeois publicness and is contrasted with the first by a presence of shared communicative norms and procedures. As free and open conditions of discourse characterize the bourgeois public sphere, so they are available *in derivative form* within alternative public spheres, as a *permeability of boundaries* between the bourgeois public sphere and its alternatives is assumed: "Bourgeois publicness . . . is articulated in discourses that provided areas of *common ground* not only for the labor movement but also for . . . the feminist movement. Contact with these movements in turn transformed those discourses and the structures of the public sphere itself from within" (Habermas 1992, 429) (emphasis added).

It bears noting that Habermas's responses call out for empirical support. Yet Habermas has offered little in the way of analysis of the discrepant aspects of emancipatory communication and exclusionary practices, on the one hand, and emergent counterpublics as responses to bourgeois publicness, on the other. This poses difficulties for those seeking to examine the role of power in its relation to publicness—its manifestations in exclusionary practices as well as its propensity to disguise its practices from those it targets or to hide its motivations from even its own practitioners—as little analytical guidance is offered with respect to how, i.e., under what conditions, power-based practices and their justifying ideologies might be made transparent to public-sphere participants (Bohman 1986, 141; Horowitz 1998, 19).

Consider, for example, the antebellum period in the United States when the South's public sphere consisted largely of slaveholders who denied the discrepancies "between [Enlightenment] ideals and certain lethal patterns of behavior . . . developed through acts of unconscious and self-deceiving compromise" (Davis 1978, 52). Denial and self-deception were perpetuated in public-sphere venues such as Southern farm journals in which pieces "were written by Southerners for Southerners, all of whom shared a common concern" and who shared the belief "that the black was hopelessly inferior to the white and, while deserving humane treatment, was created for the benefit of the superior race" (Breeden 1980, xi). Those who disagreed faced formidable obstacles, including the hegemony of law whereby it appeared to be "mere egotism and antisocial behavior to attempt to go outside the law unless one [was] prepared to attack the entire legal system and therefore the consensual framework of the body politic" (Genovese 1974, 27–28). Although it is conceivable that this monolith of thought might have been effectively broken down at some point without external intervention, it is not at all clear, given the extent of the dominant ideology—backed by a planter class that "wielded power through its monopoly on knowledge as well as property [and that] controlled the appointment and livelihood of teachers, postmasters, and village newspaper editors"—whether that point might have arrived sooner rather than later.

Habermas's claims of a common ground—the existence of derivative communicative forms and permeable boundaries between dominant and alternative public spheres—also seem to invite a suspension of belief both as to how power operates in relation to excluded other and how it is resisted (Baumeister 2003; Deveaux 2000). These claims not only seem to ignore the modes of communicative distortion that are deployed by the dominant in order to restrict the flow of communication between itself and excluded other, but also fail to appreciate the full significance of how other organizes itself in opposition, to the extent perhaps of enacting a comparatively more open and free set of discursive practices than its dominant counterpart, and this in the face of a dominant public sphere that may be in denial of the restrictive nature of its own discursive practices. Here there appears a certain irony involved in the call for analysts to view the relation of dominant and excluded other from the standpoint of what both commonly share, not from what might have rendered them distinct and oppositional or what contributes to their ongoing division. Foucault's analyses of dominant and other, as Habermas notes, may indicate an absence of shared discursive resources; but they nevertheless trace out pivotal interplays of power and resistance that produce change. Habermas's thesis, in contrast, stresses a shared commonality of discursive norms and processes available to both dominant and other, but does not provide a detailed account of how such common ground might have produced transformations either between or within dominant and oppositional public spheres.

To briefly summarize, there is validity to concerns raised that Habermas's thesis has not been attentive enough to the dialectical tensions between dominant and its resistant other. Habermas has acknowledged the validity of such claims, though without fully incorporating their contents into his overall analytical perspective. This bears negatively on the overall effectiveness of his project. For analyses of forms of otherness, the contents of their dissatisfaction as well as the kinds of normative alternative they offer— interesting in their own right—not only might shed critical light on the possible shortcomings of the dominant they oppose but also contribute to a better theoretical understanding of the possible routes emergent normative ideals may take when confronted by real power (James 2004, 59). This is to suggest that Habermas's overall analytical perspective needs to be more fully developed in light of what he acknowledges to be valid criticisms. I more fully elaborate this point in the following section.

THEORETICAL FOUNDATIONS OF THE BOURGEOIS PUBLIC SPHERE: COMMUNICATIVE AND STRATEGIC ACTION

For Habermas, a quintessential feature of the bourgeois public sphere is "all those conditions of communication under which there can come into being a discursive formation of opinion and will on the part of a public composed of citizens of a state" (1996, 446). Through public discourse, autonomous citizens openly engage one another and do so with the expectation that fellow citizens' opinions or willful decisions are true, sincerely expressed, and grounded in acceptable notions of rightness; and where such expectations appear to be violated or otherwise unfulfilled, so the public sphere provides an atmosphere wherein the sincerity, truth, or rightness of participants' discursive offerings can be openly questioned or challenged by communicative means. It is in fact the openness of the communicative process wherein validity claims are raised and contested that distinguishes this form of communication—what Habermas terms communicative action— from others: "I have called the type of interaction in which all participants harmonize their individual plans of action with one another and thus pursue their illocutionary aims *without reservation* 'communicative action' " (Habermas1984, 294).

Communicative action consists of three distinct features. First, pure symmetry is presupposed among interactants, irrespective of contradictory social forces outside the communicative process such as social inequalities, institutional goals, self- or group interests. Second, while interactants may harbor a strategic desire to motivate one another, this is achieved by rational means (as distinct from causal means such as coercion or deception), which consists of presenting one's case truthfully, sincerely, and appropriately, as well as being open to questions, challenges, or counterclaims that may emanate from other. And, third, efforts to motivate other must be done with transparency as to one's own motivations, i.e., without secrecy, deceit, or deception. Each of these three carries a prescriptive force grounded in communicative interactants' shared commitment to the background norms for uttering validity claims as well as the procedural norms meant to ensure that claims of truth, truthfulness, and rightness may be discursively put to the test within the open community.

Communicative action is contrasted with strategic action, which is of three types: openly strategic action, manipulation, and systematically distorted communication. In openly strategic action, one or more interactants attempt to bring about desired ends such as success in war or attainment of economic or political goals, but as Habermas notes, "background consensus is lacking; the truthfulness of expressed intention is not expected; and the norm conformity of an utterance (or the rightness of the norm itself) is presupposed in a different sense than in communicative action—namely, contingently" (Habermas 1979, 118). Openly strategic action, unlike communicative action, proceeds without pretense of symmetry between interlocutors but rather appears to be most frequently used in its absence—e.g., when conditions between dominant and subordinate are such that the former sees pure symmetry as a threat to the status quo and the latter feels no other communicative option is feasible.[2] Manipulation, in contrast, involves one of the interlocutors appealing to the norms that inhere in communicative action in a deliberately deceptive manner so as to influence an otherwise unsuspecting other—e.g., utterances of a statement the speaker knows to be untrue but used strategically to promote a personal or institutional interest with the hope that the hearer will fail to recognize the ruse (Habermas 1984, 272–337).

In systematically distorted communication, like-minded interactants also opt for strategic means *but without conscious awareness of so doing*.[3] That is, one or both interactants may believe they are engaging in a way that accords with communicative action's normative background conditions of truth, truthfulness, and rightness as well as the processes of rationality, openness, and transparency of motive that are meant to ensure they are put into play; but in fact they are self-deceived in that those conditions and processes have in some respect been rendered subordinate to the aims of strategic action. Cooke (1994, 148) clarifies what has been offered by Habermas in sometimes sketchy form by noting that systematically distorted communication exerts itself in "the regulation of the normative context in which discussion takes place; it regulates who is allowed to participate in which discussion, who can initiate topics, who can bring the discussion to a close, who can contribute and in which order, how the topics are ordered and how the scope of the discussion is determined, etc." (Cooke 1994, 148). Systematically distorted communication thereby disrupts all that is assumed within communicative action—viz., connections of meaning and validity, meaning and intention, speaking and acting (Bohman 1986, 336)—and does so not occasionally but systematically. Some examples are as follows:

- Institutional norms prohibit certain styles of self-expressivity, perhaps on putative grounds that some styles reflect lack of civility, though without interactants' conscious reflection upon or discussion of the restrictive nature of such norms.
- Institutional norms emphasize that truth claims must have objective standing and be delivered impartially, thereby either militating against the raising of subjective truth claims or prohibiting overtly biased representation of such, and done without interactants' conscious recognition of the restrictive nature of the practice.
- Institutional expectations are that actors regard extant law as nonfallible and so regard stated positions predicated on grounds outside of law to be illegitimate, thus sealing off inquiry into extralegal challenges to the dominant order of things, and enforced without interactants' awareness of the possible fallibility of law, need for challenges to it, or the extent to which the practice is itself restrictive.

In the preceding examples, agents may engage in an unreflective censorship of self or other—both occurring outside the bounds of dialogically produced understanding—that effectively discourages some expressive styles, truth claims, or moral views. When exercised as a matter of routine—i.e., systematically—by many or all socialized actors, such censorship may not only effectively undercut the potential for some forms of reflection or discourse but may also form the rationale for the enforcement of prohibitive entry requirements in various spheres of discourse.

Although varied forms of strategic action are most pervasive in institutional life, they also intrude into public sphere life, deployed frequently to further money, state, or other power-based interests (Elster 1998). In these cases, communicative and strategic action may become entangled with one another despite their clear distinctiveness at the conceptual level.[4] For example, interactants who engage in systematically distorted communication may proceed as if there is symmetry among all public sphere interactants when in fact there is not symmetry, with consensus thus turning out to be false consensus marked by interactants assuming themselves to be acting in accord with the norms of communicative action and without awareness of how the norms are in fact being violated. Or, perhaps some groups, in response to systematically distorted communication that deflects attention away from forced asymmetry and its harmful effects, may feel compelled to utilize openly strategic communication.

The presence of strategic action within the bourgeois public sphere is problematic for Habermas's thesis in that it seems to undercut his claim that public-sphere communication makes ideologically biased claims increasingly difficult to sustain. Both manipulation and systematically distorted communication, for example, disguise their strategic motivations. And while perhaps the former may ultimately be exposed as strategic on account of the clarity of its effects upon previously unsuspecting interactants, this is not necessarily the case with the latter.[5] For if systematically distorted communication is present, then suitable discursive conditions may not be in play to render violations of conditions or procedures of communicative action readily apparent to interactants, and thus their intuitive knowledge as communicative beings may simply not be sufficient to critically cut through the perlocutionary fog of profit, control, containment, or other by-products of systematically distorted communication. It may not be readily apparent either to participant actors or third-person observers, that is, whether public-sphere practices are being constituted through the norms of communicative action or only on the illusion of such.

Enter here the significance of otherness. Habermas, it may be recalled, emphasizes the *shared qualities* of dominant public and other and is confident that other's enactments of derivative communicative forms of otherness, combined with porous boundaries between dominant and other, ensure that the prescriptive force of the norms of communicative action will prevail. But what if systematically distorted communication seals off public-sphere boundaries while at the same time locking out those it deems to be illegitimate? From whence then the inclination on the part of interactants to identify the distortion and to critically overcome it

Table 11.1 Openly Strategic and Communicative Action

Communicative Form	*Pure Symmetry*	*Asymmetry: Uphill/Downhill*
Openly strategic action	(–)	(+)
	Violates norms of communicative action	Distorted communication as pretender to communicative action
Communicative action	(+)	(–)
	Conforms to all normative background conditions	Systematically distorted communication disguises contradiction between asymmetry and presumed norms of communicative action.

when they themselves are self-deceived *and* dismissive of excluded other? Should not analysts feel compelled to look beyond the restrictive bounds of bourgeois publicness for the challenges otherness offers? Such questions are meant to suggest that it is not sufficient to grant that other may produce "countereffects that cannot be neutralized" (Habermas 1992, 427) but to then treat other's discursive productions as mere derivations of bourgeois public sphere practices. Indeed, the hypothesis here is that other, qua excluded other, may contribute communicative forms—e.g., openly strategic communication—that might both expose the otherwise invisible workings of systematically distorted communication and invite new ways of disentangling the complex weavings of strategic and communicative action.

What is needed at this point is a stereoscopic analysis of the type called for by Habermas, but which focuses uncompromisingly on the significance of otherness in relation to bourgeois publicness. Such an analysis would be used both as a means to discover how the blinkered practices of systematically distorted communication may be illuminated in possibly unexpected ways by the very practices of those who have been locked out and whose own discursive contributions have been otherwise stymied, and perhaps as well to shine light on the subterranean passageways through which alternative discourse wends its way in the face of systematic containment.

A STEREOSCOPIC ANALYSIS OF BOURGEOIS AND COUNTERBOURGEOIS PRACTICES: THE PRESS

Focus on the mass media may potentially enhance our understanding of public-sphere practices. The press, for example, has a significant role as public-sphere participant. As an essential medium through which flows a great deal of information, analysis, and opinion, it always carries the potential to facilitate citizen engagement with issues of fact, norm, and value. Moreover, the press actively selects what is newsworthy and commands a privileged position as to how it interpretively shapes it. A challenge for analysts, therefore, is to ascertain both how the emancipatory impulses of communicative action are blunted by the demands of strategic action and how the barriers to the fulfillment of communicative action imposed by strategic action are effectively countered. Yet to restrict analysis solely to bourgeois public-sphere practices as exemplified by the mainstream press may not be adequate to the task, especially if public-sphere interactants are immersed within systematically distorted communication. A case in point is the *New York Times*, an agenda-setting newspaper frequently regarded as a standard bearer of journalistic excellence (Diamond 1994; Jones 1999; Salisbury 1980). Committed to being the "newspaper of record" (Talese 1969), its editors, journalists, and features writers are expected to conform to a clear set of institutional guidelines that for many decades have been set forth in *The New York Times Manual of Style and Usage* (1999). Consider three of the highest standards promoted in this "Holy Writ" (Shepard 1996, 306) for the newspaper's employees: First, in keeping with "the *Times*'s impression of its educated and sophisticated readership—traditional but not tradition-bound"—the manual recommends "a fluid style, easygoing but not slangy and only occasionally colloquial" (*Manual* 1999, viii). Slang, for example, is associated with flippancy and the manual cautions against its use, for "it can create the embarrassing spectacle of a grown-up who tries to pass for an adolescent" (*Manual* 1999, 307). Second, in keeping with the avowed aim to print "all the news that is fit to print," the manual upholds the *Times*'s credo (Talese 1969): "To give the news impartially, without fear or favor, regardless of any party, sect or interest involved." This entails favoring "constructions that keep language neutral, a crystalline medium through which journalists report ideas without proclaiming stances" (*Manual* 1999, viii). And third, the manual claims to "differentiate itself by taking a stand for civility in public discourse . . ." and does so by counseling respect for group sensibilities. The manual cautions against offensive or coy hints, for example, as well as slurs: "The epithets of bigotry ordinarily have no place in the newspaper. Even in ironic or self-mocking quotations about a speaker's own group—their use erodes the worthy inhibition against brutality in public discourse" (*Manual* 1999, 308).

On the surface these standards appear to be unimpeachably high and have contributed to the newspaper's credibility in the world of journalism. They help to ensure that the *Times* provides information and news analyses that are unbiased and impartial, delivered in a sophisticated style whereby the newspaper is seen to have placed itself above the fray of social conflict. Nevertheless, questions arise as to how these standards might exclude or otherwise effectively limit certain forms of discourse and thereby stifle public debate (Conaway 1999; Crimp 1990; Kim 2000). For example, does not perhaps the newspaper's emphasis on "a fluid style" as opposed to that which is "slangy" (viii) or "coarse" (240) militate against discursive styles that *are* "slangy" or "coarse"? If so, does the voice of groups that typically resort to "slang" or "coarse" language make its way into the newspaper, and if so how is it represented? By the same token, what visibility is granted to subjective truths within an institution so rigorously committed to standards of objectivity? Will overtly biased truth claims that are not conveyed impartially or that are in need of additional interpretation find inclusion within "all the news that is fit to print?" And in its unwillingness to print materials in a way that might offend some readers' moral sensibilities, might not the newspaper (however unwittingly) be aligning itself with some groups or institutions in opposition to others? What then becomes of claims or arguments that challenge, say, existing legal or institutional frameworks in ways that at the same time offend the moral sensibilities of (dominant) groups?

These kinds of questions appear especially valid when considered in light of the journalistic work conducted in at least 278 African American–owned and –operated newspapers printed across the United States (Owens 1999). The black press qua "fighting press" (Myrdal 1944, 908) has affirmed the discontent of its thirteen million readers with the mainstream press and shaped it into constructive nonviolent opposition (Tuch and Weitzer 1997). In this capacity the black press has provided information and interpretation otherwise deemed unfit to print by its mainstream counterparts. It has provided a sounding board for minority opinions that would not otherwise have been aired. And it has actively laid the semantic groundwork for critique of and active engagement with dominant groups and institutions not ordinarily found within the mainstream press. In these ways and others the black press has attempted to stimulate public dialogue not otherwise attempted by the mainstream press. Indeed, what bears noting here is that as worthy opposition to the mainstream press, the black press may offer a critical perspective on the extent to which either authoritarian or emancipatory potentials are or are not realized—a perspective perhaps not readily available to mainstream press practitioners, readers, or analysts, and especially so if they are caught up unknowingly in systematically distorted communication (e.g., Davis 2005; Huspek 2004, 2005; Ross and Camara 2005).

In what follows, I offer a brief stereoscopic analysis of the practices of two newspapers, the *New York Times* and its oppositional counterpart, the black-owned and -operated *New York Amsterdam News*. The analysis examines contrastive dimensions between the two newspapers with special emphasis on how their respective practices facilitate or restrict expression and contestation of validity claims associated with truth, rightness, and self-expressivity. More specifically, the analysis offers a critical assessment of the extent to which both newspapers provide the widest range of discursive potential in the interest of opening the public sphere to a variety of validity claims. Do the two newspapers permit stylistic diversity of self-expression? Do the newspapers provide adequate space for competing truth claims? Are normative challenges to the legal-political order given a fair hearing? These questions are addressed by a contrastive reading of both New York–based newspapers' coverage of the "same event"—here the police shooting of an unarmed twenty-two-year-old Guinean immigrant, Amadou Diallo, who was shot and killed after police officers fired at least forty-one bullets and struck him nineteen times—described as "a major symbolic event in the history of the city" (Toobin 2000, 38).

Expressivity in Styles of Reportage

Although both the *New York Times* and *Amsterdam News* raised criticism regarding the fatal shooting of Diallo, significant differences in style of coverage existed between the two newspapers. The *Times*, for example, frequently voiced criticism regarding any possible justification for forty-one shots having been fired at an unarmed person. Yet, in keeping with the *Style Manual's* guidelines, without exception reporters exhibited stylistic restraint and other "markers of civility," thereby placing the newspaper above the fray of angry street talk.

> ... things are not always what they seem at first, a truism that can be forgotten in times of passion. But it seems worth bearing in mind in the stomach-wrenching death of Amadou Diallo, the unarmed African immigrant gunned down in the Bronx by four police officers who fired an almost inconceivable 41 bullets at him ... No one is suggesting that Mr. Diallo did anything to warrant such a response, and it is obvious that something went terribly wrong. But charged words like "murderers," "massacre," and "execution" have been casually tossed around in street protests ... While the anger is understandable, it is unclear how anyone can reach such damning conclusions based upon available evidence. (Haberman 12 February 1999, B1)

In contrast, the *Amsterdam News* draws no clear line between civil and 'uncivil' speech. In editorials and analytical reports blended together in common cause as openly strategic communication, the newspaper produces a steady stream of hyperbole and invective aimed at the New York Police Department and Mayor Giuliani. With a foregrounding of 'highly charged words' of black activist leaders, references are made to the "slaughter," "execution," and "assassination" of Diallo in the context of widespread "acts of brutality" carried out by "Giuliani's storm troopers" (Tatum 24 February 1999, 12). "The New York Police Department's Street Crimes Units," states protest leader Khallid Mohammed, "are nothing more than organized death squads" (Reyes 24 February 1999, 3). And the SCU is described further as "a death squad coven of neo-fascist hit men in New York whose motto is 'We own the night'" (Baraka 17 March 1999, 12). Drawing upon the language of the street, the black newspaper refers to the "maniac in office," Mayor Giuliani, as "Fuhrer Giuliani" and "Dictator Giuliani," a "weak lily-livered monster" who, like Dracula, "wants to taste more blood" (Maddox 24 February 1999, 3; Pryce 17 March 1999, 4; Tatum 3 March 1999, 12). Over several weeks the hyperbolic attacks continued:

> Giuliani is a zero, zero in our book, for he has a license for his 40,000 minions who are called policemen to go out and murder anyone they like. It should not appear strange to you, or anyone else for that matter, that Giuliani's latter-day "storm troopers" have not slaughtered a single person who is white ... Why is it so? We cannot answer that, but if Giuliani is such an expert at dispatching Black youngsters and Black adults—many who have done absolutely nothing—why, then, is it so difficult for him to demand the holding of white policemen who have been accused of murder by eyewitnesses? (Tatum 24 February 1999, 12)

"Cussin' out," "abusing," and "reading," all of which involve "denigrating another to his or her face in an unsubtle and unambiguous manner" (Morgan 1998, 263), are "straightforward, unmitigated insults meant to be taken personally . . ." (Spears 2001, 246). Yet they are not meant to inflict emotional pain upon its target. Expressed by a historically oppressed group, the assumption is that the insult is being delivered "uphill," so to speak, and unlikely therefore to hurt as an insult might that is rolled "downhill" by a power-holding other. Nor is this directness meant to silence targeted other, but to the contrary its intention is to shake up other, to make them "fightin' mad" (Brown 1972)—mad enough perhaps even to acknowledge the sources of the "read" and, ideally, fire back an exchange. As Smitherman has noted, "Like it's not personal, it's business . . . the business of playing in and with the Word" (Smitherman 2000, 223); and the "business" here is to open up dialogue where there has been none. Calling Rudy Giuliani a "monster" or "maniac," on this view, is an invitation for the Mayor to enjoin in dialogue within a larger context where the *Amsterdam News* has been repeatedly told by the Mayor's communication director that "It is not in our interest to talk with you" (Tatum interview 2004).

"All the News That's Fit to Print": Contrastive Truths

Differences in styles of discourse between the two newspapers raise questions as to the role of truth validity claims within each newspaper. For the *Amsterdam News*, the question is whether openly strategic communication must necessarily work at cross-purposes with the offering of truth validity claims, their contents, and the normatively based procedures for questioning or challenging them. For the *Times*, a different question is posed: Can a mainstream newspaper that upholds a standard of stylistic restraint adequately represent truth claims and guarantee procedures for airing, questioning, and challenging them when they are offered up by those who transgress the newspaper's institutional-specific standards of discursive civility?

Here I note two important dimensions of contrast. First, the *Amsterdam News*' mission is to truthfully represent the world to its readers, but to do so in a way that "opens things up whether readers agree or not" (Tatum interview 2004). In this sense the black newspaper neither claims to offer all the news that is fit to print, nor does it rigidly embrace an ideal of impartiality. Indeed, the assumption of its writers and editors appears to be that the newspaper's readers—most of whom read also the mainstream press—expect biased reporting, and read the newspaper with the knowledge that another (albeit unstated) bias can be found in the counterweight of information, analysis, and opinion of the mainstream press. And it is likely for this reason that the writers and editors of the *Amsterdam News* seem unconcerned that their rhetoric might perform a manipulative role in relation to its readers. A significant difference between the two newspapers is that although both exemplify biased reporting, only one admits it while its counterpart touts high standards of impartiality. By offering truth claims that it knows are contestable, and offering them in an emotionally charged manner that is meant to stimulate open contestation, the *Amsterdam News* assumes that a community actively engaged in sorting through unambiguously biased truth claims is preferable to one that believes itself to be reading a nonbiased presentation of "all the news that is fit to print."

Second, there is some irony in that the *Amsterdam News* uses emotional language not simply to arouse its readers but also to stimulate reasoned assessment and debate with respect to officials' claims and the way they are presented in mainstream media. The black newspaper's truth validity claims, delivered in an emotionally arousing way, are meant primarily to provoke spirited and informed debate. In contrast, the *Times'* use of "constructions that keep language neutral, a crystalline medium through which journalists report ideas without proclaiming stances" (*Manual of Style and Usage* 1999, viii), may not only discourage emotional arousal but also stoke readers' fears of inflamed black citizen insurgency in real but undetected ways; for the position that excludes biased truth validity claims that are carried in emotionally highly charged constructions might well convey a conviction that such constructions exist beyond the pale of "civil" discourse and thus pose a threat to civic order.[6]

"No Justice, No Peace!" Challenges to Authoritatively Backed Norms

If challenges to societal norms and the "systemic inertia of institutional politics" (Habermas 1996, 383) are to be adequately reflected upon and publicly discussed, they must often be conveyed through mass media wherein inhere both emancipatory and authoritarian potentials. Yet the *Times'* coverage of the shooting and its aftermath, in hundreds of articles, shows a newspaper steering through the Scylla of community disapprobation and the Charybdis of state-sanctioned order. The newspaper raises criticisms with respect to forty-one shots being fired and seeks out facts that might shed light on the matter. It raises community-based grievances against the SCU's aggressive tactics, and in several analytical pieces Rudy Giuliani is called upon to open dialogue with black community leaders. Yet such probes and suggestions are offered without significant challenge to existing law and institutional arrangement. From the moment Diallo went down, for example, controversy swirled around his killers who were required by superiors to provide no verbal or signed statements, were administered no drug tests, and were permitted to leave the scene of the shooting without being interviewed. The newspaper laments the dearth of information regarding the case but in a way that always defers to the forty-eight-hour rule's umbrella of protection for police officers. In this case, the officers' attorneys advised their clients to withhold all comment until the state pressed charges against

Habermas and Oppositional Public Spheres 227

them. But this provision, too, undergoes no scrutiny: "the officers, like any other citizens, cannot be compelled to talk because of constitutional rights against self-incrimination" (Flynn 14 February 1999, A38).

The *Amsterdam News*, in contrast, combines expressive style and biased truth validity claims in an effort to press beyond the constraining parameters of existing law and institutional arrangement—in this instance as both appeared to be used to fortify a "blue wall of silence" behind which the officers were allowed to hide.

> If four policemen of African ancestry had wantonly executed a European immigrant anywhere in New York City with a hail of 41 bullets, Mayor Rudolph Giuliani would have instinctively snatched the badges from their chests and the lethal weapons from their hips before ordering them held incommunicado without bail at a local lockup. He would then assure all Europeans that punishment would be swift and certain. (Maddox 24 February 1999, 13)
>
> . . . go downtown and shoot some cracker 41 times and see what happens. (Boyd 3 March 1999, quoting Alton Maddox, 3)
>
> If the 4 police officers had shot a horse in front of the Plaza Hotel, the whole city would be outraged. (24 March 1999, AN, Boyd quoting Rep. Charles Rangel, 1)

Differences between both newspapers in this area are significant in that they may reflect either an emancipatory or authoritarian impulse. Here it is worth noting Dryzek's (1996, 476) comment that citizen pressures for greater democracy "almost always emanate from civil society, rarely or never from the state itself." And in this regard what we see is a community-based power that challenges the limits of state administrative power being channeled freely through the *Amsterdam News*, and much less so through the *Times*. In other words, discourse on existing laws and institutional arrangement is more imbued with questions and challenges in the former than in the latter.

DISCUSSION

In response to his critics, Habermas has claimed that the normative force of communicative action within the bourgeois public sphere effectively counters the objectifying strains of strategic action that emanate from and sustain intrusive state, money, or other power-based interests. The claim remains unredeemed, however, in that it lacks empirical demonstration of the mechanisms of conflict between communicative and strategic action, as well as the specific pathways by which the normative force of the former is said to eventually prevail. This is problematic for Habermas's thesis both empirically and conceptually. Historical evidence shows that long-standing exclusionary practices within the bourgeois public sphere have been eliminated neither quickly nor completely; and Habermas's own concept of systematically distorted communication also raises concern about prolonged tension between communicative and strategic action. For insofar as the presence of systematically distorted communication within the bourgeois public sphere remains unrecognized for what it is by those who routinely reproduce it, there appears to be no guarantee that it can be disentangled from, or made to eventually bow to, the normative force of communicative action.[7]

A related difficulty for his thesis is its underestimation of those who are locked out of bourgeois publicness as a result of dominant's deployments of strategic action. Although Habermas acknowledges the difficulty, he has offered little to suggest how otherness as expressed by shadow publics might best be incorporated into his thesis. His suggestion that the dominant public sphere and alternative publics share aspects of communicative action and that porous boundaries ensure some degree of blend is intriguing but underdeveloped. Does the directional flow of communicative action move from dominant to alternative, or vice versa? And through what kinds of mechanisms might the flow be either dammed up or released?

In taking up Habermas's call for a stereoscopic analysis that examines public-sphere tensions between communicative and strategic action, I have argued that consideration of alternative publics is requisite in light of Habermas's underestimation of exclusionary practices and possible misreading of the directional flow of both communicative forms. Otherness, that is, as reflected in the communicative practices of alternative shadow publics, is viewed, first, for what it may reveal as limits to realizations of communicative action within the dominant public sphere that may otherwise not be apparent either to participants or third-person observers. Second, the concentration on otherness is based on the possibility that there exist alternative tributaries of communicative practice that spring from alternative publics' ongoing struggles to speak and be heard in response to dominants' exclusionary tendencies. In this sense, otherness may not simply be a recipient of derived variants of communicative action as Habermas suggests, but rather asserts itself as a driving force that aims to remedy the silence inherent in systematically distorted communication that poses as communicative action.

The analysis can claim some success in both respects. Comparison and contrast of the *New York Times* and *Amsterdam News* coverage confirmed some of the "working hypotheses" that emerged from consideration of the former's *Manual for Style and Usage*, specifically those relevant to expressive styles, truth validity claims, and challenges to the normative bases of existing law, institutions, and policies. Consideration of the *Amsterdam News* reveals a noteworthy range of exclusions on the part of the *Times* perhaps not otherwise apparent to either its practitioners or third-person observers. Stylistic nuance, slang, and colloquialisms that have claimed a legitimate place within the African American rhetorical tradition and that are given a free rein within the black newspaper's coverage appear to find no entry point into the prestigious mainstream newspaper. Truth validity claims expressed through openly biased representations of reality of a type widely promulgated in the *Amsterdam News* are rarely if ever aired in the *Times*. And irreverent challenges to the political-legal order that are commonplace in the *Amsterdam News* are not given much of a hearing by its mainstream counterpart.

Exclusions such as these suggest a presence of systematically distorted communication at the *Times*, as tendencies to act upon the normative background conditions and procedures of communicative action are short-circuited by what appear to be an ideologically cast set of beliefs and practices. Consequently, all citizens are affected: an active community of dissenting citizens, effectively hived off from the body politic, feels compelled to voice opposition strategically in the most hyperbolic of terms; and the "majority" is deprived of hearing a range of dissenting opinion that, in J. S. Mill's terms, carries the potential to elevate public discourse via examination of otherwise unexamined principles and beliefs, as well as either to correct prevailing falsehoods or to strengthen already-held convictions of truth or rightness.

The analysis does not restrict itself solely to the discourse of other and the modes by which it is suppressed, but also draws upon Habermas's extensive work on normative background conditions and processes through which communicative action is exercised and considers the possibility that precisely those openly strategic communicative forms and offerings found in the *Amsterdam News* but given no hearing in the *New York Times* may beckon readers toward realization of a closer approximation to the ideals of communicative action than the hidden strategic forms—viz., systematically distorted communication—that rationalize their exclusion. This is not to say that the contents of the *Amsterdam News*' communicative offerings are more sincere, true, or just than those of the *Times*, as such considerations are best left for citizens to decide after reflection and debate.[8] Here emphasis is placed upon the normative background conditions and processes that are necessary if self-expression, truth, and justice are to receive a free and open hearing. And in these respects, the *Amsterdam News* appears to outperform its mainstream counterpart. In bold, emotion-arousing strokes, readers are notified where the writer fits within a universe of conflicting claims of truth and rightness. Opening salvos are launched with the intent to engage readers on the expectation that they will respond and so participate in an atmosphere of open contestation and debate. Truth validity claims, presented in a transparently biased manner, are meant not to provide closure to a set of questions or concerns but rather to crack open the confining parameters of the mainstream's impartiality and so unleash new dialogic possibilities. And claims of rightness, insofar as they challenge readers' sensibilities bound up with identifications with extant law and institutional power, strike at the very heart of collective repression, entreating subjects to reflect upon and discuss validity claims that tend otherwise to go unvoiced within a taken-for-granted legal-institutional order.

The normative force of each of these facets of communication—self-expressivity, truth, rightness—is conveyed despite a bias that is worn on the writer's sleeve.[9] In this respect, strategically advanced validity claims, whether they are harnessed to individual or group interests, may be inconsistent with the norms of communicative action only to the extent that they close off opportunities for one or both interactants to question or challenge in open and free dialogue. And as this analysis has suggested, the motives expressed in the *Amsterdam News*' coverage are transparent in ways that open up dialogic possibilities that are missing in its mainstream counterpart's tendencies to suppress any revelation of its own biases through institutional standards of civility, impartiality, and moral sensibility.

CONCLUSION

This chapter has not meant to suggest that an overhaul of Habermas's discourse-centered theoretical approach is in order, but indeed has relied heavily upon it throughout. Nevertheless, the chapter has suggested that Habermas's thesis regarding the bourgeois public sphere needs to be redirected with focus placed upon the counterpractices of those who believe themselves to be locked out from "legitimate" public discourse. Redirection is necessary not only as a precondition for discerning how sources of communicative action may perhaps have dried up within the bourgeois public sphere but also as an indispensable means of exploring real emancipatory alternatives that spring up as voices from the bottom of the well, oriented to reaching understanding, and expressed on the assumption that people's upward struggles against power and domination have not yet been completed. To state that such discourse-based alternatives are derivatives of a source of communicative action (that may or may not still be available) risks giving credence to the idea that the alternatives are secondary to the bourgeois public sphere, mere afterthoughts that are to be considered important only to the extent they share that which emerged at one historical moment in bourgeois struggles against absolutism. The analysis conducted here suggests that alternative public spheres be viewed as possible originating sources of discursive action that spring forth spontaneously from people's needs as they address unjust life conditions that confront them.

NOTES

1. Bohman (1996, 110) notes a vicious cycle that can occur when dominant groups develop practices that rationalize the exclusion of subordinate groups from public-sphere participation, and then turn silence into "consent" (Bohman 1996, 110). Others (Kim 2000; Mendelberg 2001) have discussed how pernicious ideologies are used in subtle ways that exclude subordinate

groups and are veiled in ways that discourage critical reflection among those who apply them.
2. Snyder discusses how elites may feel threatened by increased pressures to democratize as well as the strategic tactics adopted by less powerful groups in response to elites' "persuasive" attempts to forestall further democratization (Snyder 2000, 36–56). For additional discussions of the communicative tactics of excluded groups, see McAdam (1982); James (2004); Eyerman and Jamison (1991); and Herbst (1994).
3. "Whereas in systematically distorted communication at least one of the participants deceives himself about the fact that the basis of consensual action is only apparently being maintained, the manipulator deceives at least one of the other participants about his own strategic attitude, in which he deliberately behaves in a pseudoconsensual manner" (Habermas 1979, 210).
4. James suggests that Habermas's conceptual distinction between communicative and strategic action may be too brittle as an analytical device in the face of complex entanglements of the two communicative forms in empirical settings (James 2004, 85).
5. Elster (1998) offers a number of instances when resort to manipulation in the public sphere may be constrained in the face of shared communicative norms.
6. Mendelberg (2001) and Kim (2000) both offer accounts of how the "civility" of "colorblind" talk is used to discourage "uncivil" challenges that point to the relevance of race. See also Huspek's discussion of a mainstream newspaper's uses of symbolic violence in its descriptions of the "fiery rhetoric" of African-American leaders in the United States (Huspek 2004).
7. It is on account of the entanglement perhaps that so many have tended to emphasize the political force of strategic action not only as it emanates from dominant groups but from oppositional groups as well. See, for example, Joas (1988), Berger (1983), Honneth (1991), Heller (1984), and Gunson and Collins (1997).
8. Indeed, as studies by Kim (2000), Conaway (1999), Cho (1993), and Snyder (2000) suggest, there may be contexts in which the offerings of subordinate groups may fall short of expanding democracy in ways that more closely approximate the norms of communicative action. Such unhappy instances seem to be more likely when social conflict spills beyond a simple dominant versus subordinate dichotomy—e.g., when contestation between multiple ethnic groups adds to social complexity.
9. If I understand Habermas correctly, to enter a communicative context with a set of strategic interests and an intention to motivate others to adopt it is not necessarily at odds with communicative action. What sets off strategic action from communicative action is not one's interests or aims but whether or not one shows a willingness to truthfully, sincerely, and appropriately advance validity claims, to entertain other's validity claims, to respect the normative procedures of communicative action, and to emend one's position when confronted with a better argument.

REFERENCES

Alexander, Elizabeth. 1995. "Can you be black and look like this?" Reading the Rodney King videos. In *The black public sphere*, ed. Black Public Sphere Collective, 81–98. Chicago: University of Chicago.

Baker, Houston, Jr. 1999. Critical memory and the black public sphere. In *Culture, memory and the construction of identity*, ed. Dan Ben-Amos and Liliane Weissberg. Detroit: Wayne State University.

Barkley Brown, Elsa. 1995. Negotiating and transforming the public sphere: African-American political life in the transition from slavery to freedom. In *The black public sphere*, ed. The Black Public Sphere Collective, 111–50. Chicago: University of Chicago.

Baumeister, Andrea. 2003. Habermas: Discourse and cultural diversity. *Political Studies* 51(4):740–58.

Berger, Johannes. 1983. Review of J. Habermas's "Theorie des Kommunikativen Handelns." *Telos* 57:194–205.

Blaug, Robert. 1997. Between fear and disappointment: Critical, empirical and political uses of Habermas. *Political Studies* 45(1):100–17.

Bohman, John. 1986. Formal pragmatics and social criticism: The philosophy of language and the critique of ideology in Habermas's "Theory of communicative action." *Philosophy and Social Criticism* 11(4):332–52.

———. 1996. *Public deliberation: Pluralism, complexity, and democracy*. Cambridge, MA, and London: MIT Press.

Breeden, J. O. 1980. Introduction. In *Advice among masters: The ideal in slave management in the Old South*, ed. J. O. Breeden. Westport, CT: Greenwood.

Brown, H. Rap. 1972. Street talk. In *Rappin' and stylin' out: Communication in urban black America*, ed. Thomas Kochman, 205–8. Urbana: University of Illinois.

Calhoun, Craig. 1992. Introduction: Habermas and the public sphere. In *Habermas and the public sphere*, ed. Craig Calhoun, 1–31. Cambridge, MA: MIT Press.

Cho, Sumi. 1993. Korean Americans vs. African Americans: Conflict and construction. In *Reading Rodney King/Reading urban uprising*, ed. R. Gooding-Williams, 196–214. New York and London: Routledge.

Conaway, Carol. 1999. Crown Heights: Politics and press coverage of the race war that wasn't. *Polity* 32(1):93–118.

Cooke, Maeve. 1994. *Language and reason: A study of Habermas's pragmatics*. Cambridge, MA: MIT Press.

Crimp, Douglas (with A. Rolston). 1990. *AIDS demographics*. Seattle: Bay Press.

Davis, David Brion. 1978. Slavery and the American mind. In *Perspectives and irony in American slavery*, ed. H. P. Owens, 51–69. Jackson: University of Mississippi.

Davis, Olga. 2005. Vigilance and solidarity in the rhetoric of the black press: *The Tulsa Star*. *Journal of Intergroup Relations* 32(3):32–47.

Deveaux, Monique. 2000. *Cultural pluralism and dilemmas of justice*. Ithaca, NY, and London: Cornell University Press.

Diamond, E. 1994. *Behind the Times: Inside the New New York Times*. New York: Villard.

Dryzek, John. 1996. Political inclusion and the dynamics of democratization. *American Political Science Review* 90(1):475–87.

Eley, Geoff. 1992. Nations, publics and political cultures: Placing Habermas in the nineteenth century. In *Habermas and the public sphere*, ed. Craig Calhoun. Cambridge, MA: MIT Press.

Elster, Jon. 1998. Deliberation and constitution making. In *Deliberative democracy*, ed. Jon Elster, 97–122. Cambridge: Cambridge University Press.

Eyerman, Ron, and Andrew Jamison. 1991. *Social movements: A cognitive approach*. Cambridge: Polity Press.

Forester, John. 1985. *Critical theory and public life*. London: MIT Press.

Fraser, Nancy. 1990. Rethinking the public sphere: A contribution to the critique of actually existing democracy. *Social Text* 25/26:56–80.
Genovese, Eugene. 1974. *Roll, Jordan, roll: The world the slaves made*. New York: Vintage.
Gregory, Stephen. 1995. Race, identity and political activism: The shifting contours of the African American public sphere. In *The black public sphere*, ed. The Black Public Sphere Collective, 151–68. Chicago: University of Chicago Press.
Gunson, Darryl, and Chik Collins. 1997. From the I to the we: Discourse ethics, identity and the pragmatics of partnership in the west of Scotland. *Communication Theory* 7(4):278–300.
Habermas, Jurgen. 1979. *Communication and the evolution of society*. Trans. by Thomas McCarthy. Boston: Beacon.
———. 1984. *Theory of communicative action, Vol. 1: Reason and the rationalization of society*. Trans. by Thomas McCarthy. Boston: Beacon.
———. 1987. *Theory of communicative action, Vol. 2: Lifeworld and system*. Trans. by Thomas McCarthy. Boston: Beacon.
———. 1989 [1962]. *Structural transformation of the public sphere*. Trans. by Thomas Berger. Cambridge, MA: MIT Press.
———. 1990. *Moral consciousness and communicative action*. Trans. by Christian Lenhardt and Shierry Weber Nicholsen. Cambridge, MA: MIT Press.
———. 1992a. *Postmetaphysical thinking*. Trans. by William Mark Hohengarten. Cambridge, MA: MIT Press.
———. 1992b. Further reflections on the public sphere in Craig Calhoun, ed., *Habermas and the public sphere*. Cambridge, MA: MIT Press.
———. 1993. *Justification and application: Remarks on discourse ethics*. Trans. by Ciaran Cronin. Cambridge, MA: MIT Press.
———. 1996. *Between facts and norms*. Trans. by William Rehg. Cambridge, MA: MIT Press.
———. 1998. Remarks on legitimation through human rights. *Philosophy and Social Criticism* 24(2/3):157–71.
Hall, Stuart. 1997. The local and the global: Globalization and ethnicity. In *Dangerous liaisons: Gender, nation and postcolonial perspectives*, ed. A. McClintock, A. Mufti and E. Shohat, 173–87. Minneapolis: University of Minnesota Press.
Heller, Agnes. 1984. *Radical philosophy*. Oxford: Basil Blackwell.
Herbst, Susan. 1994. *Politics at the margin: Historical studies of public expression outside the mainstream*. Cambridge and New York: Cambridge.
Honneth, Axel. 1991. *The critique of power*. Trans. by Kenneth Baynes. Cambridge, MA: MIT Press.
Horowitz, Asher. 1998. "Like a tangled mobile": Reason and reification in the quasi-dialectical theory of Jurgen Habermas. *Philosophy and Social Criticism* 24(1):1–23.
Huspek, Michael. 2004. Black press, white press, and their opposition: The case of the police killing of Tyisha Miller. *Social Justice* 31(1–2):217–41.
———. 2005. "From the standpoint of the white man's world:" The black press and contemporary white media scholarship, with emphasis upon the work of W. Lance Bennett. *Journal of Intergroup Relations* 32(3):67–88.
Hutton, Frankie. 1995. Democratic idealism in the black press. In *Outsiders in 19th-century press history: Multicultural perspectives*, ed. Frankie Hutton and B. S. Reed, 5–20. Bowling Green: Bowling Green State University Popular Press.
Jagger, Alison. 2000. Multicultural democracy. In *Deliberation, democracy and the media*, ed. S. Chambers and A. Costain, 27–46. New York: Rowan & Littlefield.

James, Michael Rabinder. 2004. *Deliberative democracy and the plural polity.* Lawrence: University of Kansas Press.
Joas, Hans. 1988. The unhappy marriage of hermeneutics and functionalism. *Praxis International* 8(1):34–51.
Johnson, James. 1991. Habermas on strategic and communicative Action. *Political Theory* 19(2):181–201.
Jones, A. 1999. *The trust: The private and powerful family behind the New York Times.* New York: Brown.
Keane, John. 1988. *Democracy and civil society.* London: Verso.
Kim, Claire Jean. 2000. *Bitter fruit: The politics of Black-Korean conflict in New York City.* New Haven, CT, and London: Yale University Press.
Kochman, Thomas. 1981. *Black and white styles in conflict.* Chicago and London: University of Chicago Press.
McAdam, Doug. 1982. *Political process and the development of black insurgency 1930–1970.* Chicago and London: University of Chicago Press.
McCarthy, Thomas. 1978. *The critical theory of Jurgen Habermas.* Cambridge, MA: MIT Press.
Mendelberg, Tali. 2001 *The race card: Campaign strategy, implicit messages, and the norm of equality.* Princeton: Princeton University Press.
Morgan, Marcyliena. 1998. More than a mood or an attitude: Discourse and verbal genres in African-American culture. In *African-American English: Structure, history and use,* ed. S. Mufwene, J. Rickford, G. Bailey, and J. Baugh, 251–81. London and New York: Routledge.
Myrdal, Gunnar. 1944. *An American dilemma.* New York and London: Harper and Bros.
Negt, Oscar, and Alexander Kluge. 1993 [1972]. *Public sphere and experience: Toward an analysis of the bourgeois and proletarian public spheres.* Minneapolis: University of Minnesota Press.
Newkirk, Pamela. 2000. *Within the veil: Black journalists, white Media.* New York: New York University Press.
New York Amsterdam News
24 February 1999. Wilbert A. Tatum: Giuliani: A Monster in Our Midst, p. 12.
24 February 1999. Damasco Reyes: Protests Follow Diallo Funeral, p. 3.
24 February 1999. Alton Maddox, Jr.: No Justice! No peace! p. 13.
3 March 1999. Herb Boyd: Amadou Diallo's Homegoing: Sharpton and Cochran to Lead Case against PBA, p. 3.
3 March 1999. Wilbert A. Tatum: It's Only a Matter of Time: Giuliani's Political Demise, p. 12.
17 March 1999. Amiri Baraka: The Rise of U.S. Black-Aimed Death Squads Among the Police, p. 12.
17 March 1999. Vinette K. Pryce: Women's Scorn Lands on City Hall, p. 4.
17 March 1999. Damasco Reyes: Young Voices Echo at City Hall, p. 1.
24 March 1999. Herb Boyd: New York's Honor Roll, p. 1. New York Times
12 February 1999. Clyde Haberman: A Shooting, and Shooting from the Hip, p. B1.
14 February 1999. Kevin Flynn: Shooting in the Bronx: The Investigation; Four Officers Not Obliged to Explain Shooting, p. A38.
3 April 1999. Dan Barry and Kevin Flynn: Top Giuliani Aide Said to Experience Racial Bias by Police, p. A1
New York Times Manual of Style and Usage. 1999. New York: Random House.
Owens, Reginald. 1999. Entering the 21st century: Oppression and the African-American press. In *Mediated messages and African-American culture,* ed. V. T. Berry and C. Manning-Miller, 96–116. Thousand Oaks, CA: Sage.

Ross, Felecia, and Sakile Camara. 2005. The African-American press and the holocaust. *Journal of Intergroup Relations* 32(3):32–47.
Ruane, Joseph, and Jennifer Todd. 1988. The application of critical theory. *Political Studies* 36(3):533–58.
Salisbury, H. 1980. *Without fear or favor: The New York Times and its times.* New York: Times Books.
Shepard, R. 1996. *The paper's papers: A reporter's journey through the archives of the New York Times.* New York: Random House.
Smitherman, Geneva. 2000 *Talkin' that talk: Language, culture and education in African America.* New York: Routledge.
Snyder, Jack. 2000. *From voting to violence: Democratization and nationalist conflict.* New York and London: Norton.
Spears, Arthur. 2001. Directness in the use of African American English. In *Sociocultural and historical contexts of African-American English*, ed. S. L. Lanehart, 239–60. Amsterdam and Philadelphia: John Benjamins.
Talese, Gay. 1969. *The kingdom and the power.* New York: World Publishing.
Toobin, J. 2000 *The unasked question. New Yorker*, 76(2):38–44.
Tuch, Steven, and Ronald Weitzer. 1997. The polls-trends: Racial differences in attitudes toward the police. *Public Opinion Quarterly* 61:642–63.

12 The Rational Bases of Transgressive Rhetoric

Michael Huspek

Deliberative democracy's ideal of communicative equality guarantees all prospective participants a level playing field upon which to propose, question, and critique courses of collective action and to have their expressed ideas recognized and engaged by others (Cohen 1989; Dryzek 2000; Gutmann and Thompson 2004; Habermas 2006). This is thought to improve the quality of political life for all. It opens up to minority groups distinctive means by which to exert influence within the political order, as their voice is received and responded to on its own merits, irrespective of social rank, status or role; and, by so doing, it curbs majority tendencies to suppress minority viewpoints beneath aggregates of quantitative data as found in public opinion polls, electoral results, and apportioned representational schemes (Habermas 2006). The ideal offers up for majorities as well as minorities broadened opportunities for expanded dialogue, greater deliberation of ideas, and thus enhanced prospects for informed and reflective collective action by an enlightened public (Habermas 2006; Bohman 1996; James 2004).

At the same time, communicative rights within deliberative democracy are accompanied by obligations on the part of participants to act in a rational manner. Following Habermas (1979, 1982, 1984), processes that ensure the rights to express, question and challenge validity claims also stipulate that interlocutors conduct themselves rationally, i.e., in accordance with the rightful expectation that their claims attempt to be sincere, truthful, and appropriate (just). This, in turn, entails that interlocutors support their claims with reasons, that they recognize the claims of others, and that they compromise when warranted. These aspects of rational discourse are indispensable to deliberative democracy. They make possible shared understandings and consensus-based courses of action arrived at within an atmosphere of mutual trust (e.g., McKeon 1954; Williams 1998); and where they are absent, discourses are likely to collapse under the weight of actors' self-doubt, delusion, mistrust of others and other pathologies that germinate within atmospheres of sheer power and demagoguery (Habermas 1982).

The complementary relation of both ideals—equal opportunity participation and rational discourse—appears relatively unproblematic where deliberative democracy itself stands as already achieved ideal. Indeed, it is difficult to imagine how the ideal of equality *could* set itself up against the ideal of rational discourse, or that discourse that upholds rational standards such as openness to criticism *could* co-exist with exclusionary practices, as either course would justly earn the charge of being self-contradictory. Imperfect democracies that fall short of being fully deliberative are another matter, however, as in such instances the complementary relation of both ideals can be problematic. In the absence of full communicative equality, for example, excluded groups' appeals for recognition and engagement from already legitimated groups may go unheeded, perhaps spurring increasingly transgressive rhetorical forms and strategies that shock or offend and thereby earn the assessment that such forms and strategies violate norms of rational discourse. Such assessments, in turn, may then stand as basis for continued exclusion of the transgressors from significant zones of participation. The history of the ethnic press in the United States is a case in point (e.g., Detweiler 1922; Huntzicker 1999; O'Kelly 1982; Simmons 1998; Wolseley 1971). As minority groups' appeals for inclusion as equal communicative participants in the public sphere have often been ignored or rejected—at times even subject to violent attack (Squires 2001)—so their rhetoric has expressed a greater urgency, conveyed by hyperbole, irony, insult and other forms that appear to violate rational discourse-based expectations of truthfulness, sincerity and appropriateness. Such rhetoric has thus elicited charges of irrationality, which is suggested in Shah and Thornton's comment as to how majority audiences in the United States have perceived the ethnic minority press "as professionally unaccomplished, self-serving, gossipy, vulgar, corrupt, and a danger to the more accomplished traditional journalism of the general circulation press" (Shah and Thornton 2004, 235).

The historical experiences of the ethnic press in the United States are emblematic of the dilemma faced by imperfect democracies that aim to be more deliberative. As Dryzek states it, although we know that the rhetoric of excluded groups conveys much that can positively contribute to an increasingly enlightened populace, it also can bring with it coercion, emotional manipulation, and a host of other dangers (Dryzek 2000, 52, 67). Young, too, after making a compelling case for the significant place of rhetoric in the public sphere as necessary supplement to rational argument, then cautions that rhetoric may at times be "strategically manipulated to win the assent of others simply by flattery or fantasy and not by reason" (Dryzek 2000, 77). Now, as Dryzek and Young are both well aware, while such danger should not be underestimated, the cost of excluding some groups from deliberative arenas is itself dangerously high; for how *can* deliberative democracy satisfy the ideal of communicative equality and its commitment to inclusiveness when some groups are barred from admission? In what follows, I address the dilemma by asking the following: How *should* historically excluded groups appeal for recognition and engagement where significant channels of rational discourse have been closed off? And what *should* be the desired response of audiences whose moral sensibilities may be shocked or offended by excluded groups' transgressive rhetorical forms and strategies?

Both questions call for a normative response, which I attempt to develop in this essay. Yet it bears noting that the questions are derived from empirically situated practices of exclusion, on the one hand, transgressive response, on the other, a fuller understanding of which may serve as useful preliminary to normative queries and conclusions. To this end, I begin the essay with a brief case study of the rhetoric of the black owned and operated *New York Amsterdam News*, in relation to that of *The New York Times*, with special attention directed toward some of its transgressive elements (e.g., irony, hyperbole, insult), what motivates the transgressions, and why they persist. After the empirical preliminary, I then analyze the transgressions themselves in light of standards of rational discourse. The analysis, I go on to argue, supports the claim that although transgressive rhetoric may understandably violate the expectations of rational discourse, it by no means should be considered irrational until genuine recognition and engagement with the rhetoric reveals it to be such; nor for similar reasons should it be banished from spheres of public dialogue. Rather, it is best viewed as expression of frustration in the face of systematic inequalities, voiced in protest against ongoing practices of exclusion, and meant as an appeal for recognition and engagement as prerequisite to democratic discourse that is genuinely egalitarian and rational. Understood in this way, audiences which previously have withheld recognition and engagement are faced with the moral obligation to drop walled defenses against excluded groups, despite their transgressive rhetoric and the shock value or offensiveness it delivers. I conclude the essay by arguing that the divide between transgressive rhetoric and the perception of its irrationality can be bridged, and I suggest what the bridgework might look like.

THE CASE OF BLACK PRESS RHETORIC

Since publication in 1827 of the first African-American newspaper in the United States, *Freedom's Journal*, the black press has taken on a leadership role within the black community that has involved collecting and disseminating information otherwise absent from the white mainstream press, providing a sounding board for minority opinions not otherwise aired, and laying the semantic groundwork for critique of and active engagement with ideas not otherwise made available by its white mainstream counterpart. In this regard, the black press has met with a good deal of success as indicated by at least 278 black owned and operated newspapers printed across the United States, with a circulation of over 13 million (Owens 1999).

The black press has also sought to reach out to white majority audiences on the belief that injection of African-American points of view into public discourse might give cause for readers who are not African American to reflect upon and reevaluate their assumptions regarding race-related beliefs and practices. This strategy, however, has met with less success. Although most readers of black newspapers also read white mainstream newspapers, the same does not hold for a large majority of readers who tend not to read black newspapers either as primary source or as supplement to white newspapers (Newkirk 2000). Since many issues covered in black newspapers are not covered by white mainstream newspapers, this has left most Americans poorly informed about what is relevant to the black experience in the United States and thus poorly situated to respond to grievances rooted in that experience. This has been doubly frustrating for many African Americans. Surveys show a high degree of black reader dissatisfaction with white mainstream news coverage (Newkirk 2000, 18); and with black newspapers going largely unread by white majority audiences, African Americans view themselves as having few conventional channels through which their appeals might elicit recognition and uptake.

The black press has attempted to alleviate the frustration in two sometimes seemingly contradictory respects. First, it has positioned itself as outspoken critic of institutional structures and practices within the United States, particularly as these pertain to the black experience (e.g., Davis 2005; Huspek 2004, 2005), in order to mobilize black political protest. Second, in order to further open up possibilities for reconciliation between the races, the black press has continued to voice appeals for recognition and understanding from the majority populace (Hutton 1995). In advancing both strategies, black press rhetoric has often been transgressive, challenging dominant social and political practices but also the very discursive structures used by majority groups to legitimate such practices (Huspek 2007a). In this regard, hyperbole, irony, insult, and other transgressive modes of rhetoric have been deployed to shock or offend as a means to elicit attention and uptake from otherwise unheeding audiences. While this rhetorical strategy is understandable in light of the African-American experience in the United States, its effectiveness has often crashed against the shoals of an unheeding and unsympathetic majority populace that has raised standards of truth, civility, and moral sensibility as rationale for continued engagement. How this can play out in empirical arenas may be illustrated by a brief contrastive analysis of the rhetoric of two newspapers, *The New York Times*, and its oppositional counterpart, the black owned and operated *New York Amsterdam News*, with special focus upon both newspapers' coverage and analysis of a tragic event that had great relevance for African Americans, viz., New York City police officers' shooting of Amadou Diallo and its aftermath.

THE SHOOTING OF AMADOU DIALLO AND ITS AFTERMATH

On a February evening in 1999, four New York City plainclothes polices officers approached Amadou Diallo who was standing inside the vestibule of his Bronx apartment building, and moments after ordering Diallo to place his hands in the air, fired 41 shots and killed the unarmed, 22-year-old Guinean immigrant. The shooting, described by one commentator as "a major symbolic event in the history of the city" (Toobin 2000, 38), received a good deal of public attention and was covered expansively by news media. Yet, since there were no witnesses at the scene, and Diallo's killers withheld commentary until summoned to testify at a criminal trial almost a full year later, there was little substantive information to report. This contributed to public frustration, and the city's population divided over how to interpret the shooting and subsequent events. On one side were those who argued that there could have been no conceivable justification for firing 41 shots at an unarmed man. Their criticisms were often directed at Police Commissioner Howard Safir and Mayor Rudolph Giuliani who, presiding over a controversial "stop and frisk" policy by nonuniformed police that targeted primarily people of color in New York's low income neighborhoods, were claimed to be as responsible for the killing of Diallo as were the officers who fired the shots. Nonviolent protests were taken to the streets on a daily basis and staged for several months until the police officers were tried and acquitted in Albany, New York, some 140 miles from the scene of Diallo's death. Among those on the other side of the divide were city officials, most visibly Mayor Giuliani, who urged citizens to withhold judgment. A fair investigation was underway, he assured the public; and after criminal charges were eventually filed he insisted that the officers should be tried in a court of law, not by public opinion.

The New York Times and *Amsterdam News* tended to align themselves with the opposing sides. The former's alignment was somewhat obscured by its avowed search for a proper balance amid assurances that it sought to position itself above the fray. Nevertheless, the highly respected newspaper with nearly 1.1 million subscribers nearly always supported the views of the city's officials. Its expressions of shock and horror at the shooting were intermixed with a good deal of empathy for the officers who had pulled the trigger; its acknowledgment of highly controversial tactics used by the city's police force was offset by praise for the force's effective work against crime; and its calls that justice be served settled unequivocally upon the city's criminal justice system as the desired arbiter. In the course of choosing sides in this manner the newspaper tended also to delegitimize the opinions aired and courses of action taken "out on the street," beyond official institutional boundaries.

> . . . things are not always what they seem at first, a truism that can be forgotten in times of passion. But it seems worth bearing in mind in the stomach-wrenching death of Amadou Diallo, the unarmed African immigrant gunned down in the Bronx by four police officers who fired an almost inconceivable 41 bullets at him . . . No one is suggesting that Mr. Diallo did anything to warrant such a response, and it is obvious that something went terribly wrong. But charged words

The Rational Bases of Transgressive Rhetoric   241

like 'murderers', 'massacre', and 'execution' have been casually tossed around in street protests . . . While the anger is understandable, it is unclear how anyone can reach such damning conclusions based upon available evidence (*NYT*: Haberman 1999).

It is noteworthy in the above that the *New York Times* draws attention to "charged words" that have been "casually tossed around on the street" but fails to seriously engage their propositional contents as were no doubt expressed within context-specific validity claims. In so doing, the newspaper raises the specter of public outcry but then simultaneously dismisses its significance, which then leaves the newspaper's readers with the impression that use of such "charged words" is a condemnable act that warrants no serious consideration or engagement. Rationale for this type of practice can be located in the *New York Times Manual of Style and Usage* (1999) which sets forth institutional guidelines for the newspaper's writers. Consider three standards that are promoted in the *Manual*. First, in keeping with "the *Times's* impression of its educated and sophisticated readership—traditional but not tradition-bound," the *Manual* recommends a "fluid style, easygoing but not slangy and only occasionally colloquial" (viii). Slang, for example, is associated with flippancy and the *Manual* cautions against its use, for "it can create the embarrassing spectacle of a grown-up who tries to pass for an adolescent" (307). Second, in keeping with the avowed aim to print "all the news that is fit to print" the *Manual* upholds the *Times'* credo: "To give the news impartially, without fear or favor, regardless of any party, sect or interest involved" (Talese 1969: 29). This entails favoring "constructions that keep language neutral, a crystalline medium through which journalists report ideas without proclaiming stances" (*Manual*, viii). And third, the *Manual* claims to "differentiate itself by taking a stand for civility in public discourse" and does so by counseling respect for group sensibilities (*Manual*, 240). The *Manual* cautions against offensive or coy hints, for example, as well as slurs: "The epithets of bigotry ordinarily have no place in the newspaper. Even in ironic or self-mocking quotations about a speaker's own group—their use erodes the worthy inhibition against brutality in public discourse" (*Manual*, 308).

Such standards give the appearance of a newspaper committed to truth seeking conducted in an impartial manner and delivered in a sophisticated style that places the newspaper above the fray of social conflict. Yet there is good reason to believe that adherence to such standards limits certain forms of discourse and thereby stifles public debate (Conaway 1999; Crimp 1990; Kim 2000). Specifically, the *Times'* standards seem to exclude overtly biased truth claims that are delivered in "slangy" or "course" terms. This places those groups who do advance overtly biased truth claims in a "slangy" or "course" manner at a serious disadvantage; for the *Manual* and the practices it prescribes effectively ensures that transgressors' views do not get printed as they are expressed in the vernacular. This effectively renders transgressors dependent on reporters who may either dismiss their opinions and viewpoints outright or translate them into terms that may not do justice to their originally expressed views. The latter possibility seems more likely as indicated by the *Times'* coverage of public displays of political activism and its frequent allusions to undercurrents of danger associated with the nonviolent protests. One of the *Times'* journalists, for example, fretted that public protest of the police shooting "could inflame racial tension" (NYT: Thompson 1999), while others described the nonviolent protests as "angry demonstration[s]" that had become "nearly a daily rite" (NYT: Flynn 1999) as "fractious crowds," "sometimes unruly," and "tumultuous" (NYT: Sachs 1999) were said to be "yelling," "chanting," "demanding," "denouncing," "shouting obscenities at police" and "pumping their fists into the air" (NYT: Bumiller and Thompson 1999). One reporter stressed how a Muslim guard "swatted and screamed at those caught up in the crush" (NYT: Sachs 1999), and another noted how "those who came to wave angry banners were penned behind police barricades on Seventh Avenue" (NYT: Randolph 1999).

The implied undercurrent of danger was often complemented with an inordinate fixation upon protesters' racial composition, nationality or other characteristics of otherness (e.g., Ono and Sloop 2002): "though the crowd was mostly black and mostly female, there was a smattering of yarmulkes and Asian faces in the crowd" (NYT: Newman 1999). Such descriptions were rarely accompanied with serious reportage of the communicative contents of the protest gatherings, but rather pointed to the protesters' visible markings—e.g., "swathed in cream-colored African robes," at times wearing "turbans and sweeping white robes" and at others "gold robes and white African skullcaps" (NYT: Wilgoren 1999). The imagery is unmistakable. On one occasion protesters were said to have "danced around a drummer" and on another stress was placed upon "drumbeats of a Japanese Buddhist nun as a bus from Harlem unloaded about 40 protesters who waved antipolice placards while tramping through the mud" (NYT: Wong 1999).

Exclusion of the propositional contents of vernacular-voiced statements and expressions, along with metaphors of foreignness and racial otherness on the one hand, the threat of violence on the other, all suggest a form of coverage by the high-prestige newspaper that is disengaged from protesters and their messages. The newspaper's effort to speak on behalf of activists produces reportage and analysis that is at best superficial, at worst misleading. This leaves readers of the *New York Times* who are unexposed to alternative coverage both uninformed about how activist groups may experience the world and misinformed about how they seek to change it. This in turn contributes further frustration to activist groups and their supporters.

The *Amsterdam News*—New York City-based, with a subscription rate of approximately 50,000, and self-described as "an intrepid African American voice on controversial issues"—covered the police shooting of Amadou Diallo and its aftermath in distinctly different ways from that of its prestigious mainstream counterpart. Most indicative was the black newspaper's willingness to tap into the vernacular discourse and give it non-redacted expression in its news stories. Drawing upon the "street" perspective, the shooting was presented not as an isolated event, but rather part of an uninterrupted historical record of police lawlessness and brutality that invoked images of lynching and other acts of violence; not as an accidental tragedy, but rather a predictable outcome of a culture of racism that had been given free reign in New York's law enforcement apparatus; not as an event left to smolder beneath layers of ongoing legal and administrative procedure, but rather one that demanded an open airing by way of public protest and debate. These opposed views, moreover, were conveyed within an emotionally charged rhetoric that was conspicuously absent from the *New York Times*:

> If the 4 police officers had shot a horse in front of the Plaza Hotel, the whole city would be outraged. (AN: Boyd, quoting Rep. Charles Rangel, 1999)

> If four policemen of African ancestry had wantonly executed a European immigrant anywhere in New York City with a hail of 41 bullets, Mayor Rudolph Giuliani would have instinctively snatched the badges from their chests and the lethal weapons from their hips before ordering them held incommunicado without bail at a local lockup. He would then assure all Europeans that punishment would be swift and certain. (AN: Maddox Jr. 1999)

> . . . go downtown and shoot some cracker 41 times and see what happens. (AN: Boyd, quoting Alton Maddox, 1999)

Three rhetorical tropes are evident in the above: irony, hyperbole, and insult. Irony has long been an effective tool of black writers (Gates 1987; Fishkin and Peterson 2001), its uses aimed to plant an air of incredulousness in its readers as prelude to more serious reflection and debate. Above reference to the hypothetically slain horse, for example, is likely influenced by the uses of irony in slave narratives such as that of Frederick Douglass who, in the first paragraph of his own narrative wrote: "By far the larger part of slaves know as little of their ages as horses know of theirs, and it is the wish of most masters within my knowledge to keep their slaves thus ignorant" (Douglass 1845[1986]). Just as Douglass sought by means of irony to provoke a view of how slaves were regarded as something less than human, the *Amsterdam News* deploys the rhetorical form in order to tap into a wellspring of one group's collective memory and to appeal to another group befogged in collective amnesia to recall an age when slaves were treated on a par with plantation animals and to then use the recollection as basis for critical reflection upon the present (Baker Jr. 1999).

Hyperbole—as indicated vividly in the second of the above citations—functions in ways similar to irony in black press rhetoric (Gates 1988). High-pitched and often cast in a stylistic mode of black street vernacular, hyperbole foregoes rigorous adherence to truth validity claims aimed at empirical accuracy and instead expresses attention-getting moral outrage in response to enduring contradictions and hypocrisies of a white majority that appears blinkered by an ideology of colorblindness (Kim 2000; Mendelberg 2001). The shooting of Diallo is thus described as an "assassination," a "slaughter," an "act of brutality" (AN: Browne 1999), and an "execution" (AN: Knighton 1999) that was carried out by a "firing squad" (AN: Browne 1999), "Giuliani's storm troopers" (AN: Tatum 1999a), the "Mayor's goons" (AN: Boyd 1999), a "death squad coven of neo-fascist hit men" (AN: Reyes 1999).

Insults are also routinely deployed in black press rhetoric as indicated, for example, by reference to "cracker" in the third citation above. Typically, insults are aimed at public figures in leadership positions, as Mayor Giuliani, for example, is referred to as "a maniac in office," "Fuhrer Giuliani," and "Dictator Giuliani," a "weak, lily-livered monster" who "wants to taste more blood" (AN: Maddox 1999; AN: Pryce 1999; AN: Tatum 1999b):

> Giuliani is a zero, zero in our book, for he has a license for his 40,000 minions who are called policemen to go out and murder anyone they like. It should not appear strange to you, or anyone else for that matter, that Giuliani's latter-day 'storm troopers' have not slaughtered a single person who is white [. . .] Why is it so? We cannot answer that, but if Giuliani is such an expert at dispatching Black youngsters and Black adults—many who have done absolutely nothing—why, then, is it so difficult for him to demand the holding of white policemen who have been accused of murder by eyewitnesses? (AN: Tatum 1999).

All three tropes—irony, hyperbole, insult—are part of a transgressive rhetorical strategy of opposition to the discursive modes by which they are delivered to reading audiences in mainstream venues. And insofar as the rhetoric violates stylistics as legitimated in the *New York Times Manual*, so it appears also to violate the norms of rational discourse. Despite its transgressions, however, I believe it is a mistake either to conclude that they are irrational or that they deserve to be excluded from public spheres where rational discourse is accepted currency. This is especially true either where good faith efforts have not been made to understand the motivations for the transgressions or where genuine engagement has not been realistically offered. I shall develop this argument further below as basis for advancing the additional claim that communicative engagement with transgressors is a moral obligation if imperfect democracies are to more closely approximate deliberative ideals.

BLACK PRESS RHETORIC AS PROLEGOMENA TO RATIONAL DISCOURSE

Irony, hyperbole and insult can best be analyzed against the norms of rationality they transgress. In order to facilitate the analysis, Habermas' (1984) norms of sincerity, truth and justice are invoked here as exemplars of rational discourse within deliberative democracy. These norms take the form of presuppositions that are built into the discourse: speakers are expected to be sincere in terms of what inner states are expressed within their utterances; speakers are expected to be truthful in their efforts to represent the world; speakers' utterances are expected to be appropriate (i.e., to not violate conventional norms of propriety or decorum) in the issuance of moral claims. In contrast, black press rhetoric appears to position itself against each: irony against the norm of sincerity; hyperbole against the norm of truthfulness; insult against the moral sensibility contained in the norm of appropriateness (Huspek 2007a).

Consider again the above reference: "If the 4 officers had shot a horse in front of the Plaza Hotel, the whole city would be outraged." This statement is by no means meant to be taken literally, but rather uses irony in order to draw readers' attention to the speaker's intended meaning which emphasizes that the city has not been sufficiently disturbed by the shooting of Diallo and that the deficit of attention is likely a byproduct of enduring racial attitudes. The writer's intended meaning is conveyed by means of violating hearer's ordinary expectations within rational discourse—here specifically, the norm of sincerity. Thus, upon having their expectations disrupted, hearers might be provoked to offer a response such as "You don't really mean that do you?" or "You can't be serious!" Here, drawing upon John Searle's analysis of metaphors, we discern that the writer *intends* for his audience (1) to recognize an egregious violation of an otherwise standard validity claim and (2) to then "figure out what the speaker means" (Searle 1979, 76–116). This entails that the hearer "has to contribute more to the communication than just passive uptake—and does so by going through another and related semantic content from the one that is communicated" (Searle, 1979, 115). Should the hearer *will* the move from passive uptake to that of active engagement—admittedly a tenuous assumption (see below)—this is accomplished by resort to mutually shared background information, both linguistic and nonlinguistic, as well as powers of rationality and inference (Searle 1979, 112).

Hyperbole is no less transgressive and, as with irony, is meant to invite audiences to step beyond passive uptake and to show a willingness to engage in active dialogue. References to "execution," "firing squad" and "neo-fascist hit men" are not meant to be taken literally; nor does the writer expect that audiences, black or white, would take them so. Rather, these are meant to challenge the mainstream's conclusions, asserted for example by the *New York Times* without leaving room for debate, that the shooting of Amadou Diallo was simply a "tragedy" that occurred after "something went terribly wrong." Essential to the challenge is that it disrupt readers' ordinary understandings on the hope that it elicits active disagreement in the form of, say, "But that's not true!" or "Surely you're exaggerating aren't you?" that might then lead writer and audience alike to a more discursively shared, reflective understanding of the event.

A similar interpretation applies to variations of insult. Tropes such as "cussin' out," "abusing," and "reading" all involve "denigrating another to his or her face in an unsubtle and unambiguous meaner" (Morgan 1998, 263), and, in so doing, they violate the built-in expectation of rational discourse that utterances strive to be appropriate. Yet the tropes are not meant to inflict emotional pain upon their target. Since they are expressed by historically excluded groups, we can assume that the insult is being delivered "uphill" so to speak and therefore is unlikely to hurt as might an insult that is rolled "downhill" by privileged groups. Nor is their directness meant to silence the targeted other; to the contrary its intention is to make targeted others and those who speak in their defense "fighting mad" (Brown, 1972) – mad enough perhaps to acknowledge the sources of the "read" and, ideally, fire back an exchange.

A fuller understanding of black press rhetoric can be gained from consideration of Habermas' (1988) treatment of the world-disclosing significance of rhetoric, particularly as used in the realm of fiction. Once the rhetorical artist returns from the fictional realm, Habermas stresses, subjective wishes and desires must be pressed into the service of validity claims oriented toward shared, consensus-based understandings. The need for rhetoric therefore *recedes* in the face of other-oriented validity claims that are advanced, clarified and altered via the intersubjective dimension of dialogue so as to satisfy the general expectations of everyday practice, whether in phatic conversation or something more ambitious such as collective problem solving. Note how Habermas' view of rhetoric in the realm of fiction shares family resemblances with black press rhetoric that has often functioned historically as a group-specific *subjective* communicative form that calls for and awaits intersubjective recognition and engagement from majority audiences. Black press rhetoric's transgressive traits, on this view, are best regarded as prelude for discursive exchange of a kind that has previously been withheld. Its pitch is meant to entice an otherwise passive and unheeding audience into showing some response that, in turn, would then obligate those who have deployed transgressive irony, hyperbole and insult to more carefully defend or elaborate validity claims. This, again, would entail that the transgressive aspects of the rhetoric *recede* as subjective claims defer to intersubjective needs for shared understanding.

In imperfect democracies there are of course no guarantees that the appeals of black press rhetoric can succeed in eliciting recognition and engagement from audiences that have historically denied excluded groups meaningful access to these prerequisites of communicative equality and discourse-based rationality. However, where black press rhetoric *does* succeed – i.e., where it elicits recognition and engagement – *its transgressive ploys can be expected to recede, giving way to stylistics more in keeping with rational discourse.* Where it *does not* succeed, however, instead of progressive movement toward rational discourse, the opposite may occur whereby majority audiences, both mistakenly or willfully regard black rhetorical transgressions as violations of rational discourse and so use that view as rationale for continued nonrecognition and nonengagement. In this unhappy case, transgressive rhetoric *does not recede* in deference to the norms of rational discourse but rather *escalates within an atmosphere of increased frustration on the part of its users and more steeled resistance from its intended audiences.*

The unsuccessful outcome of transgressive rhetoric constitutes a double loss for deliberative democracy. With continued deployment of transgressive tactics, the rhetoric of excluded groups then continues to exist outside the bounds of discursive engagement with white majorities and so goes unchecked—neither effectively questioned nor challenged by stakeholders of other points of view—and thus ever susceptible to lapses into collective myth-making that may militate against the possibility for reaching shared understandings that bridge racial divides. For majority audiences, the ongoing exclusion of transgressive rhetoric creates an epistemic stunting whereby participants are deprived of valuable points of view that carry the potential for a more informed and reflective collective action.

NORMATIVE CONSIDERATIONS AND PRACTICAL BRIDGEWORK

The unsuccessful outcome of escalating transgressive rhetoric poses a strategic dilemma for its users, as there appears no obvious means by which to navigate between the poles of withheld communicative equality in the form of continued denials of recognition and engagement, on the one hand, and its own transgressive rhetoric that can potentially further alienate majority audiences, on the other. This dilemma is not caused by transgressive rhetoric, however; nor is it evident that transgressive rhetoric *should* be significantly altered or abandoned if the dilemma is to be overcome. As argued above, transgressive rhetoric is an understandable response to the systematic denial of communicative equality. It is eminently rational as an appeal for recognition and engagement along the way to genuinely rational discourse, and may on some occasions successfully achieve its goal.

This is not to glorify transgressive rhetoric, which always carries the risk of potentially alienating further those who hold up the exclusionary bar to genuine participation. Further, it bears repeating that insofar as transgressive rhetoric—at least initially—takes on something of a subjective life of its own, outside the bounds of genuine intersubjective engagement, its users may lapse into increased frustration and possible self-deception where transgressive validity claims go unchecked within a morass of ritualized, uncontested opposition where moral validity claims are neither adequately deciphered nor redeemed. Nevertheless, given the aims of transgressive rhetoric, there is sufficient warrant to argue that de-escalation of the rhetoric is called for *only if recognition and engagement are offered by significant others who have historically withheld such*. Acknowledgement of this point calls for a moral refocusing of the problem of transgressive rhetoric that involves shifting the burden from excluded groups to those whose practices and ideological justifications have enforced the exclusion.

Refocusing of the problem in the manner I have suggested is best conducted by means of speech act theory, with special emphasis upon the moral contents of interactions that involve requests, pleas, or appeals. Consider the example of a standard request:

Standard request: Will you kindly please pass the sugar?

Should the request be a reasonable one—the sugar being visibly within hearer's reach and outside of the speaker's own reach—we would expect the request to be granted. As users of a natural language, we know that requests that *can* be granted *should* be granted, unless hearer offers sufficient cause for *not* so granting: "So sorry, but my hands really are quite full right now," or "Maybe Dolores can reach it for you more easily?" Indeed, so secure are we in this knowledge, that should the denied request go without explanation, we feel justified in chastising the hearer.

There are of course requests that appear from hearer's standpoint to be unreasonable. Perhaps the sugar is clearly not within hearer's reach, or hearer knows that speaker's medical condition forbids the intake of sugar. In such a case, we'd have insufficient grounds for criticizing the hearer for not granting speaker's request. Nevertheless, the hearer can't so easily be let off the hook here; for a moral presumption built into the request is that *if the request can not or will not be granted, some stated reason must be provided*, and this irrespective of whether the request appears to be reasonable or not. Thus, where hearer withholds stated reason for not complying with speaker's request, hearer might then earn from the requester a justified moral prompt: "Okay, don't pass the sugar then; but won't you at least give me a reason why?" In sum, whether the request is reasonable or not, moral rules instantiated by the request within the communicative relationship between speaker and hearer obligate hearer to respond either by meeting the request or giving reasons for not so doing. (I believe a similar argument holds also for pleas and appeals.)

But what *is* a speaker to do if stonewalled by hearer? There are of course many options, ranging from exiting the situation to wringing hearer's neck. But probably an optimal response is communicative. Hence the following:

Hyperbolic request: Can't you see I'm absolutely dying for something sweet? Please pass me the sugar, won't you?

Insulting request: Can't you refrain from being such a selfish jerk and pass the sugar my way?

Ironic request: It's interesting that you seem to have no reservations when it comes to giving your horse a sweet treat: Do you not think you might find it within yourself to pass some of that sugar my way?

We noted precisely these kinds of transgression in the rhetoric of the Amsterdam News, understood as a strategic means to elicit uptake where straightforward appeals have gone unanswered. They violate standard expectations, and may even be found offensive to hearer's moral sensibilities. But we must bear in mind that the standard, nontransgressive request is likely to have already been issued, perhaps many times, and that these newly issued transgressive forms (1) emanate from a position of some justifiable frustration and (2) are aimed to offend hearer only incidentally as a condition for eliciting recognition and response. Thus, although their transgressive nature may likely violate majority audiences' expectations on some level, as a moral matter they deserve engaged uptake. Indeed, the real offense to the incomplete communicative interaction is not the transgressive discourse but rather the hearer's decision to deny recognition and uptake.

On this reasoning, a higher moral standing is accorded to excluded groups whose appeals have historically fallen short, and a moral call is issued to privileged groups and populations to recognize and respond to those appeals, irrespective of excluded groups' rhetorical transgressions. This should not be confused with the Hegelian view, recently recast as standpoint theory, that truth and justice *necessarily* belong to slaves, housed in their heightened consciousness that has developed out of their distinctive relation to masters; that slaves have learned to take masters' interests and dispositions into account, whereas masters have suppressed slaves' own interests and dispositions as a condition of denying slaves' humanity; and that slaves, therefore, are presumed to be better suited to develop understandings that unite masters and slaves in ways that potentially transcend the limits of their relationship. What distinguishes the view being developed here from that of the new Hegelians is the emphasis upon all that is communicative within the relationship between oppressed groups and their oppressors—an emphasis that is lacking in the Hegelian account. Although Hegelians may well be right to state that the slaves' position *may* be conducive to a higher consciousness, they are wrong to believe that this is inevitably a consequence of the master-slave relationship. Without there being genuine communicative engagement between masters and slaves, we cannot know with certainty whether the slaves' consciousness has truly transcended fear, desire for vengeance, or other emotions derived from the experience of slavery. Until, that is, slaves are recognized and engaged as communicative equals—their truth and moral validity claims being put to the test according to rules of rational discourse—any attributions of a higher consciousness are at best premature.

My argument is that deliberative democracy must ensure that the claims of excluded groups be put to the test, and that without so doing the quality of political life is negatively affected: the transgressive rhetoric of excluded groups, launched within a discursive void where validity claims elicit no uptake and thus go unchecked, may become susceptible to collective myth-making with only the weakest connections to reality; and if privileged groups and populations persist in withholding recognition and engagement, they deny themselves valuable prescriptive formulae provided by excluded groups that can point the way to a more genuine democratic order. Responsibility for implementing the conditions for shared dialogue, moreover, rests with those who historically have withheld their recognition and engagement. Requests, appeals and other speech acts conveyed in transgressive rhetoric cry out for a response. For majority audiences to withhold a response violates our most fundamental understandings as to how such speech acts generate a moral obligation to reciprocate with communicative uptake.

CONCLUSION

By way of conclusion, we might surmise how the claims conveyed in the transgressive rhetoric of excluded groups *are* best put to the test of public scrutiny within an open discursive environment. This is a task that has been undertaken by others. In discussing enclaved groups, for example, Sunstein has stated:

> It is not clear what can be done about this situation. But it certainly makes sense to consider communication initiatives that would ensure that people would be exposed to a range of reasonable views, not simply one. [. . .] An appreciation for group polarization suggests that creative approaches should be designed to ensure that people do not simply read their 'Daily Me'. (Sunstein 2001, 36)

In this regard, Bohman has recommended that deliberative democracy multiply "non-market avenues of mass public communication" as a means of "building up a vibrant political public sphere" (Bohman 1996, 141); and James has argued for state licensing practices that ensure a greater diversification of media (James 2004, 138).

These recommendations are a good start, but may not go far enough, as more far-reaching measures may be needed by which to bring alternative discourses into closer proximity with extant mainstream sources. Interesting in this regard, *The New York Times* has recently displayed on its

Internet site links to news analyses and editorial statements of major foreign newspapers such as *The Guardian* of London, *The Sydney Morning Herald*, and *The Daily Star* of Beirut. Now, the move to include black press rhetoric on its pages would not seem too much of a stretch, albeit the move *would* necessitate that the agenda-setting newspaper relax some of its stylistic requirements.

In the absence of voluntary inclusion, modest regulatory efforts may be in order. State-enforced dialogue opportunities would seem to offer no substantial intrusion into mainstream newspapers' reportage, analysis or opinion; nor would the practice *force* its readers to recognize and engage the oppositional views carried within transgressive rhetoric. It would, however, create a condition whereby more readers are brought into contact with points of view otherwise not readily available to them. And to the extent those viewpoints procure recognition and uptake, so the quality of public discourse would almost certainly be elevated. The mainstream media would find it much more difficult to mask its exclusionary reportage, as it is unlikely, for example, that the newspaper's biased coverage of political activism could withstand for long the criticisms of such emanating from its own pages. And ethnically based alternative media that have shown a penchant for hyperbole, insult, and other rhetorical tropes, finding themselves drawn into dialogues marked by genuine recognition and engagement between equals, might well feel compelled to tailor communicative forms to what has always been the expressed desire of oppressed peoples, real dialogue.

REFERENCES

Amsterdam News:
    Boyd, Herb (1999) "Amadou Diallo's homecoming: Sharpton and Cochran to lead case against PBA." 3 March.
    Boyd, Herb (1999) "New York's honor role." 24 March.
    Browne, J. Zamgba (1999) "Communities of color unite over slaughter." 17 Feb.
    Knighton, Gloria (1999) "Get the racist nuts off the squad." 3 March.
    Maddox Jr., Alton (1999) "No justice! No peace!" 24 Feb.
    Reyes, Damasco (1999). "Protests follow Diallo funeral." 24 Feb.
    Tatum, Wilbert (1999a) "Giuliani: A monster in our midst." 24 Feb.
    Tatum, Wilbert (1999b) "It's only a matter of time: Giuliani's political demise." 3 March.
Baker, Jr., Houston. 1999. Critical memory and the black public sphere. In *Cultural memory and the construction of identity*, ed. Dan Ben-Amos and Liliane Weissberg, 264–296. Detroit: Wayne State.
Bohman, James. 1996. *Public deliberation: Pluralism, complexity, and democracy*. Cambridge and London: MIT Press.
Brown, H. Rap. 1972. Street talk. In *Rappin' and stylin' out: Communication in urban black America*, ed. Thomas Kochman, 205–208. Urbana: University of Illinois.
Cohen, Joshua. 1989. Deliberation and democratic legitimacy. In *The good polity: Normative analyses of the state*, ed. A. Hamlin and P. Pettit, 17–34. London: Basil Blackwell.

Conaway, Carol. 1999. Crown Heights: Politics and press coverage of the race war that wasn't. *Polity* 32, 1: 98–118.
Crimp, Douglas (with A. Rolston). 1990. *AIDS Demographics*. Seattle: Bay Press.
Davis, Olga. 2005. Vigilance and solidarity in the rhetoric of the black press: The Tulsa Star. *Journal of Intergroup Relations* 32, 3: 9–31.
Detweiler, Frederick. 1922. *The Negro press in the United States*. College Park, Maryland: McGrath.
Douglass, Frederick. 1845[1986]. *Narrative of the life of Frederick Douglass, an American slave*. New York: Penguin.
Dryzek, John. 2000. *Deliberative democracy and beyond*. Oxford: Oxford University Press.
Fishkin, Shelley Fisher and Peterson, Carla 2001 "We hold these truths to be self-evident": The rhetoric of Frederick Douglass's journalism. In *The black press: New literary and historical essays*, ed. Todd Vogel. New Brunswick and London: Rutgers.
Gates Jr., Henry Louis. 1988. *The signifying monkey: A theory of Afro-American literary criticism*. New York and London: Oxford.
Gates Jr., Henry Louis. 1987. *Figures in black: Words, signs and the "racial" self*. New York and London: Oxford.
Habermas, Jurgen. 2006. Political communication in media society: Does democracy still enjoy an epistemic dimension? The impact of normative theory on empirical research. *Communication Theory* 16: 411–426.
Habermas, Jurgen. 1988. On the distinction between poetic and communicative uses of language. In *On the pragmatics of communication*, ed. Maeve Cooke. Cambridge: MIT.
Habermas, Jurgen. 1984. *Theory of communicative action, vol. 1. Reason and rationalization of society*. Boston: Beacon.
Habermas, Jurgen. 1982. A reply to my critics. In *Habermas: Critical debates*, ed. John Thompson and David Held, 263–269. Cambridge: MIT.
Habermas, Jurgen. 1979. *Communication and the evolution of society*. Boston: Beacon.
Huntzicker, William. 1999. *The popular press, 1933–1865*. Westport and London: Greenwood Press.
Huspek, Michael. 2007a. Habermas and oppositional public spheres: A stereoscopic analysis of black and white press practices. *Political Studies* 55, 6: 821–843.
Huspek, Michael. 2007b. Normative potentials of rhetorical action within deliberative democracies. *Communication Theory* 17, 3: 356–367.
Huspek, Michael. 2005. "From the standpoint of the white man's world": The black press and contemporary white media scholarship with emphasis upon the work of W. Lance Bennett. *Journal of Intergroup Relations* 32, 3: 67–88.
Huspek, Michael. 2004. Black press, white press, and their opposition: The case of the police shooting of Tyisha Miller. *Social Justice* 31, 1–2: 217–241.
Hutton, Frankie. 1995. Democratic idealism in the black press. In *Outsiders in 19th century press history: Multicultural perspectives*, ed. Frankie Hutton and B.S. Reed, 5–20. Bowling Green, Ohio: Bowling Green University Popular Press.
James, Michael Rabinder. 2004. *Deliberative democracy and the plural polity*. Lawrence: University of Kansas.
Kim, Cho. 2000. *Bitter fruit: The politics of Black-Korean conflict in New York City*. New Haven: Yale.
McKeon, Richard. 1954. Dialectic and political thought and action. *Ethics* 65, 1:1–33.
Mendelberg, Tali. 2001. *The race card: Campaign strategy, implicit messages, and the norm of equality*. Princeton: Princeton University Press.

Morgan, Marcyliena. 1998. More than a mood or an attitude: Discourse and verbal genres in African-American culture. In *African-American English: Structure, history and use*, ed. S. Mufwene, J. Rickford, G. Bailey and J. Baugh, 251–281. London: Routledge.

Newkirk, Pamela. 2000. *Within the veil: Black journalists, white media.* New York: New York University Press. New York.

New York Times Manual of Style and Usage. 1999. New York: Random House.

New York Times:
  Bumiller, Elizabeth (w/ Ginger Thompson) (1999) "Giuliani cancels political trip amid protest over shooting." 10 Feb.
  Flynn, Kevin (1999) "8 arrested near city hall in protest of police shooting." 23 Feb.
  Haberman, Charles (1999) "A shooting, and shooting from the hip." 12 Feb.
  Newman, Andy (1999) "Prayer in New York, protest in Washington." 16 Feb.
  Randolph, Eleanor (1999) "A long day of venting about the city's police." 28 May.
  Sachs, Susan (1999) "Anger and protest at rite for African killed by police." 13 Feb.
  Thompson, Ginger (1999) "1,000 rally to condemn shooting of unarmed man by police." 8 Feb.
  Wilgoren, Jodi (1999) "Diallo rally focuses on call for strong oversight of police." 16 April.
  Wong, Edward (1999) "Parkview: Two views of Diallo case. 25 Feb.

O'Kelly, Charlotte. 1982. Black newspapers and the black protest movement: Their historical relationship, 1827–1945. *Phylon* 43, 1: 1–14.

Ono, Kent and John Scoop. 2002. *Shifting borders: Rhetoric, immigration, and California's Proposition 187.* Philadelphia: Temple.

Owens, Reginald. 1999. Entering the 21st century: Oppression and the African-American press. In *Mediated messages and African-American culture*, ed. V.T. Berry and C.L. Manning-Miller, 96–116. Thousand Oaks: Sage

Searle, John. 1979. *Expression and meaning: Studies in the theory of speech acts.* Cambridge and New York: Cambridge University Press.

Shah, Hemant and Michael Thornton. 2004. *Newspaper coverage of interethnic conflict.* Thousand Oaks: Sage.

Simmons, Charles. 1998. *The African-American press: With special references to 4 newspapers, 1827–1965.* Jefferson, NC: McFarland.

Squires, Catherine. 2001. The black press and the state: Attracting unwanted(?) attention. In *Counterpublics and the state*, ed. R. Asen and D. Brouwer, 111–136. Albany: SUNY Press.

Sunstein, Cass. 2001. *Designing democracy: What constitutions do.* Oxford: Oxford University Press.

Talese, Gay. 1969. *The kingdom and the power.* New York: World Publishing.

Toobin, Jeffrey. 2000. The unasked question. New Yorker 76, 2: 38–44.

Williams, Melissa. 1998. *Voice, trust and memory: Marginalized groups and the failings of liberal representation.* Princeton: Princeton University Press.

Wolseley, Roland. 1971. *The black press, U.S.A.* Ames: Iowa State University Press.

Contributors

Colin Barker is Honorary Lecturer in Sociology at Manchester Metropolitan University, UK.

Lynn Comerford is Associate Professor of Human Development and Women's Studies at California State University, East Bay.

Sakile Kai Camara is Assistant Professor in the Department of Communication at California State University, Northridge.

Chik Collins is Senior Lecturer at the School of Social Sciences, University of West Scotland.

Olga Idriss Davis is Associate Professor of Communication at Arizona State University.

Darryl Gunson is Lecturer in Philosophy at the University of West Scotland.

Michael Huspek is Professor of Communication at California State University, San Marcos.

Peter Jones is Principal Lecturer in Communication at Sheffield Hallam University, UK.

Felecia G. Jones Ross is Associate Professor in the Department of Journalism and Mass Communication at Ohio State University.

Jane S. Sutton is Associate Professor of Communication Arts and Sciences at Penn State University, York.

Janice Windborne is Assistant Professor in the Department of Communication at Otterbein College.

Charles Woolfson is Professor of Labor Studies at the University of Glasgow

Index

A
African-American newspapers. See black newspapers.
American hypocrisy, 178, 79-180, 181
Amsterdam News. See *New York Amsterdam News*

B
Bakhtin, M., 41, 45–46, 52
Bell Telephone Company, 121–122, 128
Bennett, W. L., 155–167
bias
  authority-disorder bias, 168–169
  dramatization bias, 165–166
  fragmentation bias, 166–168
  personalization bias, 164–165
Black Dispatch, 139, 143
black newspapers, 174, 175–177, 179–185
black press, 8–10, 223–230, 236–246
black rhetoric, 223–231, 243–250
Black Voice News, 159–171
Blair, Tony, 17, 19, 23, 24, 26–27, 36n.12
Buffalo Star, 150

C
Chicago Defender, 174–175, 176, 177–182, 184–185
child abuse, 110
child custody
  de facto, 113
  de jure, 109
child custody law, 103
children as economic units, 85, 87, 90–92, 94–100
class, 62–64, 66–69, 73, 76–78, 119, 120–122, 125
co-custodial families, 112
consciousness, 60–62, 77
Convention on the Rights of the Child, 84–88, 90–91, 93, 97–98, 100
culture
  of North Tulsa, 138–142
  of Greenwood, 138–142, 150, 152
  of Black Wallstreet, 138, 140
cultural criticism, 137
cultural space, 137, 140
custody mediation, 104–108, 113–114

D
deliberative democracy, 1–12, 236–251
democracy, 60, 63, 64, 66, 71, 72, 74, 76, 78
democratization, 1–12
development, 86, 90, 96, 99–100
Diallo, Amadou, 223–227, 239–250
discourse, 60–63, 68–69, 72, 76–78
domestic violence, 110–111, 114
double oppression, 176
Dreamland, 150
Dungee, Roscoe, 149

E
Enlightenment, 3, 105, 109–110, 116, 191–196, 200–202
European Union, 63, 69, 75–78
Empire Star, 150

F
Fairclough, N., 18–23, 25–28, 34–35, 36n.7
family law, 103, 104
Foucault, M., 107–109, 112, 215, 217
'friendly parent' rule, 110–111

G
gender inequality, 103, 112-112

258 Index

gender roles among children, 85–86, 90, 93–94, 96, 98–100
Ghana Constitution, 86, 90, 99, 101
Ghana National Commission on Children, 91, 96, 99
girls, 119, 120–122, 125–126, 129c130

H

Habermas, J. and
 communicative action, 217–221
 communicative competence, 193, 197
 communicative reason/rationality, 196–97, 205
 discourse ethics, 191, 196–198, 200, 202–204, 209–210
 instrumental reason, 196, 202
 performative contradiction, 204–206
 project of modernity, 192–193, 199, 202, 210
 rational consensus, 193, 195, 206
 rules, 236–246
 speech acts, 194–198
 strategic action, 218–221
 universalisation, 203–204
 validity claims, 11, 195–198, 209, 212–218, 231
Harlem Renaissance, 150
Harris, R., 17, 29, 30, 32–34, 35, 36n.15,16, 37n.18, 22
Hegel, GWF, 201–202, 209–210, 249–250
hegemony, 41
Hitlerism, 178, 179, 181
Hitler's persecution of Jews, 176
Holocaust, 174, 175, 177, 179, 183, 184
Holocaust Timeline, 177–178
human rights, 85–86, 88–89, 97-99, 100
 advocacy of, 174
 abuses of, 174–176
 values, 182, 183

I

ideology, 5–6, 20–23, 26–28, 35, 40–42, 158, 169–171, 218–221
Intestate Succession, 89, 100
Iraq War, 17, 23, 24

J

Jim Crow segregation laws, 137, 141

K

Kant, I., 206, 213, 215, 223
Kristallnacht, 179, 183

L

labor protests, 60, 61, 63, 66–69, 70–74, 75–78
language, 17, 19, 20–22,24, 25, 28, 31–35, 36n.7, 37n.20
language myth, 32–34
liberalization, 65, 70, 71, 72, 78
linguistics, 19, 20, 21, 35, 36n.3, 37n.20
 critical, 20, 37n.20
 integrational/segregational, 17, 32–35
 systemic-functional, 20, 21, 27, 32, 34
Lyotard, J-F., 191, 200–202, 206, 209

M

mainstream media, 155–171, 174, 175, 177, 183, 185
majoritarianism, 155, 156–158, 163–171
Marxism, 60, 78
mediation, 104, 107, 109, 112
mediators, 105–106, 109–110
Miller, Tyisha, 159–171
moral economy, 52–54
"mother drift," 113
Muskogee Cimiter, 144
Muskogee Star, 144

N

Negro Women's Club, 143
national identity, 62, 63, 66, 72
New Labour, 19, 21, 24
neo liberalism, 65, 66, 77
New York Amsterdam News, 223–230, 238–250
New York Times, 221–230, 238–250
New York Times Style Manual, 222–230
Nietzsche, F.,121, 131, 199, 207

O

Oklahoma Star, 140
Olympics (1936), 178, 183, 184

P

Page, Sarah, 138
Paronomasia, 119, 121, 124, 129
Penelope, 123–124, 126
Philomela, 123–124
Pittsburgh Courier, 174–175, 176, 177–178, 181–185
political communication
 Analysis of, 17, 18–19, 20, 25, 26, 28, 35
postcommunism, 60, 61, 62, 63
privatization, 6, 65–66, 70–75

public sphere, 213–230

R
race relations, 137–142, 144, 145–150
rational discourse, 236–251
Rhetoric, 12, 46–47, 49, 51, 121, 123, 130
  Opposing discourse and, 128
  Space and, 123, 124–128
rhetorical trope (see also trope), 243–244, 246, 251
Riverside Press-Enterprise, 159–171
Rowland, Dick, 138–139, 150
rules,
  normative, 243–250
  violations of, 243–250

S
semiotics,, 61, 62
"serious talk", 109–110, 113
Smitherman, A.J., 138, 143–51
social imaginary, 118–124, 128–129
Soviet Union, 60, 62, 63, 64, 66, 68, 72, 77, 78
speech acts, 248–250
strikes, 67, 68, 69, 72, 74, 75, 76, 77

T
Telephone Poll, 123–124
  As loom, 119, 123–124, 126–127
  Warp threads and, 119, 121, 126, 129
  Woof threads and, 119, 124–126
Thompson, E.P., 52–54
trade unions, 67, 68, 70, 71–76, 78
trope (see also rhetorical trope), 10, 12, 119–121, 124, 129, 243–244, 246, 251

Tulsa Race Riot, 138–139, 142, 143–151
Tulsa Star, 135–138, 140, 142–147, 150–152
Tulsa Weekly Planet, 140

U
utterance, 60, 63, 69
Universal Negro Improvement Association, 142

V
Volosinov, V.N., 42, 46, 52, 60–62

W
"weavers of speech", 122, 123, 129
  as telephone women, 119, 121–128
WMD, 17, 23–24, 26
women
  authority and, 118, 123, 127–128
  bias toward their speaking, 118, 119, 121, 124, 126–128
  media and, 118, 120, 122–124, 126
  "public women" as prostitutes, 118, 120, 121, 124–129
  public women as speakers, 118, 121, 124, 127–129
  Presidency and, 118, 130
  subordination, 119, 123, 127
  as teachers, 127
  as speakers, 118, 121, 123, 126
  as weavers, 123, 124, 127
  as telephone operators, 123, 124, 127
  virtue and, 120–122, 124–125, 127
WWI, 136, 138–139, 141, 175, 176
WWII, 180

9780415849784